J.K. LASSER PRO™

ADVISING
ENTREPRENEURS

The *J.K. Lasser Pro* Series

J.K. Lasser Pro Advising Entrepreneurs: Dynamic Strategies for Financial Growth
Marc J. Lane

J.K. Lasser Pro Keeping Clients for Life
Karen Altfest

J.K. Lasser Pro Expert Financial Planning: Investment Strategies from Industry Leaders
Robert Arffa

J.K. Lasser Pro Estate and Business Succession Planning: A Legal Guide to Wealth Transference
Russell J. Fishkind, Esq. and Robert C. Kautz, Esq.

J.K. Lasser Pro Wealth Building: Investment Strategies for Retirement and Estate Planning
David R. Reiser and Robert L. DiColo with Hugh M. Ryan and Andrea R. Reiser

J.K. Lasser Pro Fee-Only Financial Planning: How To Make it Work for You
John E. Sestina

J.K. Lasser Pro Preparing for the Retirement Boom
Thomas Grady

The *Wiley Financial Advisor* Series

Tax-Deferred Investing: Wealth Building and Wealth Transfer Strategies
Cory Grant and Andrew Westhem

Getting Clients, Keeping Clients
Dan Richards

Managing Family Trusts: Taking Control of Inherited Wealth
Robert A. Rikoon, with Larry Waschka

Advising the 60+ Investor: Tax and Financial Planning Strategies
Darlene Smith, Dale Pulliam, and Holland Tolles

Tax-Smart Investing: Maximizing Your Client's Profits
Andrew D. Westhem and Stewart J. Weissman

J.K. LASSER PRO™

ADVISING ENTREPRENEURS

Dynamic Strategies for Financial Growth

Marc J. Lane

John Wiley & Sons, Inc.
New York • Chichester • Weinheim • Brisbane • Singapore • Toronto

Published by John Wiley & Sons, Inc.
Published simultaneously in Canada.

No part of this publication may be reproduced, stored in a retrieval system or
transmitted in any form or by any means, electronic, mechanical, photocopying,
recording, scanning or otherwise, except as permitted under Sections 107 or 108
of the 1976 United States Copyright Act, without either the prior written permission
of the Publisher, or authorization through payment of the appropriate per-copy fee
to the Copyright Clearance Center, 222 Rosewood Drive, Danvers, MA 01923,
(978) 750-8400, fax (978) 750-4744. Requests to the Publisher for permission
should be addressed to the Permissions Department, John Wiley & Sons, Inc.,
605 Third Avenue, New York, NY 10158-0012, (212) 850-6011, fax (212) 850-6008,
E-Mail: PERMREQ @ WILEY.COM.

This publication is designed to provide accurate and authoritative information in regard
to the subject matter covered. It is sold with the understanding that the publisher is not
engaged in rendering professional services. If professional advice or other expert
assistance is required, the services of a competent professional person should be sought.

Library of Congress Cataloging-in-Publication Data:

Lane, Marc J.
    Advising entrepreneurs : dynamic strategies for financial growth / by Marc J. Lane.
      p. cm — (The J.K. Lasser pro series) (Wiley financial advisor series)
    Includes index.
    ISBN 0-471-38947-1 (cloth : alk. paper)
    1. Entrepreneurship. 2. Business entreprises. 3. Industrial management. I. Title: At
head of title: J.K. Lasser pro. II. Title. III. Series. IV. Series: Wiley financial advisor
series

    HB615.L268 2001
    658.4'21—dc21   2001017816

Printed in the United States of America.

10 9 8 7 6 5 4 3 2 1

To my parents,
with love

Contents

Preface

What follows represents much of the professional knowledge I have accumulated over the course of nearly 30 years in helping many of the most successful entrepreneurs reach and exceed their goals. I am proud to be their friend, their lawyer, their financial advisor, and often their mentor. Their experiences and mine are probably instructive for emerging entrepreneurs and their financial advisors, and it is that premise that led me to write this book.

Advising Entrepreneurs is not an encyclopedia, nor is it exhaustive. The arcane and technical rules to which we're all subject are continually changing. They are also easily accessible, so merely compiling them is not my purpose.

This is also not a professional memoir. Although there are extraordinary tales I could tell, I will abide by the constraints of confidentiality. The stories of my clients' lives remain theirs and theirs alone. Perhaps I'll find another vehicle to relive the excitement I've experienced with clients who reached for the golden ring, grabbed it, and continue to hold it close.

Still, the secrets of entrepreneurship are worth sharing, and I do intend to share them here. My approach is strategic, first focusing on the financial issues that matter most and leading the financial advisor and his or her entrepreneurial clients on a treacherous, but irresistible journey. The nature of business is undergoing a radical transformation: More and more profitable companies are managing information rather than physical assets; their products and services are "mass-customized"; increasingly, they depend on intellectual capital; they are fast, global, and digitized.

Yet the bedrock rules remain the same. The principles of successful entrepreneurship can be taught and can be learned. My earnest conviction is that the amazing successes my clients have achieved will lay the foundation for the successes your clients can surely realize.

Marc J. Lane
Chicago, Illinois

Part One

The Financial Advisor's Role

The Regulatory and Ethical Environment

Most narrowly defined, a *financial advisor* is someone who is required to register under the Investment Advisers Act of 1940 because he is paid to give advice about investing in securities. A more expansive definition, one that includes financial planners, attorneys, accountants, financial analysts, insurance agents, stockbrokers, bankers, traditional management consultants—and even "incubators" or "accelerators," who invest in promising start-ups by providing Web development, business development services, and fund-raising assistance—would recognize that, like their entrepreneur clients, those who provide financial advice are both agents and objects of change.

After more than 20 years of wrangling, the Gramm-Leach-Bliley Act of 1999 eliminated Depression-era federal and state statutory barriers to affiliations among banks and securities firms, insurance companies and other financial service providers. The act also created the National Association of Registered Agents and Brokers to function as an agent-licensing clearinghouse in the event the Producer Licensing Model Act is not successful by November 2002 in allowing insurance agents and brokers to use their home-state licenses to conduct their business in other states.

Financial industry and financial service professionals are feeling a culture shock that will forever alter the way in which they function. Entrepreneurial and other clients are better informed and more sophisticated, and they demand cutting-edge, accurate, and fairly priced advice. At the same time, technology has made commodities of many financial services, making it increasingly difficult for financial service providers to distinguish themselves from one another.

The business models that financial service providers are pursuing compound the problem. Banks, insurance firms, and stockbrokers are gobbling up one another, and while they struggle with privacy and logistics issues, they hold themselves out as holistic healers. Lawyers, accountants, and financial planners team up, through reciprocal referral arrangements and multidisciplinary practices, to serve their clients across geographic boundaries more broadly and deeply than they could on their own.

Whether we endorse or resist these new, perhaps revolutionary formulations, they are here to stay: Financial advisors are likely to institutionalize their relationships, to focus on identifying and solving their clients' problems, and to forgo short-term profits to reinvest in their businesses and practices for long-term growth and competitiveness.

Duties of a Fiduciary

Although strategic considerations may force 21st century financial advisors to rethink their mode of practice, their duties to their clients will not diminish and, in fact, the growing complexity of the advisors' business networks give rise to new ethical challenges. Professional codes of conduct, common-law principles, and statutes spell out advisors' obligations as fiduciaries—to put the client's interest above their own, to disclose any conflicts of interest that may compromise the client, to obtain the client's consent to any such conflicts, and ultimately to protect the client.

To be perfectly clear about it, not everyone who renders financial advice is in fact a fiduciary, one in whom a client reposes trust and confidence and, for that reason, one who owes the client the highest duty of undivided loyalty. Bankers, for example, enter into arm's-length transactions with their customers and, along the way, they give advice. And insurers, who exist to sell policies, may offer their customers help with loss control. Yet, in each case, their customers recognize that the underlying business relationship is not one where the advisors are expected to hold their customer's interests above their own. And, after all, it is the consumer's reasonable expectation that triggers a fiduciary duty.

Simply put, where trust is expected, it ought to be delivered. The sometimes ambiguous example of the financial planner is instructive. Financial planning is an occupation in transition. For many years, one became a financial planner by self-designation. Now, financial planning is evolving into a profession, and its leaders, recognizing that they serve clients and not customers, embrace the fiduciary label.

The Financial Planning Association, the licensor of the Certified Financial Planner® (CFP) mark and the leading organization of financial planners, in its Code of Ethics, assumes "responsibilities to the public, to clients, to colleagues, and to employees." The code provides guidance to its members through principles it adopts relating to integrity, objectivity, competence, fairness, confidentiality, professionalism, and diligence.

Some planners contend that only advisors who work with employee benefit plans, and not those who represent the entrepreneur and other individuals, are fiducuaries. The weight of legal authority is against them: Just about anyone who gives advice and holds himself or herself out as a financial planner is required to register under the 1940 Investment Advisers Act and thus becomes a fiduciary. And the paradigm shift in the financial services industry presages that, as advisors render services collaboratively, they are likely to be held to the highest standard applying to one of them. So the consumer would reasonably expect.

Once planners acknowledge that they are fiduciaries, they may be forced to establish a process by which investment issues are made. The Uniform Prudent Investor Act, which applies to investments by trusts and trustees, deserves the attention of all investment advisors. It judges them on their performance. Accordingly, investment advisors are required to prepare written investment policy statements and document each and every step of the implementation of the policies they have adopted. After all, the client has hired a professional to bring discipline to investing and is entitled to the benefit of that bargain.

The investment advisor needs to understand the client's risk tolerance and time horizon and must develop an appropriate asset and subasset allocation. It becomes the investment advisor's job to select investments or to choose a money manager or mutual fund for each asset class. Money managers or mutual funds should be selected based on their risk-adjusted performance vis-à-vis other investments in their peer group (including performance in rising and falling markets), their adherence to investment style, and the tenure of their decision makers.

Financial advisors need to manage and control expenses. Thus, if they select load funds, it is incumbent on them to justify that decision.

Financial advisors' most central obligation is the duty of full disclosure to their clients. Disclosure usually begins at the initial client interview, which is intended to ascertain whether or not the advisor and the prospective client are a good fit. In representing entrepreneurs, the question is a particularly important and complex one since, depending on the nature and scope of the engagement, the advisor may end up rendering ad hoc advice under demanding time constraints, much of it based on instinct and intuition. Chemistry becomes critical under such circumstances, and the time to test whether advisor and client are "in synch" will long since have passed.

Initial Interview

It is imperative that an initial interview with a prospective client identify all the relevant issues. To the extent the entrepreneur has not asked all the questions she reasonably needs to have answered in selecting a financial advisor for the engagement at hand, the advisor should help her frame the issues. They will almost always include the following:

- What experience do you have? Make sure the entrepreneur knows how long you have been a financial advisor and how your experience with other entrepreneurs relates to her needs and her objectives.
- What are your qualifications? All kinds of people describe themselves as financial advisors. Make sure the entrepreneur understands what credentials you hold and exactly what qualifies you to render the advice she seeks.
- What services do you offer? Make sure the entrepreneur is aware of your licenses and expertise—and all the ways you can provide help.
- How would you approach my situation? The answer to this question will give you the opportunity to share your philosophy, but it also demonstrates how you have helped entrepreneurs with similar needs.
- Will you be the only person working with me? The entrepreneur needs to know how you work and who is on your team. If others in your

office will be participating in the engagement, the entrepreneur has a right to meet them and satisfy herself about their skills and experience. If the financial advisor will be collaborating with other professionals he selects, the entrepreneur should know that, too, and learn their backgrounds.

■ How do you get paid for your services? There should be no mystery here. The entrepreneur is entitled to know how and when the advisor is paid and should feel comfortable that the advisor's compensation is fair.

Compensation Approaches

Not surprisingly, fees are the greatest source of controversy between advisors and clients, yet advisors often have little but their instincts to rely on in formulating fees and disclosing them. Different kinds of financial advisors are likely to be compensated in different ways. Each would be prudent to document his fee structure and have the client sign off on it.

Following are some typical compensation patterns and the advantages and disadvantages of each.

Flat Fees.   Financial advisors of all stripes take on engagements for an agreed sum. Their clients have the comfort of knowing exactly what the work will cost and thus might be more inclined to authorize it. However, advisors run the risk that the engagement will take longer than they thought and they'll be obligated to "eat" some time.

Hourly Fees.   Attorneys and accountants customarily bill by the hour, and so does a growing number of financial planners. The advisor expects to be compensated for all time spent and can budget accordingly, but will not earn a premium for achieving extraordinary results. Hourly rates do not automatically avoid conflict-of-interest issues: a client may conclude that the advisor took longer or billed more to do the work than the client thought he should. To avoid any surprise, it is a good idea for the advisor and the client to develop a budget; clients prefer hourly billings only when the costs the advisor requests can be reasonably predicted and comfortably afforded.

Equity Arrangements.   More and more attorneys, accountants, and other financial advisors are providing counsel to their entrepreneurial clients for a piece of the action, that is, stock, stock options, or warrants (equity equivalents). Clients gain the advice of an advisor they might not otherwise be able to hire or retain; the clients' cash, always in short supply, can be devoted to other purposes; and advisors will be highly motivated since they have a vested interest in the venture's success. All of this can be offset by the chilling reality that the advisors' loyalty may now be divided between their clients and themselves. Some professionals have concluded that equity arrangements present a conflict of interest that cannot be overcome by disclosure and consent. Their argument is a compelling one.

Commissions. Registered securities representatives and the broker-dealers that employ them historically have been paid for their investment advice by charging a commission on the financial products they sell to their clients. So have insurance agents. The industry is moving away from commission-driven to fee-driven compensation approaches because of the potential for conflicts of interest inherent to commissions. Horror stories about "churning" and unauthorized trading tend to support that concern.

Clients should understand that advisors' compensation methods render them neither more nor less ethical than they would be were they to be paid in some other fashion. And there are good client-oriented reasons for the advisor to maintain a commission-based business. For example, many investment professionals are simply dissatisfied with no-load life and disability insurance policies and have no choice but to collect a commission when they sell the policies or mutual funds they genuinely believe to be in their clients' best interests.

If an investment professional manages his client's portfolio of individual stocks and bonds for long-term total return, the account may see little turnover, and commissions may be significantly lower than a typical management fee might be. If the advisor selects no-load mutual funds for his client, the annual fee he would need to charge, added to the funds' management fees, might well be more expensive for the client than her investment in load funds that pay a commission to the advisor. No-load fund sponsors might also refuse to send the advisor the monthly statements he needs to track the investment performance and effectively manage his clients' assets. Finally, no-load funds notoriously attract inexperienced investors who are not committed to the long term. Some analysts fear that such shareholders could force fund managers to sell holdings in down markets to make good on redemption requests born of panic.

Assets under Management. Rather than charge a commission, an increasing number of investment advisors charge an annual management fee based on the value of a client's assets. The client may perceive such a compensation method as creating incentive for the advisor to do a good job; as assets soar, so will the fee, and both the client and the advisor will prosper. In reality, the economics of asset-based fees may prove less or more fair than other approaches. The portfolio's turnover, the client's time horizon and risk tolerance, the manager's investment style, and prevailing market conditions all complicate the comparison.

Variations of These Themes. The ways in which advisors are compensated are limited only by their imaginations. Creative advisors are developing structures that combine fees and commissions, that offset commissions against fees, and that use formulas to reflect the client's investment income and net worth and the complexity of the services the advisor performs. Entrepreneurs may even negotiate bonus fees for financial advisors who are successful at consummating deals for them. So long as the client's interest remains paramount, approaches that creatively address the legitimate needs of the advisor and reward him fairly for his effort and success are to be encouraged.

Even financial advisors who may not be professionals owe their clients a duty of fairness. Thus, the National Association of Insurance Commissioners has adopted a Life Insurance Fluctuation Model Regulation to address the fact that some life insurance companies and their agents have been overly aggressive in their product design and illustration practices. The regulation prescribes industry standards to make sure that life insurance illustrations educate consumers about the important features of the products they buy and are prepared in an actuarially sound manner.

Engagement Letter

Communicating fees to prospective clients raises legal, ethical, and business issues. Although advisors of different disciplines are required to meet different criteria, virtually any financial advisor would be well served by following up his initial consultation with an engagement letter.

Its content would vary by profession but its intent would be the same—
to define the scope of the advisor's work product, to set forth how he is
to be paid, and to control client expectations.

A lawyer's engagement letter, for example, would outline the services
to be performed, how and when he is to be paid for them, disclaim any
guarantee or assurance about outcome, and set the conditions under
which he might withdraw from the engagement (if, for example, the
client is not truthful with him, fails to take his advice, or does not pay his
bills as they are rendered). Similarly, a financial planner's engagement
letter would set forth the tasks the planner and his client discussed and the
planner's estimate of his fees. The letter would be accompanied by the
planner's Form ADV, Part II, the comprehensive disclosure document
required to be given to prospective investment advisory clients under the
1940 act; it lays out the advisor's services and fees, educational and business background, conflicts of interest, and methods of analysis.

It is a good idea for the advisor to include an investment policy statement, one that lays out the client-specific risks of investing. The statement should be a product of a questionnaire designed to elicit information
about the client's investment experience and knowledge, risk tolerance,
investment time horizon, and expectations. The investment policy statement would be very helpful to the advisor should a lawsuit ever be
brought against him.

Conflicts of Interest

Correspondence throughout the course of the engagement is useful to
mitigate the risks of conflicts of interest. When there is a conflict, a possible conflict, or a perceived conflict, the financial advisor is wise to
identify it, document it, and let the client know about all the alternatives
available to her. If following an advisor's recommendation would increase the fee the client would pay, she has a right to know that, and the
advisor has a duty to come clean.

Suppose an advisor is paid based on assets under management and his
client who is approaching retirement age must decide whether to leave
her 401(k) assets with her employer or roll them over into an individual
retirement account (IRA). Or suppose the client needs help deciding
whether to pay off his mortgage or add to his investment account. The

advisor has a duty to disclose the conflict, and a duty to give her client a fair opportunity to make a fully informed judgment.

Not all conflicts are so obvious. There is the conflict of taking on more clients or more work than the advisor can handle competently. There is the conflict that results from allocating more time to one client than another. And there is the conflict advisors face as do all human beings— being more available to clients who are easier to work with. In each case the solution lies in the advisor's awareness of the issue and his consistency in being fair to his clients, to the process, and to himself.

Referrals and reciprocal agreements among financial advisors beg for full disclosure. The Financial Planning Association's Code of Ethics was derived from the Code of Ethics and Professional Responsibility of its predecessor, the Certified Financial Planners Board of Standards. It requires that CFPs disclose conflicts that "will or reasonably may impair the [CFP's] rendering of disinterested advice, recommendations or services." The principle is also found in the American Bar Association's Model Code of Professional Responsibility, which has been adopted as law in most states. It requires lawyers to avoid "even the appearance of professional impropriety" and demands that they exercise "independent professional judgment" when representing claims.

Members of the American Institute of Certified Public Accountants (CPAs) are required, under their Code of Professional Conduct, to "maintain objectivity and integrity" and be free of conflicts of interest in performing services. Where there is a conflict, a CPA can only work for a client after the client consents to the conflict, but may not perform "attest" services such as audits even with the client's consent.

Financial advisors, then, should be careful to make full disclosure to their clients:

- If they have a business affiliation with anyone whose products or services they are recommending
- If they are paid to sell someone else's products or services
- If they receive fees, commissions, or any benefits at all from anyone to whom they refer clients
- If they are affiliated in any way with a broker-dealer, a financial planner, an insurance company or agency, a law firm, an accounting firm, or anyone else who offers financial products or services

- If they are an owner of, or have any other relationship with, a firm whose products or services they recommend to clients

Risk itself presents conflict. Investment advisors who fully disclose the risk of a speculative investment may scare their clients away—and the revenue those clients represent along with them. Attorneys or accountants who discourage an entrepreneur from pursuing a flawed business opportunity act to their own short-term economic detriment. In each case, the advisors are doing the right thing for the right reason. Nothing convinces like conviction, and only by taking the high road do advisors meet their legal and ethical obligation to their clients and build the trust and rapport that are indispensable to the successful, long-term advisor-client relationship.

CHAPTER 2

Financial Management and Planning

Entrepreneurship is a subject of enormous media, academic and professional attention, and yet it is still not easily understood. To some, entrepreneurs are risk-taking innovators, drawing on the resources they can command to pursue opportunistic business growth and profits. To others entrepreneurs are the creators and bosses of a host of ventures they jumpstart, one after another, and then peddle to the public markets. Neither operating definition is particularly instructive to the financial advisor, but both provide useful insight in identifying entrepreneurial behavior and the ways in which the advisor can contribute to the entrepreneurial process.

The truth is that there probably is no "pure" entrepreneur, and each business owner harbors a risk-averse administrator within him. So it is her client's entrepreneurial behavior that should inform the financial advisor's perceptions and judgments. For that reason alone, the prototypical entrepreneur, elusive as he may be, is worth knowing and understanding.

Entrepreneurs see themselves as empowered to realize the growth they crave. Their luck is opportunity and they are out to grab it by the throat. They commit only those resources they deem indispensable to their game plan, at each of its stages, and they control their risks as best they can but with full realization that reward is a function of risk. They are action-oriented, operate with narrow decision windows, and understandably call their own shots.

When entrepreneurial characteristics surface, it becomes the advisor's mission to help her client answer the financial questions her client asks or, perhaps just as likely, fails to ask, but should: Where is my best opportunity? How do I make the most of it? What resources will I need? How can I capture those resources? Which business model makes the most sense for me?

The entrepreneur makes things happen, but the financial advisor is the agent of change.

Pre-Start Analysis

At the outset, the financial advisor helps her client define and understand both the scope and the reality of the opportunity under consideration. The advisor helps her client identify all the moving parts that will need to be integrated to exploit the opportunity successfully. Finally, the advisor helps shape a strategy to mitigate the inevitable risks, both those unique to the venture and those inherent in all businesses. The result is a business plan that, although forever subject to tweaking, will be the prescriptive blueprint from which the business will be built. Or, just as beneficially, the result will be a "no-go" decision—ironically, sometimes the most profitable of all business decisions.

The pre-start analysis begins with a candid examination of the proposed opportunity. If its scope is misperceived, an eventual launch may be fatally flawed. The financial advisor's job is to keep the entrepreneur focused, realistic, and informed. An advisor who serves only as a cheerleader, supporting the client's pipedream, can innocently cause great, even irreparable harm. The same principles apply to financial advisors for "intrapreneurs," managers of mature businesses who seek to cultivate and pursue entrepreneurial opportunities.

Evaluating the opportunity in a comprehensive and dispassionate way requires advisors to satisfy themselves about all kinds of issues, some obvious, others nuanced. Their judgment is ultimately their stock-in-trade, but it needs to be founded in demonstrable facts. Due diligence should be the product of rigorous inquiry in which all of the following questions are unequivocally answered:

- What is the demand for the product or service? It seems self-evident but too many would-be entrepreneurs miss the most important point: Unless their wares satisfy customer needs—in functionality, quality, and price—there simply is no viable basis for a business.
- What are the opportunity's size, economic life, and likely growth rate? Niche markets may prove more easily penetrable by aggressive entrepreneurs than are large markets, which are the natural domain of the big boys. What's more, younger ventures may flourish by grabbing on to an attractive chunk of a high-growth opportunity and riding its promise. Entrepreneurs can benefit from jumping into a fast-changing business at the very point in its life cycle when rewards can most handsomely be realized.
- Will the venture's profits justify the entrepreneur's investment in time and money? Obviously, more capital-intensive businesses tend to present greater risk and pay off slower than less capital-intensive businesses. The best candidates to deliver reasonable returns to their investors will forecast rapid and sustainable top and bottom-line growth, substantial recurring revenue, and the ability to withstand the onslaught of imitative competition, product substitution, and changing technology.

Assuming the opportunity passes muster, it needs to be fully exploited. Again, the financial advisor's probing questions such as those that follow will help the entrepreneur develop the optimal strategy:

- Are there really customers out there? Entrepreneurs need to demonstrate that living and breathing people would find their products or services so superior to what they're buying now instead—and so affordable—that they walk away from their current vendors to buy what the entrepreneurs intend to sell. Moreover, entrepreneurs need to establish that they will have access to the distribution channels to reach those customers and effect that very change in their buying habits.
- Will the entrepreneurs' head start be sufficient? If their product or service is the "better mousetrap," they'll need to protect it lest they lose it. While they may have a competitive advantage in pricing, in the intellectual property they will own, or in distribution relationships, sooner or later they will face one or many competitors and, for their advantage to be sustainable, they'll need to anticipate how their products or services will continue to be the purchases of choice.
- To what extent will others control the venture's destiny? In their eagerness, entrepreneurs may concede more than they should to major

customers or vendors. As entrepreneurs depend too much on the kindness of strangers, their business may prove less profitable or more risky than they bargained for.

The development of business plans assumes that entrepreneurs have or will have all the skills, cash, and other resources it takes to get into business. But the art of entrepreneurship is the art of the possible: Entrepreneurs rarely control all the resources they need to launch their ventures. It often falls to their financial advisors to help them identify and assemble what they will need but lack. Once more the advisor's insight in asking the right questions will do her client the most good.

- Which requisite skills and resources do the entrepreneurs have, and which ones do they need to recruit? The more entrepreneurs depend on others to fill the vacuum, the more vulnerable they inevitably become. But there is a competing principle: Without adequate strength in production, marketing, technology, human resources, law, and finance, the entrepreneurs' competitive disadvantage may doom their venture. So, entrepreneurs should be motivated to draw on their imagination and cajoling skills. Experienced management, for example, might be enticed by creative equity-sharing designs; or capital investments in plant, warehousing, or distribution capabilities might prudently be deferred or avoided by outsourcing or by building creative strategic-alliance relationships.
- How will unanticipated resource needs be addressed? Financial advisors can safely predict few things for their clients but it is a better than even bet that the entrepreneur's time and money will run out sooner than he counted on. Old investors are disinclined to commit good money after bad, and new investors will always want more favorable terms than investors who put money at risk before a business failed to meet expectations. Financial advisors should insist that entrepreneurs maintain—and fund—a resource contingency plan and that the plan reasonably deal with any performance shortfalls.

Entrepreneur as Manager

Once all the critical resources have been marshaled and the venture is given the green-light, the entrepreneur now becomes a manager, too. It is the financial advisor's responsibility to support management's effective and efficient use of business resources as it plans, organizes, staffs, directs and controls business operations.

Planning is the systematic way to set goals and develop the means to achieve them. The most fundamental goals of any business are to maximize its owners' wealth, to pay the interest on its debt, and to grow.

An unprofitable business cannot remain viable over the long term, and its owners and creditors are unlikely to remain committed to it. A business that cannot meet its obligations as they become due may be forced into bankruptcy and liquidation. And a business that fails to grow cannot remain competitive and, sooner or later, will succumb to the laws of the marketplace.

Beyond these most basic of goals are others, unique to each venture. The financial advisor should see to it that any goal the entrepreneur sets should be:

- measurable: "We want to see 100,000 hits on our e-commerce website . . ."
- connected to a reasonable time frame: ". . . by March 31 of next year . . ."
- achievable: ". . . which our market study supports as a perfectly reasonable goal for us."

Some plans are *strategic plans*. They comprehensively allocate business resources to achieve long-term (one year or beyond) goals and help to establish the venture's priorities. A strategic plan tries to forecast where the business may be at some future date and how it can best get there.

Other plans are *functional plans* that support the strategic plan. They are targeted to the needs and opportunities of a specific aspect or operating area of the business and might include a personnel plan or a capital equipment plan.

The functional plan that is of greatest interest to the financial advisor is one or another *financial plan*, which might be prepared for many different purposes. One typical approach is for the enterprise to ascertain the costs associated with implementing each functional plan and consolidating all of them into an overall company budget. The budget is then used by the entrepreneur and his financial advisor to develop the company's financing requirements.

Different business plans for various needs must be based on specific and attainable goals. The financial advisor has a crucial role in the development of such goals and in the planning they support.

Once business plans have been drafted, the entrepreneur is obliged to *organize*, or set up the organization to carry them out. Here, too, the financial advisor has a very important contribution. In the case of the entrepreneurial start-up, the financial function may in fact be carried out entirely by the business owner and his financial advisor. As the organization grows and becomes more complex, the financial advisor will monitor financial plans and determine how best to obtain the funds to carry them out.

The entrepreneur's *staffing* function involves recruiting and retaining the best people to implement the business plan. Objective educational, training, and skill requirements and a job description need to be developed for each position. Often, particularly in the company's early stages, the financial advisor is called on to help the entrepreneur describe, identify, interview, and hire the most capable personnel.

The entrepreneur is called on to *direct*. His leadership distinguishes and, perhaps above all other factors, accounts for his success. Directing the financial aspects of the business is accomplished through the budgeting process and, as one would expect, the financial advisor is a key source of guidance in allocating the financial assets of the business among its various operational areas.

The quality of *controlling* the business often separates the successful venture from the failures it leaves behind. The process has three parts:

1. Setting performance benchmarks
2. Comparing the company's performance against such benchmarks
3. Taking prompt and decisive action to bring performance to benchmark levels

The process is a perpetual one, continually revisiting and resetting benchmarks, measuring the company's performance against them, and taking corrective action to improve future performance. As with all controls, financial control starts with the establishment of standards. Then, it contrasts actual revenues and expenses with the standards, flags any problem areas, and takes appropriate curative action. Financial control also includes the development of internal auditing procedures to protect the company's financial assets. Financial controls can only be implemented once strategic and functional financial plans are in place.

Evaluating the Enterprise

Financial management and planning are difficult to undertake when the "base case" is a new or fledgling enterprise with little or no operating history. The process can be even more complicated for the financial advisor whose counsel is sought by a growing concern. In such a case, the advisor's first step needs to be fact-finding. He needs to be brought current—and quickly—about any issue or problem that may bear on the advice he gives. Although advisors of different disciplines may emphasize one or another aspect of the entrepreneurial client's financial history, the following audit letter may be a useful model in eliciting the facts and documents the advisor will want to review. Since entrepreneurs are likely to have interests in more than one business, the letter is drafted expansively to probe into all the relationships that might prove relevant to the advisor's engagement.

Today's Date

Mr. Courage O. Convictions
One Silicon Valley Tower
Palo Alto, CA 94103

Dear Mr. Convictions:

Set forth below is a list of the documents and information I would appreciate the opportunity to review pursuant to my "financial advisor's audit" of the business entities with which you have a relationship (hereinafter referred to individually as an "Entity" and collectively "the Entities"). After reviewing such documents (or copies of them) and information as may exist, I'll be happy to get together with you at your convenience and offer my recommendations to you.

1. *Role in Entity.*   For each Entity, please provide a narrative of your role and activities in the Entity; whether or not you are compensated for such role; and, if so, how. In addition, please provide a description of each Entity's business, activities, and operation and how each of the Entities relates to the others in terms of both ownership and activities.

(continued)

---

2. *Entity Organizational and Governing Records*
    2.1 For corporate entities:
         (a) The corporations' original certificates of incorporation, together with all amendments to date.
         (b) The bylaws of the corporations, as currently in effect.
         (c) Minutes of all meetings of boards of directors, executive committees, and any other committees of the boards of directors and of the shareholders of the corporations since their date of incorporation.
         (d) The stock transfer ledgers of the corporations and the forms of the corporations' stock certificates.
         (e) Certificates of authority to do business in any state or country other than its state or country of incorporation.
    2.2 For limited liability companies:
         (a) The articles of organization, together with all amendments to date.
         (b) The operating agreement among the members, and all amendments to date.
         (c) Any and all management agreements.
         (d) Minutes of all meetings of the managers, members, or committees since the dates of organization.
         (e) Records showing membership, ownership interests, and any profits or other economic interests.
         (f) Certificates of authority to do business in any state or country other than its state or country of organization.
    2.3 For trusts:
         (a) The trust agreements, as amended to date.
         (b) Any letters of direction tendered to the trustees since the trusts were settled.
         (c) Any and all notices received from the trustees since the trusts were settled.
         (d) Any assignments of beneficial interests tendered to the trustees since the trusts were settled.
3. *Governmental Regulations and Filings*
    (a) Any reports filed by the Entities and any significant correspondence to or from any state or federal regulatory agencies during the past five years.
    (b) Any material governmental permits and licenses of the Entities.
4. *The Entities' Loan Agreements and Other Financial Arrangements*
    (a) All documents and agreements evidencing borrowings, whether secured or unsecured, by the Entities, including loan and credit agreements, promissory notes, other evidences of indebtedness, and any and all guarantees executed in connection therewith.

(b) All financing documents of any other entity that may contain covenants or restrictions that may be relevant to you or the Entities.

(c) All bank letters or agreements confirming lines of credit.

(d) All documents and agreements evidencing other material financing arrangements, including sale-and-leaseback arrangements, installments purchases, and the like.

(e) All correspondence with lenders (including entities committed to lend) for the past three years, including all compliance reports submitted by the Entities or their independent public accountants.

(f) Computations demonstrating compliance with covenants in existing financing documents.

(g) The Entities' financial statements, whether audited or unaudited (including reviewed statements or compilations), for the past five years, including all notes and schedules thereto.

(h) Copies of all the Entities' domestic and foreign income tax returns for the past three years.

(i) Copies of all the Entities' state and local income tax returns for the past three years.

(j) Information with respect to any Internal Revenue Service or other governmental audit of the Entities and the results of each audit.

(k) An aged accounts receivable and payables list for the Entities at the end of the most recent month and at the end of each of the past four quarters.

5. *Material Agreements*

(a) All agreements, contracts or commitments relating to the employment of any person by the Entities (including collective-bargaining agreements), and any bonus, deferred compensation, pension, profit sharing, 401(k), stock option, employee stock purchase, retirement or other employee benefit plan, including:

  i. Personnel policy manuals and literature relating to all current programs and benefits and programs expected to be proposed in the future

  ii. All current and past summary plan descriptions and all other documents provided to employees regarding the plans

  iii. Financial statements of each plan and related audit reports

  iv. A schedule describing all unfunded liabilities under any pension or other employee benefit plan

  v. Actuarial reports for each defined-benefit pension plan

  vi. Tax returns, reports, determination letters and other communications or filings with the Internal Revenue Service, the Department of Labor, and the Pension Benefit Guaranty Corporation (including Form 5500, "Annual Return/Report of Employee Benefit Plan").

(continued)

(b) All agreements, indentures, or other instruments that contain restrictions with respect to the payment of dividends or any other distribution in respect of any corporation's capital stock.

(c) All agreements, contracts, or commitments relating to capital expenditures or the sale, distribution, or purchase of any products or services.

(d) All material licensing agreements, franchises, and conditional sales contracts to which you or any of the Entities is a party.

(e) All loan agreements and all documentation relating to loans or advances to, or investments in, any other person; or any agreements, contracts, or commitments relating to the making of any such loan, advance, or investment.

(f) All guarantees in respect of any indebtedness or any obligation of any other person (other than the endorsement of negotiable interests for collection in the ordinary course of business).

(g) All management service, consulting, executive employment, or any other similar contracts.

(h) All joint venture and partnership agreements to which you or any of the Entities is a party.

(i) All mortgages to which any of the Entities is a party or which cover property leased by any Entity.

(j) Deeds to all real estate owned in whole or in part by you or the Entities, copies of title reports and title policies relating thereto, and copies of all surveys of any such property.

(k) All agreements, contracts, or commitments limiting your freedom, or the freedom of any of the Entities, to engage in any line of business or to compete with any other person.

(l) All agreements, contracts, or commitments not entered into in the ordinary course of business that involve $10,000 or more and that may not be cancelled without penalty within 30 days.

(m) All agreements, contracts, or commitments that might reasonably be expected to have an adverse impact on the business or operations of any of the Entities.

(n) Any contracts, instruments, judgments, or decrees that materially adversely affect the business practices, operations, or condition of any of the Entities or any of its assets.

(o) All leases of real property and all leases of any substantial amount of personal property to which any of the Entities is a party, either as lessor or lessee.

(p) A schedule of all insurance policies of the Entities.

(q) A schedule of all patents, patent applications, trademarks, service marks, trade names, Internet domain names, brands, and copyrights owned or licensed by the Entities.

(r) Principal documents relating to any acquisitions or dispositions of businesses by the Entities in the past five years or currently proposed for the future.

(s) All contracts or agreements with or pertaining to any of the Entities and to which directors, officers, managers, or owners of interests in the Entities are a party.

(t) Any documents relating to any other transactions between any of the Entities and any director, officer, manager, or owners of the Entities.

(u) All documents pertaining to any receivables from or payable to directors, officers, managers, or owners of the Entities.

(v) All contracts relating to any Entities' securities to which any of the Entities is a party, including stock option plans, stock option agreements, and stock redemption, cross-purchase or other buy-sell agreements.

(w) Any documents pertaining to any preemptive rights outstanding with respect to any securities of any of the Entities.

6. *Miscellaneous*

(a) A schedule of, and documents relating to, all material litigation, administrative proceedings, or governmental investigations or inquiries, pending or threatened, affecting you or any of the Entities.

(b) All letters from the Entities' independent public accountants to any of the Entities in the past three years regarding such Entities' control systems, methods of accounting, and the like.

(c) All letters from any of the Entities' attorneys to the Entities' independent public accountants in the past three years regarding litigation in which the Entity is or may be involved.

(d) All consent decrees, judgments, other decrees or orders, settlement agreements, and other agreements to which you or any of the Entities is a party or is bound, requiring or prohibiting any future activities.

(e) Any recent analyses of the Entities prepared by investment bankers, management consultants, accountants, or others, including marketing studies, credit reports, and other types of reports, whether financial or otherwise.

(f) A schedule of major suppliers and customers, giving annual dollar amounts purchased or sold.

(g) Any financial projections, budgets, and business plans prepared by or for the Entities for the past three years and for any future periods.

(h) The most recent brokerage account statements issued to you and the Entities, setting forth their respective investment holdings.

(continued)

(i) Any other documents or information that, in your judgment, are significant with respect to the business of the Entities or that should be considered and reviewed in order to evaluate accurately the financial condition of the Entities.

Once we have received the foregoing documents, or your advice (where applicable) that they do not exist, we will undertake our analysis. During the course of that process, we may find the need to review additional documents, in which case we will so advise you.

Thank you for your assistance. We eagerly look forward to working with you.

Cordially,

Your Financial Advisor

Eventual Harvest

Once the venture achieves success, the entrepreneur's personal objectives or the needs of the business may require that its value be harvested. Outside investors may be pushing to cash out. Key employees may want to pursue other opportunities. Profits may have peaked. The venture may demand a huge new capital outlay to remain competitive or reach the next stage of growth. Or the entrepreneur's interests or circumstances may suggest that now is the time to move on. Whatever the reason, the financial advisor will turn to the task at hand, maximizing her client's return on investment.

Businesses can be harvested in a variety of ways:

- Most obviously, the business can be liquidated and its proceeds (net of liabilities) can be distributed to its owners. But liquidation sees good will—the company's "going concern" value—evaporate.
- The company or its assets can be sold to key employees, often requiring the selling entrepreneur to finance their purchase and to continue to bear some or all of the risks of the venture.

- The company can be sold to an unrelated third party, ideally one who sees the venture as complementing its preexisting business in a significant way—and, for that reason, is willing to pay a premium, an up-charge beyond what the company might otherwise be worth—to pursue a strategic vision.
- The company can issue and sell new shares in the public markets and thereby establish a fair market value for the company's stock. Concurrently or at some later date, the founding entrepreneur and his early investors can also sell the shares they own in a secondary offering.

However a harvest is engineered, its ultimate success turns in large measure on the care taken by the entrepreneur and his financial advisor throughout the life cycle of the business. Seemingly inconsequential early decisions may, for example, protect the entrepreneur's tax status, preserve the venture's intellectual property, or check a would-be competitor. Thus, the entrepreneur's financial plan is not an academic exercise, but a prudent investment whose quality can be substantially impacted by the talent, attention, and foresight of the financial advisor.

Part Two

Shaping the Venture's Financial Structure

3

Using the Tools of the Accountant

Entrepreneurs' substantial investments in money, time, energy, and reputation entitle them to reasonable profits, profits that are more likely to become theirs if they understand and use the tools of the accountant. Before entrepreneurs launch their ventures, they need to know how many units must be sold or how much revenue must be realized before they turn a profit. For that reason, a clear understanding of the enterprise's break-even point is imperative.

Break-Even Analysis

The venture's break-even quantity (*BEQ*) is computed by dividing its fixed costs (*FC*) by the difference between the price (*P*) it charges per unit and the variable costs (*VC*) of production. Expressed as a formula, the calculation is

$$BEQ = \frac{FC}{P-VC}$$

A few words about each of the components are in order. Fixed costs are the costs of running the business that are not related to sales and, in fact, are incurred even if there are no sales. These include items such as, rent, insurance, advertising costs, and administrative salaries. Price is what the company charges for its products or services. Variable costs (or costs of goods sold) are those costs directly tied to the manufacture or procurement of the products or services the company sells. For manufacturers, variable costs include the costs of raw materials, production labor, and production machinery. For sales organizations, variable costs include the price of merchandise, freight, and insurance in transit.

The break-even formula will establish the number of units that must be produced during a given time period for the venture to break even. But the formula can tell the entrepreneur much more than that.

Within the equation is the calculation $P-VC$, which represents the *contribution margin*, the amount of profit the company will make on each unit sold in excess of the break-even quantity—or the amount the company will lose on each unit of production by which it falls short of the break-even quantity. Revenue can also be developed using the formula, simply by multiplying the sales price by the quantity sold ($P \times Q$).

The BEQ formula can be modified to determine the unit sales needed to turn a profit. Here is the modification:

$$\text{Total quantity} = \frac{FC + \text{Desired net profit}}{P-VC}$$

Suppose the entrepreneur needs to know how much revenue, or how many break-even dollars (*BE $*), will be required for the venture to break even. The formula only needs to be adapted to express the contribution margin as a percentage of sales, as follows:

$$BE\ \$ = \frac{FC}{1-(VC/P)}$$

Yet, the entrepreneur still lacks the requisite information to validate her business plan. She may understand that she needs to estimate or forecast her venture's sales and that the sales forecast will drive the pro forma income and, in turn, projected financial statements. It is those statements that will allow the entrepreneur to gain comfort that her venture will be a viable one; to develop internal budgets; to recruit equity capital and debt; and to fine tune and, ultimately, to realize her financial objectives.

Forecasting Models

A forecast of sales and revenues is a supportable estimate of future demand for a business's products or services. It is the result of a careful and deliberate process involving one or more models. Forecasting models may be judgmental, time series, or causal.

Judgmental Forecasting Model

Employing a judgmental model, the entrepreneur forecasts sales based on expert opinion using historical analysis, market research, or the Delphi method—the use of a panel of experts to obtain a consensus of opinion about a new product or service for which no reliable data exist. Although judgmental models are qualitative, they lead to a quantitative conclusion about the dollar volume of sales expected to be made during a given time frame.

Time Series Forecasting Model

Time series models look at a company's or the industry's historical records to forecast future sales. If the company believes that recent sales performance is the best predictor of future sales, and that each successive time period equally influences the prediction of future sales, a moving average model will probably be used. The entrepreneur computes average sales for a number of recent periods, adds them together, and then divides the total by the number of periods. That average becomes the forecast for the next period.

If the entrepreneur believes that a moving average too simplistically extrapolates results, other time series models are available to forecast future sales more accurately. The weighted moving average model, for example, assumes that more recent periods are better predictors of future sales than earlier periods and assigns weights to each measuring time period. The exponential smoothing model uses a smoothing constant, represented by the Greek letter alpha (α), to adjust a forecast based on the company's judgment about the relationship between the sales in one period and the next. The linear regression model is most often used for intermediate and long-term forecasts; it is based on a sophisticated statistical method known as least squared regression.

Causal Forecasting Model

Causal models take into account the general condition of the economy as it impacts company revenues. Causal models can be very complex, using so-called multiple regression analysis. To cite one obvious example, if building permits increase, contractors may take comfort that their business should improve. But most entrepreneurs are acutely sensitive to the macroeconomic factors that affect their businesses for good or bad.

A basic sales forecast is the starting point in developing a pro forma income statement, a projected income statement based on the forecast. The pro forma income statement determines the company's expected future profitability and seeks to validate or challenge the entrepreneur's vision.

Assuming the entrepreneur's is a start-up business and thus lacks historical records, the pro forma income statement begins with an estimate of sales and reflects costs of goods sold as a percentage of sales based on industry standards. Each and every operating expense figure must be accounted for on the pro forma income statement, and each of them must be realistically verified.

Analyzing Financial Statements

Once the entrepreneurs' confidence in the venture is confirmed through careful and continual forecasting, their job, of course, has only just begun. At all times, they need to know where they are at, where they are going, and how they are going to get there. They will also always be concerned about how they are measuring up against the competition, as will their financial advisor, their lender, and their investor. From the venture's earliest stages on, all of them will analyze its financial statements and, for their special purposes, draw inferences about its financial health.

The three primary methods of analyzing financial statements are *vertical analysis*, *horizontal analysis*, and *ratio analysis*.

Vertical Analysis

Vertical analysis takes a single variable on a financial statement and measures other variables against it. On the income statement, the financial report that summarizes sales and revenue for a period of time, the analyst divides each expense category by net sales to learn what percentage of net sales is being consumed by that expense. If advertising or payroll represents a greater percentage of net sales than it did the previous year, management can take corrective action and bring costs back into line. Vertical analysis can also help entrepreneurs price their products because, over time, patterns can be discerned among net sales, overhead, and profitability.

Vertical analysis of a balance sheet—the financial report that summarizes the company's assets, liabilities, and ownership interests in excess of assets over liabilities—divides balance sheet items by total assets, which shows entrepreneurs just how much of their company's assets are tied up in equipment or receivables, or obligated to lenders through bank loans or trade payables. Again, management can identify areas where corrective action might be warranted, such as pursuing more aggressive collection efforts or reducing inventories.

Horizontal Analysis

Whereas vertical analysis looks at only one financial statement and relates one of its components to another, horizontal analysis spots percentage increases or decreases in an account over time. If, for example, the entrepreneur, comparing one income statement to the next, notes a slide in net profit in spite of a spike in the gross sales, she needs to dig deeper and find out why. An increase in cost of goods sold might signal problems in the company's pricing policy.

The approach works just as well in analyzing percentage changes in successive balance sheets. If the entrepreneur sees cash shrink while receivables and inventory climb, she should not be surprised to find total liabilities grow too, while her equity stake deteriorates because

$$\text{Assets} - \text{Liabilities} = \text{Owner's Equity}$$

and she should prudently use what she has learned to take corrective action. Thus, she might redouble her collection efforts, but also might reconsider her inventory and pricing decisions.

Ratio Analysis

Vertical and horizontal analyses look within the entrepreneurial venture itself, whereas ratio analysis subjects it to a reality check by comparing its trends to those of other firms in the same business. A ratio shows the relationship between variables expressed as a factor. There are many kinds of ratios worth calculating and then measuring against industry averages or other benchmarks to see how the enterprises compare.

Facts and figures on the competition are readily available. Industry reports and trade journals are good sources. So is *The Value Line Investment Survey* and companies' annual reports or their SEC Forms 10K, available online from the Securities and Exchange Commission's Electronic Data Gathering and Retrieving System (EDGAR); its address is *http://www.sec.gov/edgar.shtml.*

Some of the most popular and useful ratios are liquidity, activity, leverage, and profitability ratios.

Liquidity Ratios

Liquidity ratios show how much of a firm's current assets are available to meet short-term creditors' claims. Current assets are cash and other assets that will be converted into cash during one operating cycle. An operating cycle is the sequence of buying or manufacturing products, holding them as inventory, selling them, waiting to be paid for them, and ultimately receiving cash from customers.

Liquidity ratios are of greatest importance to investors and creditors. The *current ratio* divides total current assets by total current liabilities (debts that will become due within one year):

$$\frac{\text{Current Assets}}{\text{Current Liabilities}}.$$

Industry averages vary, but a current ratio of two or higher is usually a reliable indicator that the company can comfortably pay its short-term bills.

The *acid test ratio* extracts inventory from current assets,

$$\frac{\text{Current Assets} - \text{Inventory}}{\text{Current Liabilities}},$$

and thus measures the company's ability to pay its short-term bills without liquidating its inventory. This is a particularly telling measurement for companies that have highly seasonal sales or rapidly changing product lines. For such firms a healthy current ratio might conceal a problem lurking in inventory that might not easily or quickly be sold.

Activity Ratios

Activity ratios measure how efficiently a company is managing its assets.

The *inventory turnover ratio* shows how efficiently the company is moving its inventory. The ratio divides the company's cost of goods sold by its average inventory (at cost).

$$\frac{\text{Cost of Goods Sold}}{\text{Average Inventory}}$$

and reveals how many times a year the company moves its average inventory. By dividing 365 (days in a year) by inventory turnover, management also learns the average number of days stock is held in inventory. Depending on the company's cash flow, it may need financing to carry its inventory for that length of time.

Another activity ratio is *accounts receivable turnover*, which demonstrates how fast the company is turning its credit sales into cash.

$$\frac{\text{Credit Sales}}{\text{Accounts Receivable}}$$

Accounts receivable turnover, in turn, is used to determine the company's average collection period.

$$\frac{\text{Days per Year}}{\text{Accounts Receivable Turnover}}$$

Other activity ratios are the *fixed-asset turnover* ratio, which shows how efficiently fixed assets—property, plant, and equipment   are being used to generate revenue.

$$\frac{\text{Net Sales}}{\text{Fixed Assets}}$$

and the *total-asset turnover ratio*, which demonstrates how efficiently the company deploys all its assets to generate revenue.

$$\frac{\text{Net Sales}}{\text{Total Assets}}$$

In each case, income statement and balance sheet items are compared. Unless the company is buying new equipment each year, one would expect to see fixed-asset turnover consistently improve because fixed assets automatically decline as depreciation is deducted from all long-term operating resources except land.

Leverage Ratios

Leverage ratios measure how much of a company's assets or net worth are financed with debt. Putting it another way, leverage ratios show how much of the company's assets really belong to its owners and how much are subject to the claims of creditors. The *debt-to-equity ratio,*

$$\frac{\text{Total Liabilities}}{\text{Owner's Equity}},$$

indicates what percentage of the owner's equity is debt, or for every dollar of equity, how many dollars the firm owes to others. The *debt-to-assets* ratio,

$$\frac{\text{Total Liabilities}}{\text{Total Assets}},$$

demonstrates what percentage of the company's assets are owned by its creditors. Both the debt-to-equity and the equity-to-assets ratios are based on information found on the balance sheet.

Profitability Ratios

Profitability ratios allow entrepreneurs to judge how well their ventures are performing. They also help potential investors and creditors evaluate how much of their investment would likely be returned from the company's earnings or the growth in value of its assets. If the company's liquidity ratios, activity ratios, and leverage ratios all pass muster, management and others concerned about the company's well-being look at its profitability in the context of industry averages or other relevant benchmarks. Dun & Bradstreet Credit Services' *Industry Norms and Key Business Ratios* is one good source of such information.

The *gross profit margin ratio* shows how much gross profit (sales revenue of goods sold less costs of goods sold) is generated by each dollar of net sales (gross sales less returns).

$$\frac{\text{Gross Profit}}{\text{Net Sales}}$$

Both numbers come from the income statement.

The *operating profit margin* ratio demonstrates how much each sales dollar generates in operating income, earnings before interest and taxes.

$$\frac{\text{Operating Income}}{\text{Net Sales}}$$

In contrast, the *net profit margin ratio* reflects the payment of all obligations, including interest and taxes.

$$\frac{\text{Net Profit}}{\text{Net Sales}}$$

The *net return on assets ratio* (ROA) or *return on investment* (ROI) helps potential investors decide whether the company is an attractive place to invest compared to other alternatives. It tells the investor how much the company earns on each dollar of its assets after it pays interest and taxes.

$$\frac{\text{Net Profit}}{\text{Total Assets}}$$

Both the income statement and balance sheet must be used to calculate ROA.

The *return on equity ratio* is probably the single best indicator of the quality of management's performance. It tells the entrepreneur exactly how productively the company's resources are being put to work by calculating how much each dollar of the shareholder's investment is generating in net income.

$$\frac{\text{Net Profit}}{\text{Total Assets} - \text{Total Liabilities}}$$

Again, both the income statement and balance sheet are used in the calculation.

Ultimately, ratio analysis focuses on how well the company has achieved entrepreneurial efficiency, that is, obtaining the highest possible return with the fewest resources. This efficiency is especially difficult for the typical entrepreneur whose current liabilities are payable periodically in lump sums but whose revenues are sporadic. Managing the venture's working capital, the difference between its current assets and current liabilities, becomes critical to survival.

Managing Cash

On the asset side, entrepreneurs should be concerned about the way their cash, marketable securities, accounts receivable, and inventories are managed.

Cash is most easily and profitably managed by depositing it in banks. Not only can it then earn interest, but a paper trail of receipts and disbursements can most simply be maintained through bank statements and cancelled checks. If a creditor or the IRS requires proof of payment, the entrepreneur can easily comply. Paying by check also allows entrepreneurs to take advantage of float. Disbursement float is the money earning interest in a bank account after a check has been written but before the check clears the bank. Throughout the year entrepreneurs may write hundreds of thousands—or even millions—of dollars of checks. The longer it takes those checks to clear, the more interest entrepreneurs collect on funds until they are disbursed.

As creditor, entrepreneurs want to speed up collections. When they are on the other side of the check-clearing transaction, they are shortchanged by collections float, the time between their receipt of a check from a customer and its clearing, when interest-earning funds hit their accounts.

There are two ways to reduce the impact of collections float. The first is the use of lockboxes, post office boxes set up throughout the company's market area to receive customers' checks. Each day, or several times throughout each day, a designated local bank will collect the checks received in each box, deposit them, and, immediately upon clearing, wire the proceeds to the company's primary bank for deposit to its account. It is easy to see that transit time can be shrunk enormously and so can collections float. In addition, quickly concentrating assets in one bank can result in lower bank service charges. But lockboxes only make sense for companies with very high transaction volumes necessary to overcome the substantial bank charges involved. A break-even study (see Break-Even Analysis) will establish whether lockboxes are worth the company's consideration.

Another way to reduce collections float is electronic funds transfer (EFT), which moves money from the customer's bank account to the company's bank account via computer. The most familiar example of EFT is the automatic teller machine (ATM) where a customer inserts a bank card into a machine, punches in his or her personal identification number, and effects a purchase or cash transaction. Again, funds are transferred immediately and collections float is minimized.

Ironically, maintaining too much cash on hand and in banks can also present a cash-management problem. Rates of interest earned on checking or savings accounts carry an opportunity cost. Cash in excess of a company's short-term liabilities should be invested in U.S. Treasury or agency securities, corporate bonds, stock, or other investments. The returns on such investments can be far superior to that of bank interest.

How the company's portfolio is allocated between stocks and debt instruments primarily depends on how quickly cash will need to be made available to meet business obligations. Over the short term, say five years or less, stock prices are too unpredictable to count on. But, over time, stocks strongly outperform bonds and treasuries; they consistently beat inflation; they have extraordinary recuperative powers when markets correct or when the economy suffers a recession; and they enjoy irresistible tax benefits: profits are not taxed until a stock is sold, and even then at preferential capital-gain rates; and dividends are 70 percent exempt from income tax received by investors that are C corporations (see Corporation in Chapter 4).

Portfolio managers take different approaches in selecting stocks when they seek higher-than-market returns. Some favor technical analysis, which looks at price and volume statistics as the key to the direction of price movements. The theory is that stocks and the stock market as a whole move in discernible trends until they unequivocally signal a change in course.

Others rely on fundamental analysis and tend to be value investors or growth investors. Value investors select stocks based on their perceived earnings potential and rule out new issues, concept stocks, and growth stocks. Growth analysts, on the other hand, focus on companies whose profit margins and returns on equity are likely to contribute to rapid expansion.

Market timers try to time buys and sells to the phases of the market. They look at prevailing interest rates, business activity, and industrial production, for example, and draw conclusions about the probable direction of the market.

Most portfolio managers are impressed by companies that boast low price-earnings, price-to-cash flow, and price-to-book value ratios, especially those whose stocks are among the lowest priced in their respective industries.

It is no secret, though, that the traditional benchmarks against which stock values are measured have recently seen a tectonic shift. Whereas stocks have historically traded at price-earnings ratios in the teens, by 2000 stocks in the S & P 500 traded on average at 32 times their cumulative trailing 12-month earnings, and the tech-dominated NASDAQ at an incredible 294 times earnings.

Dividends tell a similar story. In 1990, S&P companies paid their shareholders cash dividends amounting to 3.1 percent of share prices. A decade later, with stock prices having rocketed, dividends were down to 1.2 percent.

And consider the price-earnings-growth (P/E/G) ratio, the company's price-earnings ratio divided by its earnings growth rate. Long a favorite measurement employed by investment analysts, P/E/G compares a company's stock price with the profit it might eventually generate to support that price. Companies whose price-earnings ratios are lower than their growth rates have a P/E/G less than one and were once thought to be attractive buy candidates. By 2000, the S&P traded at a P/E/G of almost three. P/E/G no longer helps analysts, unless they are prepared to use a growth number five years out.

So, how are high-growth companies valued today? Or, more accurately, how are their prices justified under what Federal Reserve Board Chairman Alan Greenspan has labeled a "new paradigm"? The answer lies in jettisoning the traditional tenets of stock valuation. Without endorsing its merit, let's identify the component parts of the new valuation methodology. This construct bears little or no relationship to the way an entrepreneurial venture is valued while it remains in private hands (see Chapter 11). But it is the stuff dreams are made of, particularly for entrepreneurs who set their sights on a public offering (see Chapter 18).

The business cycle has obviously not been repealed, and cautious analysts may gag on some of the following principles, but other, more aggressive commentators remain perfectly comfortable in promoting them:

- Cash is king. Cash earnings—earnings reported on a company's cash flow statement, but with short-term goodwill expenses added back to earnings—is still popular as the basis for valuing high-growth companies. Goodwill is the price one company pays to buy another less the liquidation value of the acquired company's assets. It is supposed to be amortized over many years but companies prefer to show higher profits and thus goose up the barter value of their stock. Cash earnings let them do just that and gobble up companies using fewer of their high-price shares. The investment community seems to be going along with the game.
- Investment analysts also justify higher stock prices by relying heavily on cash flow, net earnings with noncash charges such as depreciation and amortization added back. It is not unusual for a go-go company to have decent earnings before interest, taxes, depreciation, and amortization (EBITDA), but at the same actually report a loss. If the analyst has high hopes for the company and its share price, cash flow is the number he may emphasize in his valuation.

- But suppose a fledgling, yet well-positioned company has neither current earnings nor cash flow to gloat about. Almost every company has sales, and sales are always a positive number. For that reason, the most bullish analysts are more and more inclined to hype companies' price-to-sales ratios.
- Some companies, Internet start-ups notably among them, have only minimal sales. In those cases, supportive analysts are quick to highlight a company's business model or even the momentum of escalating stock prices instead of its internals. Latch on to a survivor, it is argued, and you will latch on to a winner.

Whichever philosophy the entrepreneur adopts in managing her company's cash in excess of short-term liabilities—and whichever investment style gains her confidence—she should be encouraged to put idle funds to work and monitor the performance of this important current asset.

Managing Receivables

Receivables also require careful management and most businesses, to stay competitive and profitable, must establish and administer a sensitive credit and collection policy. Offering credit to customers can increase sales. But, especially for early-stage ventures, the costs of maintaining a credit department can offset the benefits of any incremental revenue it generates. For that reason, many companies turn to *factoring*, selling accounts receivables to a firm that buys them at a discount. Although the entrepreneur would forgo a part of her sale price to the factor, she would nonetheless receive payment immediately and in cash and avoid any risk of collectibility.

Credit card sales work much the same way. The company permits its customers to pay for merchandise with MasterCard or VISA, for example, takes each day's credit transactions to the bank that honors them, and receives a discounted sum of cash without delay. The hassle of billing, processing, and collecting become someone else's.

Those companies that decide to grant credit need to identify their customers to whom credit will be granted. The shorthand test of creditworthiness is the "six C's": character, capability, capacity, collateral, context and conditions (see Creditworthiness in Chapter 7). The customer needs to demonstrate a good bill-paying history, provide favorable credit references, and allow the company to check those references by signing a suitable release.

The credit application must disclose income and cash flow more than sufficient to meet the customer's obligations, including those that would result from the company's extension of credit to the customer. It may also require the customer to post marketable assets that can be sold to pay off the debt should the customer default.

The credit limit the company sets for the customer, or the amount of credit it will allow the customer, will be determined in part by the customer's credit reputation. Credit references will be important to check and so will the customer's credit rating from a commercial credit agency such as Dun & Bradstreet.

In addition to screening credit risks carefully and limiting the amount of credit available even to a creditworthy customer, the company should establish commercially reasonable terms. Cash and trade discounts will be dictated largely by industry standards and should motivate customers to meet their obligation to the company promptly.

The credit function then needs to be controlled. Steps must be taken to see that customers are in fact paying their bills as agreed or, if not, the company's credit policy needs to be tightened.

Too often collection problems are the result of poor invoicing. Invoices need to be prepared in a timely manner and mailed as soon as they are prepared. Timeliness will avoid customer complaints that invoices were received too late for them to take advantage of discounts or to run through their accounts payable systems.

Invoices also need to disclose everything the customer expects. All terms and conditions should be clearly disclosed, and any collateral documentation should be sent along with the invoice.

One way to analyze the effectiveness of the company's credit and collection procedures is to look at its accounts receivable turnover. Let's suppose, for example, that the company's credit customers are required to pay their balances in full within 60 days after a transaction. If the company has $3 million in credit sales and $1 million in accounts receivable, its accounts receivable turnover would be $3 million divided by $1 million, or three. Dividing 365 days in a year by three tells us that the company's collection days are 121.7, more than double the 60-day requirement. Under those circumstances the company would be well advised to revisit its credit criteria and collection process.

Managing Inventory

The last category of current assets is inventory, and inventory management can be particularly challenging. For retail or wholesale trade and manufacturing concerns, inventories, including raw materials, work-in-process, and finished goods, may represent one-quarter to one-half or even more of a company's total assets. There must always be sufficient inventory on hand to meet customer demands, but not so much that company cash is unnecessarily tied up or that the company is stuck with obsolete or short shelf-life products that can never be sold.

Good inventory control demands that lead times required for materials and services be held to a minimum. This objective, in turn, suggests the importance of careful production and purchasing planning.

Pegging inventory at optimal levels is a natural byproduct of the sales forecasting process. Requesting longer-term order forecasts from larger customers will allow the company to serve them better and control the costs they pay. It may also allow the company to avoid interest and obsolescence costs.

But healthy and continuing dialogue with key customers will not anticipate and solve all the company's inventory problems. Just as the company reasonably seeks information from its customers, it should furnish purchase forecasts to its vendors and may thereby shorten supply lead times and insure the availability of the supplies it needs.

It is often helpful to isolate the 5 percent or 10 percent of inventory stock numbers or stock keeping units that are likely to make up about 75 percent or so of total costs. These are the items where one's management time and energy—in negotiating contracts, obtaining competitive bids, and establishing internal controls—deliver the greatest return. Even a small saving on the purchases of these items can enormously increase profits and reduce inventory costs. These items, too, are the ones management should be most concerned about with regard to optimizing the size of the order and the stocking of inventory.

Inventory modeling helps minimize the total cost of ordering and carrying merchandise. To develop an inventory model, the entrepreneur first needs to establish:

- The total annual demand for an item (D).
- The total ordering cost for the item, including the value of an employee's time for entering an order, the cost of receiving and checking

an order, the cost of placing the order in storage, and the cost of accounting for and issuing a check (*F*)

- The unit cost or price of the item (*P*)
- Carrying cost per period (including rent, insurance for the goods and obsolescence), expressed as a percentage of *P* (*C*).

The economic order quantity (EOQ) formula helps the entrepreneur keep overall inventory costs down. It balances order costs against storage costs and computes the most economic quantity to order. The formula is expressed as the square root of 2*DF*/*PC*.

As handy as EOQ is, it should not be relied on blindly. If, for example, customer demand is small or storage space scarce, orders that are smaller than EOQ may need to be placed. On the other hand, if vendors require minimum orders or if quantity discounts are available, orders bigger than the EOQ may be justified.

Managing Liabilities

Just as current assets demand careful management, so do current liabilities, which include short-term debts, accrued liabilities, and accounts payable.

Short-term debts are those that must be paid within the current accounting period. They include bank lines of credit and notes payable (which come due during the current year) as well as current payments on long-term debt.

There is one primary rule here, and that is to finance short-term assets with short-term debts, and long-term assets (those whose lives exceed one year) only with long-term debts and equity. That way, the entrepreneur is always assured that, when a short-term obligation comes due, there will be sufficient cash, or assets readily convertible to cash, to pay them.

Accrued liabilities include payroll taxes, employee benefits, property taxes and sales taxes. These expenses are notorious for getting business owners into more trouble than they bargained for: Although corporations usually shield their owners from liabilities, officers of business corporations, as "responsible persons," can be saddled with certain IRS debts owed by the business.

Businesses are collection agencies for the government, whether for payroll taxes withheld from employees' pay or sales taxes collected from consumers. And penalties can compound at lightning speed. To avoid the problems that have brought down many otherwise viable businesses and their owners, the best advice is to pay as you go. As obligations accrue, set the cash aside to meet them, and the entrepreneur will always have cash on hand to satisfy accrued liabilities when they are due.

Accounts payable present enormous opportunities for saving and for greater profits. Payables can include any kind of expense, but inventory purchased on credit often represents the biggest single line item. Such purchases are often eligible for discounts offered by vendors, discounts that can materially reduce the cash payments the company needs to fund.

Typically, discounts fall into three separate categories: trade discounts, cash discounts, and quantity discounts. Entrepreneurs should try to avail themselves of each discount they can and at the highest level.

1. *Trade discounts* are deducted from products' list prices when the buying company agrees to perform certain services that the selling company would otherwise be required to perform, such as delivery, installation, or advertising. Such discounts are often expressed as a series or chain, such as 30/20/10. The company should recognize that, even if it were to perform all the services that might be delegated to it, the discount is not the total of each separate discount—30 percent plus 20 percent plus 10 percent, or 60 percent off list price. Instead, the discounts are successively claimed, one at a time against the last computed net price.

    Thus the calculation would afford the buyer 30 percent off list (70%), 20 percent off that number (55%), and 10 percent off that number (50.40%). The net cost rate factor is 50.40 percent. Subtracting the net cost rate factor from one provides the single equivalent discount.

    The net cost rate factor also can be determined by multiplying the complements of the trade discounts. The complement is found by subtracting the number from one.

2. *Cash discounts* encourage a buyer to pay promptly. They are offered on an invoice in terms such as 2/10, net/30. The company is invited to take 2 percent off the invoice if it pays within 10 days. If the company pays in more than 11 but less than 30 or fewer days, the invoice is payable net—that is, in the stated amount. If the invoice is not paid within 30 days, it is understood that interest will be added to the unpaid balance as the parties

have agreed. The company may be better off borrowing money from a bank or tapping into a preexisting credit line to take advantage of a cash discount.

3. *Quantity discounts* help vendors increase their own cash flow by giving discounts to large-quantity buyers, either on a one-time, single-quantity basis, where the discount is available to purchasers of large single orders; or on a cumulative basis, where the discount is available to purchasers of stated quantities over the vendor's fiscal year. Single-quantity discounts may be attractive to the entrepreneur who is motivated to reduce the company's finished goods inventory while improving throughput and cash flow. However, if the company's overall cost of inventory is not improved by ordering in quantity, it would be well advised to limit its purchases, rather than draining precious cash merely for the privilege of serving as the vendor's warehouse. Cumulative discounts build loyalty among small-business customers who cannot justify complying with a vendor's single-quantity discount requirements.

Managing Capital Assets

The entrepreneur is forever striving to generate high returns on both short-term and long-term investments. Investments in capital expenditures (assets whose useful life is one year or more) help grow revenues that will make the company more profitable in the future. For most companies, capital assets were once confined to plants, real estate, and equipment. Now, entrepreneurs' most important assets may be intangible—their trade secrets, their patents, their trademarks, their copyrights, their Internet domain names, their brands, and their processes. Entrepreneurs not only need to protect all their capital assets, but also need to understand their real worth and see them generate profits.

Whether or not a capital asset should be acquired turns on a simply stated question: Will the benefits the entrepreneur receives over the asset's life be more than the cost of buying or building the asset and maintaining it over its life? Applying the test is not easy. For one thing, entrepreneurs need somehow to quantify the increased efficiency the asset will foster. For another, they need to consider what tax benefits might be associated with owning the asset; after all, writing off an asset's cost through depreciation or amortization enhances cash flow and, if the asset is financed, interest expense is tax-deductible and creates still more tax savings.

The capital budgeting decision, then, compares costs and benefits. Several methods help entrepreneurs mix and match the variables. Each of the following methods requires entrepreneurs to forecast future cash flows resulting from higher revenue, greater efficiency, and tax benefits.

Payback. The payback method merely divides the cost of an asset by the annual after-tax benefit it is forecasted to generate. The result is the number of years it is expected to take for the company to recoup its investment. Although a payback approach offers the beauty of simplicity, that is ultimately its major drawback. Since the payback technique completely ignores the time value of money, it is only helpful to the entrepreneur if the investment will likely be recovered in short order, and the entrepreneur will have intuitively known that to be the case, anyway.

Accounting Rate of Return. The accounting rate of return compares the forecasted average annual income from an asset with its average annual cost. Again, rate of return is computed exclusively on income and fails to consider the time value of money or the present value of future cash flows. Consequently, forecasted returns are apt to be grossly exaggerated.

Net Percent Value. With net percent value (NPV) the time value of money is taken into account. The technique involves the discounting of all future costs and all future benefits to their present value.

Interest rate assumptions are a key determinant of the analytical result. Because of the wide variability of rates, the entrepreneur who relies on the NPV method of capital budgeting should be encouraged to take it a step further and subject it to sensitivity analysis, alternatively modifying interest rate and other variables in her assumptions. In that way the entrepreneur will gain the benefit of a range of results from which to draw inferences and make informed judgments.

Profitability Index. A variant of NPV, the profitability index has the present value of a capital investment's benefits divided by the present value of its costs. If the answer is greater than one, the asset is worth acquiring.

Two shortcomings are worth noting. First, the two present-value numbers are tougher to calculate than they are to describe. Second, if any cash flow or interest rate assumption is even slightly off the mark, the results will be enormously skewed.

Internal Rate of Return. The internal rate of return (IRR) technique looks at the asset's actual rate of return and uses the time value of money in the calculation. Criticized for its complexity, IRR requires interpolation, finding a value between two known values. Another, more substantive criticism: It isn't practical. Whereas the NPV method assumes that cash flows are reinvested at the company's "hurdle rate," the minimum rate of return the company has established for its capital investments, IRR unrealistically assumes that cash flows are reinvested at the IRR rate.

Capital budgeting analysis is constrained by two unavoidable facts of life. The first is mutual exclusivity. Even if each of three computer networks passes muster under cogent NPV scrutiny, the company may only need one such network. Selecting one precludes any further consideration of the others.

The second is capital rationing. The entrepreneurial venture will have finite resources. Even though positive NPVs can be demonstrated for each of a dozen new retail locations, the entrepreneur will eventually be faced with the real-life challenge of selecting among them.

Entity Design Choices

Even before the entrepreneur opens his doors, he will be wise to select a business unit: a sole proprietorship, a general or limited partnership, a C corporation, an S corporation, or a limited liability company. (The "C" and "S" designations refer to Subchapters C and S of the Internal Revenue Code, which provide different tax rules for these two categories of corporations.) Sometimes the choice of business form is dictated by external factors: High exposure to legal risks, for instance, may suggest a corporation or a limited liability company with their insulation from personal liability; a tax-sheltering or income-shifting objective may favor a limited partnership. Or the business unit may be freely selected by a savvy entrepreneur who is acutely sensitive to the legal, tax, and operational results of his decision.

Whatever prompts the selection, the entrepreneur should know its consequences and make the most of his choice by maximizing its strengths and mitigating its weaknesses. In particular, the entrepreneur should consider the different tax treatments applicable to the alternative ways in which he can operate his business. Before any decision is made, the financial advisor will want to consider the relevant tax issues.

Tax Considerations

The entrepreneur may overlook the dramatic impact his choice of entity may have on the access-to-capital and cost-of-capital issues with which he is probably struggling. His financial advisor should sensitize him to the significant tax implications of his choice and the direct impact on both the availability and cost of capital. Tax-related variables that bear on the choice-of-entity decision include the following:

1. *Taxability of Income.* Look at the tax rates, the brackets, and whether the entrepreneur will save by having a separate entity that pays relatively low rates on its first increments of profits.
2. *Deductibility of Losses.* Can losses generated by the business be used to offset all other sources of income, just active or passive income, or active and portfolio income? Is the use of losses deferred through a mandatory carryforward?
3. *Organization of the Business.* Can assets be transferred to the business without tax? Can the organizational expenses be amortized, or written off as deductions against ordinary income without waiting for a liquidation of the entrepreneur's interest?
4. *Family Tax Planning.* Does the form of the business make it possible to split the business income among the entrepreneur and his family members in order to achieve savings in income, gift, and estate taxes?
5. *Special Allocations.* In a group enterprise, can certain individuals receive the benefit of an allocation of a disproportionate amount of income, deductions, or losses?
6. *Fiscal Year.* Can the business choose a different fiscal year from that of its owners? If so, can income or loss be accelerated or deferred advantageously between individual owners and the business?
7. *Fringe Benefit Deductions.* Are expenses for medical reimbursement plans, group term life insurance, and accident and health insurance plans fully deductible against business income?
8. *Loans.* On loans from the owners, will the business be able to deduct interest against income from all sources? Do the loans increase the tax basis or the amount at risk on the part of the lender-owners in order to provide tax advantages?
9. *Leases.* Will rental payments on property leased from owners of the business be deductible against business income from all sources?

Can the owners take accelerated depreciation deductions on leased property?

10. *Liquidation.* Will there be a double layer of taxes on gains upon liquidation, one layer at the level of the business itself and another at the owner's level?

11. *Passive Losses.* Can passive losses be deducted in the year they are incurred and against active or portfolio income as well as against passive income.

12. *Alternative Minimum Tax.* Is the tax position of the business clouded by the book income preference on corporations and other factors relating to the alternative minimum tax?

Sole Proprietorship

A *sole proprietor* is a person who independently conducts an unincorporated business for profit. The proprietorship is created at will without legal documentation. For this reason alone it is clearly the easiest and cheapest way to start and run a business, and it may be the best way for some entrepreneurs to get started. Ordinarily, all an entrepreneur needs to begin operating as a sole proprietor is compliance with local assumed-name and licensing statutes. Since the enterprise has no legal identity apart from its owner, centralized management can be absolute. There are no directors, no officers and, indeed, no co-owners to impede free-swinging decisionmaking.

Sometimes the price of all this independence can be surprisingly high. The entrepreneur will need to assess the following four hidden costs.

1. A proprietorship leaves the entrepreneur exposed to unlimited personal liability. The business is the entrepreneur's alter ego, and judgments entered against it are his to pay. Of course, the entrepreneur can insure himself against a multitude of hazards, but some risks are wholly uninsurable, and liability for debts is boundless.

2. Since a proprietorship is nothing more than its owner, it dies with him, leaving its assets less its liabilities to his heirs. The prospect of the owner's death or incapacity can cloud dealings with would-be creditors, customers, and employees.

3. Proprietors cannot take full advantage of many of the deductible fringes enjoyed by corporate shareholder-employees.

4. In general, tax planning opportunities are minimal. Inasmuch as the law does not recognize a proprietorship as a distinct entity, the proprietor is taxed on his total business income, whether or not that income is drawn on for personal use. And taxed income may not be controlled by engineering compensation to the owner. Moreover, a parade of tax deductions are lost to the proprietorship, including the amortization of organizational expenses and the business deduction of passive losses from investments, both of which, by contrast, can create savings for a C corporation.

Partnership

The *general partnership* may offer the entrepreneur greater latitude in business planning. An association of two or more persons to conduct a business for profit as co-owners, the partnership is a legally recognized entity. As such, it offers its owners flexibility in sharing operating responsibilities and decision-making authority. Where partners neglect to negotiate and resolve these issues up front, the Uniform Partnership Act will presume equality in both rights and obligations.

The partnership form can offer great tax opportunities to its owners. The business is a tax reporter, but not a taxpayer. Every year it files an informational return with the IRS, spelling out each partner's proportionate share of profits, gains, losses, deductions, and credits. Each partner then treats those items as if they were realized or incurred by him directly. The big tax advantage is the partnership's limited ability to allocate income and expense items among the owners to achieve the best overall tax result.

In negotiating allocations, note that a partner's share of income is taxed to him even if he does not receive it. Any income retained by the partnership merely increases a partner's tax basis in his partnership interest, reducing his taxable gain on its ultimate sale. A partner's share of losses (including capital losses) is personally deductible, but he may not deduct more than the adjusted basis (before reduction by any current year losses) of his partnership interest at the end of the partnership year in which the loss is incurred. This adjusted basis is the capital contribution, or the original purchase price, of the partnership interest (less any withdrawals) plus accumulated tax earnings that have not been withdrawn.

Another tax plus is the partner's privilege to deal with the enterprise as a separate legal entity. The partner can lease or sell property or loan money to the partnership, all with controllable tax consequences.

Even with all these benefits, the general partnership is subject to the following three criticisms:

1. Like the proprietor, the partner is open to unlimited personal liability and, still worse, is liable for the business acts and omissions of his copartners.
2. Any partner can contractually bind the enterprise, since each is its agent. Without a clear-cut agreement, lines of authority can blur, and management by committee can swiftly become no management at all.
3. Under the Uniform Partnership Act, when the partnership agreement does not otherwise provide, a partnership is subject to dissolution at the death or withdrawal of any partner. A new partner can be admitted only with the consent of all the existing partners. Although the termination and admission rules can be varied to some extent by the terms of a partnership agreement, it is still not unusual for a partnership to be subject to an inadvertent termination under the tax laws or to encounter difficulties in transferring interests. The result may be that a partnership looks fragile to potential backers and employees.

To mitigate these defects, new partnership forms have evolved:

- The *joint venture* is simply a short-term general partnership created for a limited purpose. Since the venture ends at the conclusion of a specific project, issues of continuity of life and free transferability become moot.
- The *limited partnership* historically is the entity of choice for real estate investors, and now is a popular device for tax-efficiently shifting a venture's future appreciation to an entrepreneur's children (see Income-Shifting Techniques in Chapter 17). One or more general partners manage the business and remain personally liable for its debts. The other partners are limited in liability to the extent of their investments. They have no rights in management and may transfer their interests (as provided by contract) without dissolving the partnership. Deductible partnership losses are allocated among the general and limited partners in ways designed to maximize offsets against taxable income from the partnership. A limited partnership is formed when a Certificate of Limited Partnership is filed with the appropriate state office, generally the Secretary of State (or Department of Corporations).

- The *family partnership*, like the limited partnership, is a vehicle for splitting income among family members to use up zero tax brackets and gain other tax advantages. A high-earnings taxpayer gives a partnership interest in his business, if capital (and not service) is a material income-producing factor, and pays the applicable gift tax. Future income is allocated between the donor (the entrepreneur) and donee (his family member), allowing reasonable compensation for services rendered to the partnership by the donor, and a lower overall tax liability is possible. However, losses must also be allocated to the donee, creating a possible tax detriment. The partnership may not be recognized for tax purposes if the donor (1) has too much control over the distribution of income or assets needed in the business or the sale of a donee's interest; (2) exercises excessive managerial decision making; or (3) does not treat the donee as a partner, either operationally or in business relations with the public. Moreover, the compression of tax rate brackets and the "kiddie tax" on minors under age 14 have reduced or nullified the family partnership advantages in many cases. Further, if the donee of a family partnership interest is a minor, the minor must be competent to manage his or her own affairs and be recognized as a partner for tax purposes, and the interest must be held by an adult trustee or guardian, who can be the donor, acting for the sole benefit of the child.

The partnership relationship is complex. The entrepreneur should be encouraged not to back away from the controversies that will invariably arise. Instead, he should opt for candor. He must seek out the hot issues and bargain for his best position *before* he gets into business. He will have gained all that is rightfully his, with honor and without the pain of friction among partners. The following issues are worth resolving and reducing to contract form:

- *Partnership's Name.*   There may be legal restrictions that limit the entrepreneur's choice, and he needs to steer clear of any name that is deceptively similar to that of an existing business.
- *Nature of the Business.*   The entrepreneur needs to identify and avoid any conflict in goals. Since a general partnership obligates him for the business acts and omissions of his copartners, it is wise to limit the scope of the partnership's business activities by consent.
- *Duration of the Partnership.*   A partnership can end on a predetermined date, or it can last indefinitely. Either way, a partner might withdraw from the enterprise at any time, without notice, and even in

violation of contract. The entrepreneur should specify a fair liquidated-damages amount to which he would be entitled upon a partner's premature exit.

- *Contributions.* The partners decide who will contribute what and when. They may allocate the income from the partnership's eventual sale of a contributed asset to compensate for any difference between its tax basis to the partnership (carried over from the contributing partner) and its fair market value at the time of contribution. Such an arrangement avoids favoring partners who contribute appreciated property.

- *Sales, Loans, and Leases.* To avoid disparities between tax basis and fair market value, any of the partners can sell their assets to the partnership at their fair market value and individually realize taxable gains and losses. Or the partner can lend money to the partnership, which can then buy equivalent assets elsewhere; the partner will realize interest income, and the interest payments are deductible by the partnership. A third option is that the partners can consider leasing property to the partnership; the partnership can deduct the rent payments, and the partners' lease income may be reduced by deductible depreciation.

- *Distributions and Withdrawals.* Unless all the partners agree otherwise, no partner will be entitled to a guaranteed salary from the partnership. Each will be taxed solely on his allocable share of profits less his allocable share of losses, whether or not the difference is actually distributed to him. The partners should spell out the profit-and-loss split in detail, as well as any rights to distributions. Beyond living expenses and personal tax liabilities, they may want to limit both income distributions and capital withdrawals and let the partnership use its money to grow.

- *Partners' Rights and Duties.* Remember that each partner is legally liable for the acts of the partnership. Each partner has a right to know what the partnership is doing and an obligation to fulfill his decision-making responsibilities. The partners should carefully delineate managerial responsibilities and set up a settlement procedure to resolve conflicts in judgment.

- *Dissolution.* The partners should set out notice requirements for dissolving the partnership and procedures for winding up the partnership's business. They should agree about the distribution of assets and the payment of liabilities upon dissolution.

- *Continuity.* The admission of new partners requires the consent of all existing partners. They should agree on consent mechanics and, more important, on a "buy-sell" approach. A buy-sell agreement can be a near-perfect answer to the structural problems arising out of a partner's death. The surviving partners are assured of the right to buy a deceased partner's interest, generally with life insurance proceeds, and they retain control of management. The decedent's estate is assured of a fair price (computed by formula), one that will hold up for federal estate tax purposes (see Chapter 12).

Corporation

A *corporation* is a business structure that is legally recognized as an artificial person. The law's view that a corporation is an entity separate and apart from its owners inescapably leads to the conclusion that it is liable for its own debts and taxes. This simple thesis reaps special benefits that include the following:

Insulation from Personal Liability. A sole proprietor is liable for all his business debts, and a general partner is responsible for the claims of business creditors when partnership assets do not provide full coverage, but a shareholder's liability is limited to his investment. And, although shareholders are often called on to pledge their personal credit in borrowing business funds, trade creditors and employees with wage claims cannot reach investors' assets. Moreover, shareholders are usually shielded from all business tort liability.

More Favorable Tax Treatment. The tax features of corporations should be evaluated in the different ways set out in Tax Considerations at the beginning of this chapter. Major factors favoring the corporate form include the attractive tax treatment that applies to family gifts of stock, with income-splitting potential; to qualified employee benefit plans; and to the payment of premiums for certain insurance programs. And, although top income tax rate brackets may not be lower for corporations than for individuals, the corporation as a separate taxpayer begins paying taxes at the lowest rates. (Professional service corporations, however, are taxed at the highest-bracket rates on all income.) Profits not distributed to shareholders—up to $250,000 ($150,000 for certain personal service corporations) or even more—can be accumulated in the corporation, and passive investment losses can be offset against income from all sources. When a corporation is formed, the general rule is that no gain or loss need be recognized by either the corporation or its shareholders, even if assets with appreciation in market value are transferred to the new entity, so long as the transferors control the corporation, and the same rule enables tax-free transfers of assets to the entity after it is formed.

Continuity of Business Life.   When a proprietor dies, his business may die with him. When a partner dies or withdraws from a partnership, its business is disrupted and endangered. Yet, a corporation may be perpetual, despite the death of an owner or his sale of shares. This stability alone may be enough to keep employees feeling secure and creditors calm. What's more, the corporation offers its owners the greatest range of estate-planning possibilities (see Chapter 17).

Centralized Management.   All general partners have an equal voice in decisionmaking, and each is bound by the business acts of the others. A corporation's shareholders, on the other hand, appoint directors to set basic company policy; the directors, in turn, effect that policy through the officers they appoint. In small corporations, shareholders, directors, and officers may be the same people. In larger corporations, officers and those they supervise may be structured into their own bureaucracies, or into freewheeling task forces overlapping organizational lines to solve short-term problems. Simple or complex, the corporation is a decision-making form noteworthy for its systematic delegation of legal responsibilities. One result that is important to the entrepreneur is that liabilities will not ordinarily flow through to its owners.

Free Transferability of Interests.   The sale of a partnership interest will not ensure the purchaser's admission to the firm on equal footing with his predecessors; a change in membership requires the partners' prior approval. To convey his interest to a newcomer, a corporate investor needs only to sell his shares and deliver the certificates that represent them. He need not undermine the business or compel its dissolution.

But the entrepreneur should anticipate some problems: The securities laws may severely restrict transferability, and, even if he is legally able to sell his interest, he ought not to count on a ready market for it. Should any shareholder want out, his coshareholders are the likeliest purchasers. All the shareholders should agree in advance about the terms of any eventual buy-out and they will be sure to receive a fair price.

Where it exists, free transferability is a detriment as often as it is a benefit. If the business is heavily dependent on the rapport the principals have developed, the entrepreneur should consider a contract to restrict transfers to outsiders.

Compensation Mechanisms. A corporation's equity interests are evidenced by certificates representing shares of its stock. Different classes of stock have different rights and afford the corporation flexibility in allocating its ownership.

Common stock is the most frequently used form of equity security. The rate of return on common stock is not fixed. Instead, dividends are declared at the discretion of the corporation's board of directors and are based on the corporation's economic performance. Common stock is the most speculative form of investment, but it holds the greatest potential for returns.

Preferred stock, on the other hand, resembles a debt instrument. It carries a contractually fixed rate of return that does not fluctuate with the economic performance of the corporation. Holders of preferred stock have a claim against corporate assets superior to that of common shareholders in the event the corporation liquidates. Both common and preferred stock can be voting or nonvoting.

Since the corporation is the only type of business entity that can issue stock, it is the only way to provide Employee Stock Ownership Plans (ESOPs), Incentive Stock Options (ISOs), other stock options, stock bonus plans, stock purchase plans, stock appreciation rights, or "phantom" stock plans. Often these plans give employees strong growth incentives without necessitating immediate cash outlays (see Chapter 15).

Against the advantages, the entrepreneur also needs to consider a few detriments of the corporate form of business.

Nondeductible Dividends. If the corporation employs its shareholder-owners and pays them reasonable compensation, income tax deductions can be taken by the corporation for those payments, which in a sense can be used instead of dividends as a way to distribute corporate earnings. Thus, the rule that dividends are not deductible often has application only when it becomes necessary to liquidate the corporation—for example, if the owners can neither continue the business nor find any buyer for it. At this point, the nondeductibility rule may necessitate a double layer of taxes on the same income: once at the corporate level in the year earned, and then at the shareholder level when they receive a liquidation distribution.

Unreasonable Compensation. If family members are on the corporate payroll but do not really earn the amounts they receive as compensation, the compensation will likely be held to be unreasonable. The result will be the same as if dividends were declared in the amount equal to the excess over a reasonable amount of compensation, with the shareholders receiving taxable income in that amount and also possibly being liable for gift taxes as if the family members were donees of the same amounts. Marital, annual, and lifetime exclusions can usually enable the entrepreneur to avoid gift taxes if other gifts are sufficiently limited (see Federal Tax Rules in Chapter 17).

Piercing the Corporate Veil. If a corporation's owners disregard legal formalities, a court may treat the corporation as its owners' alter ego, and the corporation's capacity to shield its owners from personal liability for business debt may be destroyed. The shareholder-owners should never manipulate their own affairs and those of the corporation without observing the legal boundaries between them. Thus, putting corporate money in an individual bank account or vice versa without documenting a loan or other shareholder transaction as though it were undertaken at arm's length can have a devastating result, as can other failures to respect the separate identity of the corporation.

Administrative Considerations. Corporations involve more complex administration than other business entities, with annual reports, shareholder and director meetings, and other requirements, depending on the applicable state corporation law.

The advantages of incorporating may be impressive, but what does it really take to incorporate? The corporate game is one of many formalities, and all of them are meaningful. They include the following steps:

- *Executing Certain Contracts.* The entrepreneur and his fellow investors sign a comprehensive subscription agreement, setting out the purpose and structure of the new corporation, their agreement to contribute specific assets, and the proposed issuance of corporate stock and notes. They also sign employment agreements, detailing the duties and rights of shareholder-employees, including their compensation. In addition, they will probably sign a buy-sell agreement, restricting the sale of shares to outsiders and obligating the corporation or its shareholders to buy the stock of a deceased shareholder on the basis of a prescribed formula, typically with life insurance proceeds (see Chapter 12).
- *Picking a State.* Normally, the state in which the business will operate is the state in which to incorporate. If the shareholders contemplate

interstate activities or a fancy equity-and-debt mix, they might consider Delaware or a state having a Delaware-type corporation law. Here are ten good reasons to pick Delaware (or a state with a similar corporation law):

1. There is no corporate income tax in Delaware for companies doing no business there, no tax on shares held by nonresidents, and no inheritance tax on nonresident shareholders.

2. The private property of shareholders is protected from liability for corporate debt (shareholders' liability is limited to their stock investment), and officers and directors may be indemnified.

3. Shareholders and directors may meet outside Delaware, or meet by conference telephone calls, video or Web conferencing, and keep corporate books and records outside the state.

4. Only one incorporator is required, and that incorporator may itself be a corporation.

5. A Delaware corporation may be perpetual, and it can operate through voting trusts and shareholder voting agreements.

6. Directors may make and alter bylaws, and they may act by unanimous written consent in lieu of formal meetings.

7. Delaware has no minimum capital requirements. A corporation may issue shares—common and preferred, even in serial classes—without par value, fully paid, and non-assessable, for consideration or at a price fixed by the directors. They may determine what portion of the consideration received goes to capital and what part to surplus. And the directors' judgment about the value of the property or services is conclusive.

8. A Delaware corporation can hold the securities of other corporations and all kinds of other property, both in Delaware and outside the state, without limit. It can also purchase its own stock and hold, sell, or transfer it.

9. All different kinds of businesses can be conducted in combination.

10. Dividends can be paid out of profits as well as out of surplus.

■ *Requesting IRS Rulings on Any Questionable Tax Aspects of the Incorporation.* Especially when one incorporates an existing business, it may be a good idea to seek a Treasury Department opinion of the transaction before it is consummated. The Internal Revenue Code's philosophy is to recognize no taxable event in the incorporation of a going concern when incorporators transfer their business assets to the new corporation, receive stock or securities in exchange, and retain control, but, in certain circumstances, the shareholders may cautiously secure a ruling to that effect.

- *Drafting the Charter—the Articles of Incorporation.* Once filed with the Secretary of State in the state of organization, the Articles of Incorporation become the corporation's governing instrument.
- *Holding the First Shareholders' Meeting.* The shareholders will elect the initial directors at the first shareholders' meeting; Shareholders meetings must be held at least annually thereafter.
- *Holding the First Directors' Meeting.* The first directors' meeting is held to elect officers; to adopt the bylaws (the rules of internal management); and to approve the corporate seal, the stock certificates (and their issuance), the transfer of property, and the opening of the corporate bank account. The directors will conduct the affairs of the corporation at frequently held meetings. Both shareholders' and directors' meetings should be recorded by minutes, or the principals will be hard-pressed to prove the meetings ever took place.
- *Issuing Stock.* The directors must okay the corporation's issuance of stock as provided in the subscription agreement. The actual sale or distribution of corporate stock is regulated by both the states and the federal government. Most initial issues will qualify for an exemption from registration (see Chapter 5). The shareholders should be sure theirs does. In any case, the twin principles of fair dealing and full disclosure must characterize any sale.

  When issuing stock, the directors should consider an election under Section 1244 of the Internal Revenue Code. The election protects the shareholders' right to an ordinary loss deduction should the stock become worthless.
- *Requesting a Corporate Taxpayer ID Number.* The corporation must request a taxpayer ID number from the IRS and file IRS Form 2553 (Election by a Small Business Corporation) by the 15th day of the third month of the corporation's tax year, if it is electing Subchapter S status (as opposed to regular, or Subchapter C status).

Subchapter S of Chapter 1 of the Internal Revenue Code allows certain small corporations to be taxed much as partnerships are, allowing them to enjoy the advantages of the corporate form without incurring income tax liability at the corporate level. During its early, lean years, a corporation may make the S election, permitting business losses to flow through to its owners and, at the same time, preserving the benefits of corporateness. Following are the five requirements for the Subchapter S election:

1. At the outset, the corporation must have no more than 75 shareholders. (A husband and wife are considered one shareholder.)
2. Individuals, estates, qualified plans, charitable organizations, or certain types of trusts must own all the stock.
3. Citizens or resident aliens must own all the stock.
4. It must be a domestic corporation and not a member of an affiliated group eligible to file a consolidated tax return.
5. The corporation must have only one class of stock, but differences in voting rights are allowed.

Subchapter S is not for everyone, but if the foregoing tests are met, some advantages may be available but possibly subject to even greater detriments. The determining factors will usually be the considerations of whether the corporation is expected to be profitable in the first years, levels of compensation to shareholder-employees, the different rates of tax on retained and distributed earnings, and the deductibility of payments for fringe benefits. The entrepreneur should be aware of the following principles:

- *Tax Rates and Brackets.* An S corporation's net income flows through to its shareholders, and the only taxes are those on the individuals, usually at slightly lower rates than those applicable to C corporations. However, while top-rate brackets may be higher for C corporations than for individuals, a C corporation as a separate tax entity can usually provide some rate reduction for the first-bracket levels of its earnings.
- *Use of Losses.* If a corporation is expected to have net losses from operations (other than from passive investments) in its first years, the S election permits those losses to pass through to shareholder-employees, who, if they have materially participated in running the business, can then deduct the losses against income from other sources. However, if the losses are passive at the corporate level or derived from passive-type investments, then the losses can be so deducted only against passive income, notwithstanding the material participation of the shareholder in the S corporation. Flow-through losses are deductible only to the extent of the shareholder's basis in stock or debt of the S corporation, and there is a special limit on the

deductibility of losses derived from expensing certain depreciable assets. And the pass-though of losses reduces the shareholder's basis in his stock, creating the potential for later taxes on any future gains. Frequently, for corporations expecting first-year losses, an S corporation election is initially advantageous, but after a year or so, a revocation of the election is indicated, either because net profits are achieved or the limits on loss deductions kick in.

- *Effect of Losses on Stock Basis.*   While the pass-through of losses in an S corporation results in a reduction of the shareholders' stock basis, that effect can be overcome if the shareholders hold their stock until death, at which point a step-up in basis to the then-current market value is permitted. In the event one or more shareholders expect to sell their stock, however, precise financial calculations will probably be necessary in order to assess the merit of the S election.

- *Fringe Benefits.*   A partner is not an employee for tax purposes and is not eligible for some of the fringes that corporate owner-employees enjoy. On the other hand, the costs of some S corporation fringes for shareholder-employees who own more than 2 percent of its stock may not be deductible, even though they would be deductible if paid by a regular (or C) corporation.

- *Loans.*   The amount of partnership loss a partner may personally deduct is generally limited to the cost of his partnership interest plus his pro rata share of partnership liabilities. His loans to the partnership increase the partner's basis for absorbing losses only by his share of the liability. In contrast, an S corporation shareholder may deduct his share of the corporate net operating loss up to the cost of his stock plus any corporate debt to him. Therefore, any valid loan from a shareholder to the business directly increases his tax basis for absorbing losses.

- *Income Recognition.*   A partner must report his share of partnership income and losses. If a partnership interest is sold before the year's end, the purchaser earns taxable income from the time of transfer. S corporation distributions, however, are taxed as dividends in the year a shareholder receives them. Any taxable income remaining in the corporation is taxed to the shareholder in his tax year within the corporation's tax year (or in the year in which the corporation's tax year ends). Such "undistributed taxable income" is shared by those shareholders who own stock on the last day of the corporation's tax year, so S corporation shareholders can redistribute income among themselves or to new owners through the use of good-faith year-end stock transfers.

- *Tax Year.* In general, neither S corporations nor partnerships can elect to use a taxable year that is different from that of their owners. C corporations that are not professional service corporations are not so restricted, providing opportunities for acceleration and deferral as to both income and expenses as between the corporate entities and shareholders.

Limited Liability Company

The newest and an enormously popular entity choice is the *limited liability company* (LLC). Like a corporation, an LLC is a legal entity that can sue and be sued; buy, sell, own, and deal with property; enter into contracts; and engage in business just as any other entity can. As a separate entity, its debts are its own and its owners, called "members," can be shielded from the debts and liabilities it incurs. Any individual or entity can be an LLC member.

An LLC is a creature of the state, as is the corporation. Articles of Organization, analogous to Articles of Incorporation, are filed with the Secretary of State in whichever state the LLC is organized. An LLC can be run directly by its members or by one or more managers, comparable to directors, they elect. Managers can be members or they can be hired hands. They can be individuals, partnerships, corporations, or even other LLCs. And when an LLC is manager-managed, no member (unless he also happens to be a manager) can bind the LLC contractually.

An Operating Agreement lays out all the particulars about governance, and it begs for negotiation. The Operating Agreement will identify all the members and what they are contributing to the company. If the LLC is to be run by a manager, it will spell out his authority as well as his compensation. It will describe how the manager is elected and how and when he may be replaced.

Unless the Articles of Organization or the Operating Agreement provides to the contrary (and they can provide just about anything), the manager is elected by a majority of the members and he will be liable to them only for reckless misconduct or gross negligence. The entrepreneur will be wise, then, to impose specific responsibilities on any manager and prescribe meaningful consequences and remedies should any of those responsibilities not be met.

If the LLC is to be member-managed, any member can bind the entity contractually, just as any general partner can bind a partnership. The difference is that no member has any personal liability for an LLC's obligations; all he stands to lose is his investment in the company. And, although every member has "apparent authority" to act on the LLC's behalf—and bind it contractually to third parties—a member who acts without the actual authority of the company is still answerable to his comembers and can be forced to make the LLC whole for his indiscretion.

As a general rule, a majority of members can authorize any act on behalf of the LLC. The exceptions, where unanimity is required, include amending the Articles of Organization or the Operating Agreement, authorizing any act that violates the Articles of Organization or the Operating Agreement, or shifting from a member-managed approach to manager-managed approach or vice versa.

The Operating Agreement mirrors a partnership agreement in that it can allocate tax attributes and cash distributions disproportionately among members. LLCs also follow the partnership rule that, when such issues are not specifically addressed in an agreement, equity will demand equality: All members will share equally.

The financial advisor should guard against the inadvertent dissolution of the client's LLC. Unless there is a written agreement to the contrary, the death, incompetence, bankruptcy, resignation, or withdrawal of any member can trigger dissolution and, with it, a taxable event to all the other members. Such an eventuality should surely be avoided through the careful drafting of the Operating Agreement.

The Operating Agreement should also deal with the attempted transfer of member interests. Unless the Operating Agreement provides otherwise, a member simply may not sell his interest unless all the other members agree. In some states, an attempted sale will result in a valid transfer, but unless all the other members accept the transferee as a replacement member within 90 days, the LLC will automatically dissolve! In other states, Nevada notably among them, an attempted transfer without immediate acquiescence by the remaining members will not force the LLC to dissolve, but it will limit the transferee to a profit interest and it will deprive him of a vote as a member. Suffice it to say that the Operating Agreement ought not to be regarded as an optional document; it should be deliberately negotiated and sensitively drafted.

From a tax perspective, the LLC can decide whether it prefers to be taxed as a corporation and foot its own taxes or to be taxed as a sole proprietorship or a partnership and pass its income along to its owner or owners who then declare the profits as part of their taxable income. The choice is made through compliance with "Check-the-Box" regulations. These regulations have almost entirely obviated the tricky requirements of the *Kintner* case, which taxed any entity as a corporation unless it failed to meet at least two of the four tests of corporateness—free transferability of interests, continuity of life, limited liability, and centralized management.

The LLC offers smaller companies enormous flexibility in ownership, in governance, and in tax planning. Following are a few of them:

- The LLC can flow tax costs through to its owners, as an S corporation does, but without any restrictions on the number of its owners.
- LLCs offer their members a broader range of choice than S corporation shareholders enjoy in allocating income and losses among themselves.
- LLCs can distribute appreciated property to their members tax-free; S corporations cannot do the same for their shareholders.
- An entrepreneur can be an active member of an LLC without running the risk of incurring personal liability, whereas a limited partner becomes a general partner, fully liable for the partnership's debts, once the partner actively participates in the management of a limited partnership.
- Since any trust can be a member of an LLC, entities can be created where ownership slowly and comfortably passes to the next generation while the founders continue to call the shots.
- Increasingly, LLCs, spurred on by institutional lenders who demand single-purpose entities, are effective vehicles to own and operate real estate.

Table 4.1 compares the various legal forms of organization available to the entrepreneur.

It should be obvious that the entrepreneur's choice of business structure ought not to be a decision by default. The selection of the optimal form for the entrepreneur's ventures should pragmatically relate, in detail and in depth, to the law's newest opportunities and the entrepreneur's income needs and tax and business objectives.

Table 4.1 Comparison of Legal Forms

Characteristic	Proprietorship	General Partnership	Limited Partnership	C Corporations	S Corporations	LLC
Ownership rules	One owner	Unlimited number of general partners allowed	Unlimited number of general and limited partners allowed	Unlimited number of shareholders allowed; no limit on stock class	Up to 75 shareholders allowed; only one class of stock allowed	Unlimited number of members allowed
Management	Sole proprietor manages the business	The general partners have equal management rights, unless they agree otherwise	The general partner manages the business, subject to any limitations of the Limited Partnership Agreement	Board of Directors has overall management responsibility, and officers have day-to-day responsibility	Board of Directors has overall management responsibility, and officers have day-to-day responsibility	The Operating Agreement sets forth how the business is to be managed; a manager can be designated to manage the business
Capital contributions	Sole proprietor contributes whatever capital is needed	The general partners typically contribute money or services to the partnership, and receive an interest in profits and losses	The general and limited partners typically contribute money or services to the limited partnership, and receive an interest in profits and losses	Shareholders purchase stock	Shareholders typically purchase stock in the corporation, but only one class of stock is allowed	The members typically contribute money or services to the LLC, and receive an interest in profits and losses

(continues)

Table 4.1 (Continued)

Characteristic	Proprietorship	General Partnership	Limited Partnership	C Corporations	S Corporations	LLC
Personal liability of the owners	Unlimited personal liability for the obligations of the business	Unlimited personal liability of the general partners for the obligations of the business	Unlimited personal liability of the general partners for the obligations of the business; limited partners generally have no personal liability	Generally, no personal liability of the shareholders for the obligations for the corporation	Generally, no personal liability of the shareholders for the obligations of the corporation	Generally, no personal liability of the members for the obligations of the business
Tax treatment	Entity not taxed, as the profits and losses are passed through to the sole proprietor	Entity not taxed as the profits and losses are passed through to the general partners	Entity not taxed, as the profits and losses are passed through to the general and limited partners	Corporation taxed on its earnings at the corporate level and the shareholders have a further tax on any dividends distributed	Entity not generally taxed, as the profits and losses are passed through to the shareholders	Entity not taxed (unless chosen to be taxed), as the profits and losses are passed through to the members
Documents required for formation	Assumed name filing	General Partnership Agreement Local filings, if partnership holds real estate	Limited Partnership Certificate Limited Partnership Agreement	Articles of Incorporation Bylaws Organizational Board resolutions Stock certificates Stock ledger	Articles of Incorporation Bylaws Organizational Board resolutions Stock certificates Stock ledger	Articles of Organization Operating Agreement

5

Private Placements

I f the entrepreneur seeks to raise money by selling securities, including common or preferred stock, LLC or partnership interests, promissory notes or other rights, she might not realize that federal law could require the registration of the offering with the U.S. Securities and Exchange Commission (SEC). The federal securities laws and companion state laws, which add another layer of regulation, are intended to protect investors. These laws limit the way securities can be offered and sold, and they generally mandate that financial statements and voluminous disclosure documents be filed with the SEC and state regulators. The initial public offering (IPO) process is both expensive and time-consuming, and where it can be safely avoided, it should be. That's where private placements come in.

Private placements, as distinguished from public offerings (see Chapter 18), are those debt or equity securities that are made available to relatively few investors and thus can qualify for an exemption from registration. Those investors might be the entrepreneur's relatives, friends, or business colleagues. They might be "angels," other passive investors who are impressed by the company's prospects. Or they might be venture capitalists (see Chapter 6) who see the possibility of a future IPO or strategic acquisition (see Chapter 16). Whoever an investor may be, the financial advisor should confirm that he shares a common exit strategy with the entrepreneur so that neither of them is ultimately disappointed about the time horizon of the investment or the mechanism by which the investor is cashed out.

Federal Exemptions

1g are federal exemptions on which the entrepreneur may rely. In each case, certain minimal filing requirements nevertheless apply.

Rule 504

Rule 504 under Regulation D of the Securities and Exchange Act of 1933 was the product of a collaborative effort by the SEC and the states' securities regulators to exempt qualifying small securities issues from registration. Privately held businesses other than investment companies may sell up to $1 million of securities over a 12-month period to any number of investors without federal registration. The issuer must file a Form D with the SEC within 15 days after the first sale of a security under the offering.

Rule 505

Under *Rule 505*, both public and private issuers other than investment companies or those that have been found to have violated specific securities laws may sell up to $5 million of securities over a 12-month period to any number of accredited investors and as many as 35 nonaccredited investors, generally without federal registration, but substantial disclosure to nonaccredited investors is required. In light of the antifraud provisions of the federal securities laws, any information required to be disclosed to nonaccredited investors should probably be disclosed to accredited investors, too. The scope and form of the disclosures vary with the size of the offering. The issuer may not engage in a general solicitation or advertisement in seeking out investors. Again, Form D must be filed with the SEC within 15 days after the first sale of securities.

To determine whether the exemptions in Rules 505 and 506 (discussed below) apply, the entrepreneur must understand the term *accredited investor*. Regulation D enumerates eight categories of accredited investors:

1. Institutional investors (e.g., banks, brokers or dealers, and insurance companies), including Employee Retirement Income Security Act (ERISA) plans with total assets in excess of $5 million
2. Private business development companies (as defined in the Investment Advisers Act of 1940)
3. Tax exempt organizations that are defined in Section 501(c)(3) of the Internal Revenue Code with total assets in excess of $5 million

4. Certain "insiders" of the issuer, such as directors, executive officers, and general partners (these persons need not meet the financial criteria set forth in items 5 and 6)
5. Any person whose individual net worth or joint net worth with that person's spouse at the time of purchase exceeds $1 million
6. A person who had an individual income in excess of $200,000 in each of the two most recent years or joint income with that person's spouse in excess of $300,000 in each of those years, and has a reasonable expectation of reaching the same income level in the current year
7. Any trust, with total assets in excess of $5 million, not formed for the specific purpose of acquiring the securities offered, whose purchase is directed by a "sophisticated person" (see the discussion of Rule 506, immediately following)
8. An entity in which all the equity owners are accredited investors

Rule 506

Rule 506 is clearly the most advantageous exemption to seek, if the issuer can qualify: Without federal registration both public and private issuers may sell any amount of securities to any number of accredited purchasers and to as many as 35 nonaccredited but sophisticated purchasers.

And what does "sophisticated" mean? Each purchaser who is not an accredited investor either alone (or with his purchaser representative) must have such knowledge and experience in financial and business matters that she is capable of evaluating the merits and risks of the prospective investment, or the issuer reasonably believes immediately prior to making any sale that such purchaser comes within the description. To determine whether a prospective investor is accredited or sophisticated, legal counsel should require the completion of a questionnaire that the issuer should retain as evidence of compliance. As in the case of a Rule 505 offering, substantial disclosures need to be made to nonaccredited investors and should prudently be made to all investors. Once again, Form D must be filed with the SEC within 15 days after the first sale of securities.

Rule 701

An exemption from federal registration is available to private companies that offer stock or stock options (see Chapter 15) to employees, directors, officers, consultants, and advisors as part of their compensation.

Intrastate Offering

Federal registration is avoidable for offerings and sales solely within the issuer's state of incorporation as long as the issuer does substantial business in that state and the securities are not later transferred outside the state. Practical compliance problems render the intrastate offering exemption less than foolproof.

Regulation A

Although exempt from registration, *Regulation A* offerings require the filing of an offering circular for sales of less than $5 million of securities. Because Regulation A only allows issuers to raise a relatively small amount of capital, yet the issuers still need to comply with substantial disclosure requirements, it is not a popular way for growing companies to raise money.

Small Corporate Offering Registration

Not technically an exemption, *Small Corporate Offering Registration* (SCOR) offers companies with $25 million or less in annual revenue a reasonable alternative to an IPO. SCOR allows for stock offerings of $1 million or less that bypass the federal bureaucracy altogether. The issuer registers by answering 50 basic questions about its finances and management, and only the states in which stock is offered get involved in administering the offering.

The entrepreneur should understand that claiming exemptions carries with it several traps for the company. They include the following:

- Merely offering securities in the right dollar amount to the right buyers is not enough to keep the entrepreneur safe. For an exemption to apply, the company needs to follow all the technical rules (only the most important of which are recited here and even those have been simplified). A careful account must be kept of just who has been solicited, whether all of them are qualified purchasers, and who has been sent a Private Placement Memorandum. Failing to meet all the requirements, however arcane they may be, can trigger the investors' right of recision (to get their money back) as well as civil and even criminal sanctions. For all these reasons, involving a competent securities lawyer in the process is indispensable.

- When an issuer and its security are exempt from federal registration requirements, they remain subject to other federal laws, most notably antifraud laws. Both the company and its officers and directors are subject to harsh penalties if, when securities are sold, the company makes an untrue statement of a *material* fact (one that should make a difference to the investor), fails to disclose material information to an investor, or provides misleading information to the investor. The prudent financial advisor will insist on a full disclosure of all the risks that matter and discourage any effort to exaggerate an investment's promise.

- Federal exemption does not guarantee state compliance. Each state has its own securities laws and regulations and, although federal exemption generally preempts any state registration requirement, state filing requirements and antifraud rules still apply.

- The financial advisor should be especially concerned about the client's inadvertently running afoul of a state's laws. Not only do some states define a security in broad and unexpected ways, even including, for example, certain contract rights, commitment letters, and profit-sharing certificates, but there may even be a question about which state's laws apply: an investor may be a resident of one state, physically present in another, and invest in a third—and any or all interested states may claim the transaction as subject to their jurisdiction.

- The issuer should be careful to avoid advertising the investment or generally soliciting would-be investors unless the offering is exempt under both federal and all applicable state laws. Otherwise, the offerings may become public and disqualified from the exemption on which the issuer is relying.

- The financial advisor should be aware that offerings can be integrated and exemptions thus jeopardized or lost. So, exempt offerings to be made less than six months apart ought to be resisted as should sales to incidental investors shortly before or after an exempt offering is undertaken. Such sale can be linked to the exempt offering by regulators, who then find that all sales, taken together, fail to meet the requirements of the exemption.

- The issuer needs to inform investors that the law imposes restrictions on their resale of exempt securities, generally for a period of two years. Failing to police resales can itself put a security's exemption at risk. A legend on the face of securities should set forth all the restrictions that apply.

Private Placement Memorandum

The best way to guarantee that the issuer is satisfying its disclosure duties and complies fully with antifraud standards is by preparing and distributing a Private Placement Memorandum to all prospective investors. Although a Private Placement Memorandum is not required in small offerings to only sophisticated investors who can fend for themselves and know the right questions to ask, using a memorandum for all investors is a good way to safeguard the issuer, should any investor later argue that all material information about the company and the offering had not been available.

The Private Placement Memorandum's content tracks that of the business plan (see Business Plan in Chapter 6) but should be sensitively drafted to allow prospective investors a fair opportunity to arrive at an informed judgment about the company, the offering, and how well the offering meets her investment objectives. A start-up should disclose the special risks of a new venture; a company raising second- or third-round capital (immediately following *seed* capital) should describe its business, its history, and its management, and it should disclose historical and projected financial data and the uses to which it intends to put the funds it raises.

For most exempt offerings (excluding those relying on Rule 504 and made only to accredited investors), the Private Placement Memorandum will include information usually found within an offering circular. Beyond that, it is a good idea to protect the issuer by disclaiming the accuracy of projections and preserving the confidentiality of the information being disseminated. Typically, the Private Placement Memorandum includes the following contents.

Checklist for Contents of a Private Placement Memorandum

1. Cover page
2. State securities legends
3. Suitability standards for investors
4. Summary of the securities offering
5. Risk factors
6. Capitalization of the company
7. Use of proceeds
8. Dilution
9. Plan of distribution
10. Selected financial data

11. Management's decision and analysis of financial condition and results of operation
12. The business of the company
13. Management and compensation
14. Certain transactions (between the company and its shareholders, officers, directors, or affiliates)
15. Principal shareholders
16. Terms of the securities offered
17. Description of capital stock of the company
18. Tax matters
19. Legal matters
20. Experts
21. Documents available for inspection
22. Financial statements
23. Projections
24. Exhibits

Once the prospective investor has reviewed the Private Placement Memorandum and elects to proceed, the investor should be asked to complete and sign a Subscription Agreement. The investor's submission of the agreement constitutes an offer to buy the securities the company is selling. And, through the subscriber's representations it contains, the agreement should insulate the company and its principals from a host of legal liabilities. The investor will warrant that she has received, read, understood, and relied on the Private Placement Memorandum in rendering her investment decision; she has the knowledge and experience necessary to evaluate the investment or has relied on others who do; that any other documents she has asked to review have been furnished by the company; and that she acknowledges that the securities are to be sold under a securities-law exemption and, as such, are not freely transferable. The agreement will then have the subscriber hold the company harmless from any liabilities it might incur should the subscriber breach any of her warranties.

The Subscription Agreement also performs another function. It should include a questionnaire that, when completed by the subscriber, evidences her qualification under the exemption on which the company is relying. The questionnaire is likely to elicit information about the subscriber's investment experience, sophistication, income, and net worth. With the subscriber's responses in hand, the company can establish, as it is obligated to do under law, a reasonable basis for its decision about the subscriber's suitability to invest in the exempt offering.

Venture Capital

L et's dispel a myth before we get started. Few venture capitalists are in the business of funding innovative start-ups. Although some specialize in putting money into companies at their earliest stages and others invest in acquisitions and buyouts, most provide follow-on funding for adolescent companies in industries they like.

Let's also make no mistake about it: If venture capital (VC) isn't the last resort for capital-hungry entrepreneurs, it's a close second. Banks aren't in the market because usury laws prevent them from charging an interest rate commensurate with the risks of the venture. Generally, they'll only finance hard assets, a commodity in short supply in our information-based economy. And the capital markets aren't a fertile place to seek funds either, even with the creation of new "development-stage company" securities, because operating practices and regulations designed to protect the investor effectively shut out the early-stage entrepreneur.

VC, then, fills the gap between the traditional sources of funding for innovation—government, corporations, charge cards, and home equity lines—and the friendlier banks and capital markets, which cater to the seasoned concern. The venture capitalist usually represents a company's first equity financing from an outside source other than friends or relatives.

Venture Capital Marketplace

Venture capitalists are of many stripes. Some invest in specific industries, often high-tech; others invest in any venture that meets their risk-return criteria. Most are only interested in companies located near their home bases.

Of course, there is the individual investor, the so-called "angel" or "adventure capitalist," who is more likely than anyone to fund the true start-up, an enterprise launched by a person with a viable business idea but no track record.

Then there are private VC partnerships or limited-liability companies, which themselves have attracted funds from pensions, insurance companies, and banks. They invest both their money and their managerial skills in young companies where, on average, they can expect to realize annual returns of at least 30 percent. Privately owned, independent VC firms are the largest single source of institutional equity capital.

There are also public VC funds that do the very same thing but look to the equity markets to raise money to invest. As public companies they are obliged to disclose their activities and operations, a treasure trove of data for entrepreneurs looking for just the right match among venture capitalists.

Corporate VC funds are in the same line of business as private and public funds, but are guided by a strategic mission. Some target ventures that offer some synergistic mesh with their own businesses and provide capital to prime the pump for an eventual acquisition. Others adopt the opposite strategy, seeking out diversified portfolios of totally unrelated businesses. The corporate venture fund's involvement can be a mixed blessing for the entrepreneur: a healthy source of money, infrastructure, and expertise in planning, personnel, marketing and financing, but at the expense of a traditional culture that may well clash with that of the venture.

Small Business Investment Companies (SBICs) and Specialized Small Business Investment Companies (SSBICs) are privately capitalized VC firms licensed and regulated by the Small Business Administration (SBA). To qualify for SBIC funding, the venture must meet net-worth and net-income restrictions.

Finally, more than half the states provide seed or early-stage capital to companies that can't raise it elsewhere. The states hope to profit from their investments, but they also seek to attract entrepreneurs and, with them, jobs. In most cases, states will invest only modest sums in new companies, typically between $100,000 and $500,000.

Not surprisingly, finding the right venture capitalist involves some research. Attorneys, accountants, Economic Development Centers and, Small Business Development Centers are good sources of leads. So are directories published by industry groups such as the National Venture Capitalists Association in Arlington, Virginia, *Pratt's Guide to Venture Capital Sources* (Venture Economics, Inc.), *Venture's Guide to International Venture Capital* (Venture Magazines, Inc.), *Who's Who in Venture Capital* (John Wiley & Sons), *Handbook of Business Finance & Capital Sources* (Dileep Rao), and *Venture Capital at the Crossroads* (Harvard Business School Press).

Venture capitalists are not only looking for healthy returns on their investment, they also seek to keep their risks at tolerable levels. So they generally avoid early-stage companies where technologies are unproven and market needs not yet established. They also stay away from later-stage companies, characterized by consolidations and slowing growth rates.

Their targets, then, are high-growth companies where venture capitalists are betting on management's ability to execute and where an eventual IPO provides a predictable exit strategy (see Chapter 18). The ideal entrepreneur is in a "hot" business area, delivers sales at a fast clip, is persuasive to outside investors, has a good résumé, is a team player, understands the cost of capital, and isn't offended by the typical deal structure. He also has a winning business plan.

Venture capitalists require a meticulous written description of everything they need to know about the company to make an informed investment decision. Developing a business plan is also a useful exercise for the entrepreneur, forcing him to reckon with the tough issues he faces.

Business Plan

The following is an outline of the topics a clear, carefully constructed business plan will address; the narrative presentation should be followed by detailed supporting schedules and exhibits.

- *Executive Summary.* The executive summary contains the business concept and opportunity; the company's products or services; the company's markets and potential markets; and the company's strengths and sustainable competitive advantages.
- *Description of the Business.* The description of the business contains the company's history; its identity; its goals; an analysis of its products

or services; its intellectual property; its unique competencies; the deficiencies it needs to address, and its plans to do so; its markets; and its sales and profit expectations.

- *Market Analysis.*   The market analysis covers the industry description and outlook; regulatory and economic environment; the company's competition; positioning and market share; customer identification; and alternative sales projections.

- *Market Strategy.*   The market strategy covers the size and attractiveness of the company's target market; the company's short-term and long-term dollar, unit, and market-share goals; and a specific marketing program for each product or service, including any new technologies and products that might affect the competitive environment.

- *Management Team.*   The management team description covers the company's board of directors and key managers; their credentials; their compensation; and any company plans to enhance the management team.

- *Operations.*   Operations covers the company's facilities, plant, and equipment; outsourcing and vendor relationships; and present and future capacity.

- *Financial Condition and Projections.*   Financial condition and projections contain the company's financial history; its current financial condition; its debt and equity structure; its capital needs and an analysis of how new funds would be allocated; income statements, cash flow statements and balance sheets projected for the next three years; a summary of the company's insurance policies; and any significant tax considerations.

The business plan will whet the venture capitalist's appetite—or not. If all goes well, it will become the first step in a broad and deep dialogue between the entrepreneur and the venture capitalist, each of whom may draw upon the might of outside experts and professionals who, working together, will strive to create a fair and workable relationship between the company and its new funding source.

The Venture Capitalist's Valuation Process

The venture capitalist's assessment of the company will in large measure turn on its "risk adjustment" to the company's earnings projections, which invariably will be scaled down. The venture capitalist will make judgments about all kinds of risks the company faces, for example, that the company might not have the technical skill to execute the business plan, that management might not be able to produce or market the company's products successfully, that the company may require more financing than it anticipates to bring its products to market, that the company might not be able to turn a prototype into a marketable product, or that the company's products might rapidly become obsolescent. The higher the risk the venture capitalist perceives, the higher return she will demand.

Once the venture capitalist satisfies herself about the viability and potential of the company, she will price its investment opportunity, and the haggling will begin in earnest. The venture capitalist's goal will be twofold: to agree to a low present value for the business, while providing incentives to management, and to anticipate the company's future financing needs.

The venture capitalist's starting point will be the company's likely value at the end of the investment term. (See the discussion of the way in which entrepreneurial businesses are valued at Evaluation Methods in Chapter 11.)

Suppose the venture capitalist estimates the company will be valued at $100 million in five years. With the level of risk the venture capitalist sees, she demands a 40 percent compounded annual rate of return. The company, let us assume, has requested $5 million in VC.

The venture capitalist will then discount the company's value to determine its value today. The formula is:

$$PV = FV/(1 + r)^n$$

where

PV is present value,
FV is future value,
r is the investment's required rate of return, and
n is the number of years in the investment period.

The company's present value is $100 million$/(1 + .40)^5$, or $18.6 million. So, to realize a 40 percent return on her investment, the venture capitalist will expect $5 million/$18.6 million, or 27 percent of the company's equity. Depending on the risk they perceive, venture capitalists usually look for returns over five years of 5 to 10 times the capital they invest. A return of five times one's investment represents an annual return of 37.97 percent; a return of 10 times one's investment represents an annual return of 58.49 percent.

Venture Capital Agreement

When the venture capitalist begins her due diligence, or evaluation process, she may ask for a "lock-up" agreement, preventing the entrepreneur from negotiating with any other possible funding source, typically for 60 to 90 days. Since the venture capitalist will not have committed to anything yet, the entrepreneur should seek to avoid such an agreement or at least limit its term.

The deal can take many forms, some of which are listed here, but it always insulates the venture capitalist on the downside and affords her the opportunity to enjoy upside participation as the company prospers:

- The venture capitalist's security of choice is a preferred equity position, usually convertible preferred stock (see Corporation in Chapter 4). It mimics debt, favoring the venture capitalist in the event the company fails; the venture capitalist will have a right to be made whole from the company's assets before management's common shares entitle them to anything. But the venture capitalist's interest will also convert into common stock when risk has abated and common shareholding becomes attractive.
- The VC agreement will protect the venture capitalist in other ways, too. It will probably grant the venture capitalist the right to block any major decisions, such as the timing of an IPO.
- The VC agreement will certainly include ratchets or antidilution clauses. Ratchets lower the price at which venture capitalists can convert their securities into common stock, increasing their share of equity holdings and saddling the entrepreneur with the dilutive impact of issuing cheap stock. With "full" ratchets, the price of the venture capitalist's common stock is reduced to the lowest price any share of common stock later fetches. With "weighted" ratchets, the conversion rate becomes the weighted average price of all outstanding common shares. The difference between the two can be enormous, particularly if the company issues only a few cheap shares. The entrepreneur should be counseled to carve out of the calculation any below-market shares granted to key employees or others who will improve the venture's opportunities for success.
- The venture capitalist's risk is mitigated in still another way: Venture capitalists invest in groups, diversifying their portfolios and sharing

the work. The entrepreneur is well served by a VC package that includes a number of VC firms, all endorsing the company and its prospects.

■ On the other hand, the venture capitalist will probably have reserved the right to buy more shares once the company demonstrates success, at an established, below-market price.

Employment Agreement

Although the venture capitalist will cut a tough deal, she doesn't hold all the cards. Indeed, some deal terms are negotiable and the savvy entrepreneur should know about them.

First, there is the entrepreneur's employment contract, an integral component of the financing arrangement. The venture capitalist will want to come to terms about the compensation a founder will be paid and the circumstances under which he may leave the board. Yet, the venture capitalist is buying into the company, not necessarily buying the entrepreneur, at least for the long term.

As the company grows, the venture capitalist may prefer to supplement the founders with professional managers possessing new, different, and arguably more relevant skills. Over time, the founders may be deemed expendable. If the venture capitalist is buying a controlling interest in the company or the right to control it later, the entrepreneur might want to protect his employment by negotiating a contractual term, perhaps of two to five years. Earlier termination should be only for "good cause," and that term should be defined narrowly in the employment agreement. One trap to avoid: A long-term employment agreement may keep the entrepreneur at the helm even if the company's growth has stalled or if a better opportunity has surfaced. A liquidated-damages clause, permitting the entrepreneur to buy his freedom for a specified price during the term of his employment agreement, may solve the problem.

The employment agreement should do some other things for the entrepreneur, too. It should provide for an adequate severance package, including extended health insurance benefits. It should require the company to give the entrepreneur notice if the agreement isn't to be renewed or if it's not to be renewed on the same terms. It should restrict the entrepreneur's postemployment competition only by prohibiting his solicitation of the company's customers and his enticement of its employees and not by depriving him of his right to earn a livelihood in the same industry. And, finally, it should give him an option to sell his shares back to the company at a price based on an agreed formula.

Shareholders' Agreement

The VC arrangement will also require the founding shareholders to enter into a shareholders' agreement with the venture capitalist; and that agreement, too, can benefit from some targeted negotiation. It is here, for example, where the venture capitalist's preferred equity position takes shape, and it deserves special attention. For one thing, some agreements give a venture capitalist a right to receive back not only her whole investment should the company liquidate, but also a share of any net liquidation proceeds. This kind of double-dipping can actually motivate the venture capitalist to force the company to liquidate, even though the company is healthy. And the venture capitalist may control the decision to liquidate. However the shareholders' agreement is drafted, care should be taken to ensure that the venture capitalist and the entrepreneur are both pulling for the same result, a profitable company whose survival—and the exit strategy ultimately pursued—benefit both.

One other nuance often neglected as preferred equity positions are negotiated is that mergers may be defined as liquidations, entitling the venture capitalist to a cash payout. The effect is to deprive the company of any real ability to merge, or unwittingly to grant the venture capitalist a chip she can play to her benefit, at the entrepreneur's expense, should an attractive merger opportunity ever present itself.

The shareholders' agreement should be fair. The venture capitalist is likely to require that the company's financial statements be audited by a national accounting firm; that new managers be hired in operational areas that might benefit from them; that one or more of her nominees be elected to the company's board of directors; and that certain kinds of business decisions, such as the company's merger or liquidation, will require her approval, even though she may own only a minority of the company's outstanding shares. The entrepreneur, if he will have only a minority stake, can demand the same rights for himself—to appoint a specific number of board members or to block important decisions.

The shareholders' agreement can serve still another purpose for the entrepreneur. Recognizing that venture capitalists rarely fund companies without other venture capitalists joining them, the entrepreneur should anticipate that any one of them could someday hold him hostage. If venture capitalist consent is required before an important company decision goes forward, as it inevitably will be, the entrepreneur shouldn't cut a deal that lets any single venture capitalist have a veto right. Instead, the entrepreneur should try to deal with the venture capitalists as a group and define consent as the approval of a majority of the venture capitalists.

Finally, both the shareholders' agreement and the business understanding behind it need to reflect the reality that one day the venture capitalist will need to cash in her investment, whether through an IPO or otherwise. As the company matures, new high-risk, high-return investments are likely to make more sense for the venture capitalist. At the same time, the entrepreneur can't allow the sudden withdrawal of capital to sabotage the company's business or force its growth rate to slow. Sensitively seeing to it that the company and the venture capitalist have compatible objectives is perhaps the most critical prerequisite to their coming together, and that commonality of interests should be the basis of the bargain they strike.

7

Bank Loans and Debt Alternatives

Before worrying about the mechanics of obtaining a loan, the entrepreneur should test whether or not she really needs one. Ideally, traditional debt financing should be prompted by a justified desire to build on a venture's success and to pursue its natural opportunities.

The entrepreneur may want to limit her and other investors' equity investment, now that operating results warrant doing so, by taking some money off the table. She may see a need for more working capital as her business grows. She may want to fund a new product or market expansion or the purchase of a strategically compatible and complementary business (see Chapter 16). Or she may want to refinance or recast preexisting debt because her banking relationships or prevailing interest rates permit or require it.

Characteristics of Debt

Debt is not always to be preferred over equity. Companies that are saddled with high interest costs have a tougher time making money than those that aren't: Not only do interest payments raise a venture's break-even point, but higher debt-service obligations may be an insurmountable impediment to continuing growth. Indeed, the higher the company's debt-to-equity ratio (representing its leverage), the less inclined a new creditor is to extend credit.

Debt can also tie management's hands. Owners of entrepreneurial firms are usually obliged to guarantee commercial loans personally and may be required to pledge nonbusiness assets to secure repayment. In addition, they frequently find themselves bound by restrictive covenants to limit the range of management prerogatives so that the creditor can gain comfort that the loan will be repaid on time and in full along with the interest and fees that have been negotiated.

Finally, debt is not equity. It must be paid back as and when agreed, no matter how the business or the company fares. So, debt carries with it a special kind of risk, a special kind of obligation that is not owed to pure equity investors. Yet, debt is an integral part of most balance sheets. It affords the entrepreneur extraordinary economic benefits she will never find when selling equity interests.

For one thing, the interest expense the venture incurs on its debt (but not principal repayments, of course) is tax deductible by the venture. When interest costs offset the entity's taxable income, the government is effectively subsidizing its growth by reducing its real cost of borrowing.

Interest and principal obligations are predictable and budgetable. The entrepreneur can plan for them and plan around them. Even when rates float with prime or bank reference rates, the interest rates charged banks' best customers, interest rate caps can be used to limit a borrower's interest expense.

Most important, debt holders are not business owners and do not share the wealth the entrepreneur creates. No matter how successful the business becomes, the lender will never walk away with more than the dollars he loaned and the interest he charged. Never will the lender have a claim against the equity of the business that would dilute its owner's stake.

Sources of Debt Financing

There are many sources of debt financing, each occupying its own market niche. Early on, the entrepreneur may have tapped her personal credit cards to the max, taken out a home equity line of credit or a second mortgage on her home, or borrowed from friends and family members who love and believe in her. In time, she may also consider commercial banks, finance companies, investment banks, savings and loan associations, insurance companies, pension funds, and other institutional lenders.

Each lender will have established its own lending and underwriting criteria. Some will make relatively small loans; others, large ones. Some will favor certain industries and geographic locations. Each will have its own favored types of loans, approved purposes for which credit will be extended and, of course, its own peculiar way of doing business.

A *cash-flow* lender, usually to be found at a commercial bank, is probably the most conservative of the breed. He looks at a company's historical profits to see whether it is likely to maintain the cash-flow coverage to support the loan's timely repayment and its timely payment of interest. Ironically, although the cash-flow lender is as tough as they get, his borrower is so impeccably creditworthy, she may not even require collateral. The cash-flow lender's reliance on past and consistent profitability will discourage most early-stage companies from currying his favor.

Asset-based lenders may prove to be a better fit for the entrepreneur. They are typically associated with unregulated commercial financing companies, and loan money against hard assets such as inventory, receivables, or equipment. Asset-based lenders are frequently called on to fund working capital, inventory, and asset acquisition needs. They are known for bearing more risk than their bank-based brethren and are paid higher interest rates for that privilege. For the entrepreneur whose growth has outpaced her working capital or whose operating track record is scant or spotty, the finance company that underwrites primarily against the liquidation value of collateralized assets may fit the bill.

Then there is the *secured* lender. Although he is probably housed at a commercial or regional bank, his mind set is somewhere between that of the cash-flow lender and the asset-based lender. While he is not unmindful of cash flow and profitability considerations, he may be more concerned about asset values and collateral coverage. Secured loans are deemed riskier and more expensive to administer than cash-flow loans since borrowers may not have lean balance sheets or enviable operating histories. For that reason, secured loans are usually priced higher than cash-flow loans, and they are subject to some procedural safeguards, too.

The central features of a secured loan are a borrowing-based formula and the lender's control of the company's cash. The formula may, for example, allow borrowing of up to 75 percent of the company's collectible receivables and up to 50 percent of its finished goods inventory. Payments from customers may be collected through a lockbox and used to reduce debt. Re-advances are available when the company re-quests them, but always subject to the formula. Secured loans are usually one to three years in term and provide for prepayment penalties, intended to guarantee the bank's profits should the borrower end the relationship earlier.

Finally, the *hybrid* lender offers mix-and-match financing opportuni-ties. He will cut a deal with the borrower for virtually any combination of secured debt, unsecured debt, revolving term debt, and even equity financing. Hybrid lenders understand cash flows, know how to under-write, and earn fixed, variable, and sometimes profit-tied compensation for each financing component they provide or deliver.

Creditworthiness

Whoever the lender may be, he will concern himself with the so-called Six Cs of Credit, the general underwriting criteria that test the entrepre-neur's eligibility for a loan. The Six Cs of Credit are:

1. *Character.*   Is the borrower trustworthy? What is her personal and business credit history? What do her suppliers say about her? How long has she been in business? What is her standing in the community? These questions will be answered by the entrepre-neur's business plan and the personal and business references she furnishes.

2. *Capability to Manage the Business.*   Does the entrepreneur know what she is doing? What are her education, her professional back-ground and her previous business experiences? How successful has she been as a business owner? An entrepreneur with limited experience improves her odds of obtaining a loan if she is a fran-chisee of an established business or if she is associated with a more seasoned manager.

3. *Capacity.*   How will the loan proceeds be used? How will they be repaid? How soon can the business be reasonably expected to generate positive cash flow? How soon will it show a profit? How large will that profit be? Will profits be lasting? Will assets be financed by debt or purchased with equity? The answers will come from the entrepreneur's and the company's financial state-ments and tax returns.

4. *Collateral.* If all else fails, what other sources of repayment are available? The company's projected cash flow and a schedule of its and the entrepreneur's assets will answer the question.

5. *Context of the Business.* Which market condition, economic factors, employee or supply problems, or legal concerns might sabotage the business's strategy? The entrepreneur who introduces a new product or service for which there is obviously a demand is more favorably viewed by a lender. So is one with a sustainable competitive advantage, one who operates within a market composed of small independent businesses, or one who runs a business in a category that has a historically low failure rate.

6. *Conditions of the Loan.* How much money is the entrepreneur seeking? What will it be used for? How long will it be needed? Lenders prefer to make loans when the items they fund are identifiable, of lasting value and, should there be a default, easily marketable.

Types of Loans

In debt financing, as elsewhere, form follows function. A loan's purpose will indicate its design and often its best source.

Term loans, for example, may be useful to fund facilities expansion or the acquisition of another business. Since they often run three to seven years, they are deemed to pose a higher risk than shorter-term loans. Accordingly, they are subject to stricter underwriting and bear higher interest rates. The lender may also protect its interests through compensating bank account balance requirements, which will beef up loan yields; restrictive covenants, limiting management compensations and perks; and annual account reviews.

A capital loan is a very common form of term loan, one used to finance the purchase of equipment. Since most entrepreneurial ventures simply cannot afford to pay for high-cost capital assets out of their cash flow, they rely heavily on capital loans.

The concept is a simple one. The bank (or insurance company or other fixed-asset lender) makes a five- to seven-year loan secured by a security interest (historically called a lien) on the equipment the company purchases. If the borrower fails to meet her obligations to the lender, the lender can repossess and sell the equipment and go after the borrower for any shortfall.

Leasing

The main purpose of obtaining a term loan is to gain the use of a fixed asset such as machinery or equipment, which, of course, the entrepreneur does not intend to sell at a profit, and therefore, doesn't really need to own. Consequently, she might entertain leasing the equipment and avoiding debt obligations. Leasing is an attractive alternative for the cash-strapped business since it offers a quicker approval process and looser credit requirements than those typical of a bank loan. Moreover, lease payments are generally tax deductible. Finally, through leasing, the entrepreneur hedges her bet that the equipment she is acquiring won't become obsolete or obsolescent sooner than she expects.

Leases are usually structured under a sale-and-leaseback arrangement or as an operating lease. Either way, the entrepreneur gains the advantage of off-balance-sheet financing, where neither the asset nor the liability is recorded on the company's balance sheet.

A third choice, although a less common one, is the capital lease, where the asset's ownership is actually transferred to the company, the lease is noncancelable and other technical requirements are met. Under such circumstances, both the asset and the liability become balance sheet items.

Leasing is generally more expensive than borrowing, but may provide more leverage than the use of conventional debt, and is often an easier way to finance assets one at a time. Equipment vendors and banks both provide lease financing, but early-stage companies might find vendors more motivated and their deals less expensive than those of banks.

When leasing the entrepreneur will concern herself with many of the same issues confronting borrowers: How long a term is available? What upfront fees attach? Are monthly payments affordable? Can the lease be terminated early and, if so, at what extra cost? In addition, one extra possibility comes into play: Will the vendor allow the company to buy the equipment outright and, if so, when and on what terms? Typically, a purchase option may exist at the end of the lease term, either at fair market value or with a fixed price stated, perhaps a percentage of the original purchase price.

Working Capital Funding

Growing entrepreneurial companies may find themselves in continuing need of more equipment and more working capital. But banks, they will learn, are disinclined to offer large amounts of long-term financing with relatively long repayment terms. So, entrepreneurs in an expansionary mode may be wise to keep nonbank alternatives in mind for their evolving long-term financing needs.

Whereas long-term debt may help the venture finance major capital needs, short-term working capital alternatives, including revolving lines of credit, accounts receivables financing, and inventory financing, will bridge cash shortfalls occasioned by fast-growing sales or unanticipated expenses. A revolving line of credit allows a creditworthy company to borrow up to a set amount and pay interest on only that portion of the line that remains outstanding at any given time. An unsecured arrangement, the revolving line of credit may need to be "cleaned up," or repaid, for 30 days during a one-year period, and the line itself might mature in two years, and then, if needs dictate, converted into long-term debt. Banks typically charge interest (tied to the prime or reference rate), fees (50 to 100 basis points each year on the total amount committed), and compensating balances (5 percent to 50 percent of the loan commitment held in a non-interest-bearing account at the lending bank). Any fee or balance deficiencies will be converted to hard-dollar costs and invoiced to the company at regular intervals.

Although a line of credit may be unsecured, financing the company's accounts receivable presents another alternative to funding working capital needs, especially for the less creditworthy entrepreneurial venture. The quality of the collateral is immediately at issue: the receivables must be current, collectible, and neither concentrated in too few debtors that their creditworthiness is a major cause for concern nor too many debtors that enforcing rights against them becomes economically infeasible. As goods are shipped, a bank or finance company advances funds to the borrower based on an agreed percentage, perhaps 80 percent, of those receivables that have satisfied underwriting criteria. As receivables are liquidated by the borrower, the bank or finance company debt is paid down; as new sales are made, the borrowing base is recalculated. As one might expect, the costs of administering an accounts receivables financing program can be high and so can the interest and service charges that attach to it.

Even more expensive, but the only reasonable choice for some entrepreneurial concerns, is the *factoring* of their receivables. Here, the lender, which actually buys the company's receivables as they are, assumes the burden and all the risks of collection. Factoring allows the entrepreneur to avoid the hassle of credit management, but at a price.

There are two typical factoring patterns.

1. Maturity factoring has the financial institution pay the company an agreed sum each collection period based on credit limits that have been established for each customer. The factor charges the company interest on any paid, but uncollected amounts, as well as a commission, ranging from 0.5 percent to 1.5 percent of the factored invoice. Maturity factoring helps companies collect their receivables and guard against bad debts.
2. Old-line factoring, on the other hand, merely has the financial institution lend funds to the company before receivables have been collected. Customarily, 70 percent to 90 percent of invoice values (reflecting bad pay and slow pay accounts) are fronted at an interest cost of 1 percent to 3 percent above the prime or reference rate.

Factoring can be "with recourse," where the borrowing company guarantees any deficiencies, or "without recourse," where the factor bears the whole risk of late payment or nonpayment. Either way, factoring can be a useful tool as the company seeks to increase working capital turnover, to sidestep the risk of bad debts, and control the costs of credit and collections.

One entrepreneurial opportunity is worth noting: Receivables can be pledged to raise capital without incurring a financial-statement liability. The trick is to design the pledge as a sale. As long as a transfer (even with a guarantee) to a lender involves the company's give up of all economic benefit in the receivables, Financial Accounting Standards Board Statement Number 77 will sanction the reporting of such a pledge as a sale.

Just as receivables can be used as collateral to secure short-term working capital debt, so can inventory, especially hard commodities and nonperishable goods. Inventory financing is generally of three kinds:

1. A *blanket inventory advance* has the bank lending against inventory and possibly receivables, too. The lender claims a security interest against all the borrower's assets it deems marketable and carefully monitors transactions on at least a monthly basis.
2. *Floor planning* has the bank buying its customer's inventory and allowing the customer to hold it under a trust receipt arrangement at its own premises or a public warehouse. As assets are sold, the proceeds pay down the trust receipt the bank has issued. Again, the lender monitors inventories closely to insure that proceeds are properly applied as the company makes sales of collateralized inventory.

3. *Warehousing financing* is similar to floor planning, but requires that the collateralized goods be stored and sealed at a bonded public warehouse and the receipt is held by the lender. Although field warehousing adds a cost to the transaction, it also tends to give a bank greater comfort about its loan and may render marginal inventory items bankable.

Selecting a Banker

It is usually not a banker that the entrepreneur selects, but the bank where he works. Nevertheless, the banker's talent is tapped on the same personal basis as any other professional's. The entrepreneur has a right to rely on her banker as an expert and experienced business counselor who plays an important role in the success of virtually any venture.

Ironically, the entrepreneur may choose her bank as she would a commercial (as opposed to professional) firm to perform services, on valid criteria such as these:

- *Services and Location.*   The entrepreneur may need a bank that offers specific services, such as payroll processing or a night depository. And if a bank is geographically convenient, so much the better.
- *Size.*   The entrepreneur will want a bank big enough to fulfill her needs, now and in the future, yet not too big to take an interest in her growth.
- *Reputation.*   A bank can be a major source of business contacts, and therefore the entrepreneur will want to enjoy the benefit of her bank's good relations with others in the community and elsewhere.
- *General Lending Policy.*   Loans are a bank's foremost product. The entrepreneur will want to know that the bank's lending policy will not exclude her, and, for example, whether it extends letters of credit to small-business owners, or short- term loans on accounts receivables or warehouse receipts.

On a closer analysis, a bank must meet the same expectations the entrepreneur has for any professional. The bank's management philosophy, a philosophy manifested in its attitudes and policies, must dovetail with the entrepreneur's needs before a banker may be added to the professional team. The entrepreneur should interview a banker just as she would any professional, and satisfy herself as to the following criteria:

- *Is the banker interested in the venture?* The bank that's on the entrepreneur's side has declared itself in favor of the small business. And the banker to select is the one who is eager to grow with the venture.
- *Is the banker familiar with this type of business?* A banker's knowledge of a business can go a long way toward offsetting his natural conservatism. And his experience and insight can prove to be valuable resources for the entrepreneur.
- *Is the banker progressive?* Without question, the entrepreneur will need a bank that extends credit to people in her position at a reasonable rate of interest. If all the bank's assets are in readily liquidated securities, management is probably very conservative and tough on loans.
- *How much help is the banker willing to offer?* When a bank cannot lend the entrepreneur money, it should be able to find someone who can, such as a bank-owned SBIC (see Other Federal Opportunities in Chapter 8) or another VC source (see Venture Capital Marketplace in Chapter 6). A bank should also be willing to provide the entrepreneur with credit information on customers and suppliers. And it should want to make operating recommendations to help the business grow successfully.

Once the entrepreneur has found a banker she can count on, she should start at once to build a productive relationship. The more the banker knows and cares about the entrepreneur, the more valuable he will become as a player on the professional team. And, wearing his money-seller's hat, he will eventually be more receptive to a loan request.

The entrepreneur should visit the banker frequently and keep him fully and candidly informed about the business. The banker will be glad to receive all the hard information the entrepreneur cares to share with him—annual financials, budgets, anything that helps tell the story. The entrepreneur should demonstrate her confidence in the future, but acknowledge any business shortcomings, too. The banker, who may well know about any problems before the entrepreneur reveals them, will appreciate her honesty and astuteness. And he will welcome the opportunity to offer the advice that the entrepreneur just might need. What's more, the entrepreneur will be bolstering her banker's faith in her good character, a wise investment against the day she really needs money.

Surprisingly, bankers are very reluctant to lend money to those who urgently need it. A strong, durable relationship with one's banker can guard against an abrupt turndown.

Negotiating a Bank Loan

When an entrepreneur is after a bank loan, she should adopt the following bargaining posture:

- The image the entrepreneur projects is critically important. Since everyone loves a winner, she should come on like one. She should hide any feelings of desperation. And she should act as if there is no doubt about her eligibility for a loan: the only purpose for meeting is to agree on the loan's terms.
- The entrepreneur should back up her confidence with all the detailed data she can muster. Bankers love facts and figures, so the entrepreneur should submit recent balance sheets, profit-and-loss statements, sales and profit projections (contemplating the use of loan proceeds and their payback), and personal financials. And she should put a ribbon around the package with positive research summaries and favorable publicity.
- The entrepreneur should not hide the negatives; they'll be discovered anyway. Instead she should lay all her cards out and, as best she can, explain the missing aces.
- The entrepreneur should know what kind of loan she wants and shoot for it (see Types of Loans earlier in this chapter).
- The entrepreneur should negotiate for a loan as she would for anything else. She should ask for more than she needs so she can maintain a fallback position. And she should avoid off-the-cuff answers to hard questions. She can always defer to her financial advisor, her partner, or her board, and can, with the benefit of time to plot a course, come back with a well-conceived counterattack.
- The entrepreneur should not be blinded by the appearance of success. Getting a loan is not her purpose; getting the loan she needs with a reasonable interest rate, over a reasonable term, with only reasonable strings attached, is.

Negotiating just the right loan is something of an art. First, of course, is the question of cost—and not merely interest, where there may be little room for movement. For example, when negotiating a variable-rate loan, the prudent borrower will demand a *ceiling*, above which the rate will not go. In exchange, she may be obliged to accept a *floor*, below which the rate will not fall.

But interest doesn't tell the whole story. The costs of a loan will also be increased by points or fees charged at closing, quoted as a percentage of the total loan. Realistically, points should be amortized over the loan's life to evaluate their economic impact.

Commitment fees also increase loan costs. They are charges to keep a line of credit available to a bank customer and usually run between 0.25 and 0.50 percent of the unused portion of a credit line.

Prepayment penalties should also be considered. Once the customer strikes a deal with the bank, the bank is entitled to the profits for which it has bargained. Should the customer pay off a loan prematurely, the bank may recoup the profits it would have earned had the loan remained on the books through the agreed maturity date. Often a "yield maintenance formula" is used to compute the benefit of the bank's bargain.

Finally, *float days* add to loan costs. Float days represent the time between the day the secured or asset-based lender receives payment and the day the borrower is credited for that payment. Typically, the bank receives the borrower's funds one to three days before they are deemed received for interest calculation purposes.

Not only do incidental costs of a loan add to its burden, other contractual provision may reduce the amount of money available to the borrower, thereby squeezing her cash flow. One such provision is a compensating balance requirement. The bank's strategy is to require the borrower to keep cash on deposit in noninterest-bearing accounts as a condition of the loan. Lost interest should, of course, be regarded as additional interest expense. The borrower would be wise to negotiate a credit against any compensating balance requirements equal to the amount of any predictable float, the difference between book and balances occasioned by uncleared checks.

So, if a bank charges 11 percent interest on a loan but requires that the borrower's checking account not fall below 15 percent of the loan balance, then the company is permitted to use only 85 percent of the credit extended. The real rate of interest becomes about 13 percent: .11/(1 − compensating balance), or .11/.85 = 12.94 percent.

Lenders may also play discounted-interest games, collecting interest and finance charges up front. Doing so, however it may be sold or described, merely reduces the company's available cash on hand.

Just as bad but just as common, the bank may credit the company's receipts against its account only after some arbitrary period of time. The technique is called *check-clearing float* or *holds* and, by whatever name, slows receivable turnover and increases the company's capital costs.

Issues other than interest and related loan costs can also be very important to the entrepreneur. One such issue is the extent to which collateral needs to be pledged. Although a lender will grab all the protection it can, and having collateral in place may facilitate further borrowing, the conventional wisdom is that the borrower should only pledge that which is commercially reasonable and no more. As the loan is paid down, the collateral should be released, having served its purpose.

The entrepreneur should clearly understand that, even were she to lose her collateral, she may not be off the hook. Should a lender take control of pledged assets, both the borrower company and the entrepreneur (to the extent of any personal guarantees) will still be liable for the balance due on the loan as well as any legal fees and court costs incurred by the bank.

To the extent personal assets are pledged against a business loan, they should be specifically identified. If corporate stock is pledged, the default provisions of any collateral agreement should be carefully scrutinized to avoid the bank's claim to control over the company.

Banks usually look for personal guarantees by the owners of a privately held business, especially one that cannot boast a long history of creditworthiness. Such guarantees are required as much for psychological as for business reasons in that they demonstrate the commitment of ownership. The entrepreneur should be disabused of any notion that signing a very limited guarantee or none at all undermines her credibility. In all events guarantees should be drafted as narrowly as possible and their release should be self-executing as the company meets its obligations and achieves agreed revenue and profit targets.

The entrepreneur will also be well advised to negotiate comfortable repayment terms. Often a bank will acquiesce in an arrangement where the borrower pays interest only for a year or two and then starts to retire principal. At the same time, an effort should be made for the bank to permit prepayment of some or all of the loan without a penalty. That way, should prevailing interest rates fall, the borrower can refinance the loan with another lender or, just as likely, the same lender.

Loan documents often impose tough restrictions on future borrowing, hampering the pursuit of growth opportunities. Similarly, the bank may demand that financial ratios be maintained (see Analyzing Financial

Statements in Chapter 3). Ratios that are out of kilter do in fact signal a troubled loan, so the banker's concern is not unjustified. But thought should be given to any difficulties that might be encountered in maintaining the ratios the bank may demand. And the company should always reserve the right to correct a ratio imbalance before a loan is declared in default. Constraints on future borrowing and financial-ratio restrictions should be accepted only after careful deliberation and never merely to get the loan.

Negotiating a loan is by no means a simple matter, and boilerplate documentation rarely suffices. The entrepreneur or her financial advisor should raise any concerns about a loan's structure early on, when her bargaining power is greatest. She should fully understand the proposed loan's likely impact on the venture. It is, after all, the entrepreneur, and not the banker, who should run the business. And never should any deal term be left undocumented. Recollections may vary; bank employees may depart; and the entrepreneur's trust in the institution ought not surpass the institution's trust in the entrepreneur.

CHAPTER

8

Government Funding

The role of government in financing the entrepreneurial venture is not easily characterized. On the one hand, politicians and regulators talk a good game. They know that the growth and expansion of small businesses are largely responsible for the unprecedented strength of the U.S. economy, for the remarkable technological innovation that has buoyed the American standard of living, and for the reliable and consistent creation of private-sector jobs.

On the other hand, government is slow to act and slow to react. It is often and justifiably perceived as antibusiness, arbitrary, capricious, and bureaucratic. The entrepreneur who seeks a government loan may be discouraged and frustrated by the reality that government loans are subject to all the requirements of bank loans (see Chapter 7) with political strings attached. In fact, the government may only be willing to become a lender or guarantor of last resort after a bank has declined a loan request.

Nonetheless, government programs are the largest single source of funds made available to business for growth and expansion. Such programs are forever evolving and aren't easy to master. But, for the entrepreneurs who qualify, they are clearly worth the effort.

Federal, State, and Local Funding Sources

State and local governments may offer direct loans and even grants for fixed-asset purchases, construction, inventory, or infrastructure improvements. Business promotion and other state agencies provide direct financing assistance to small business through the Small Business Micro Loan Program, Minority and Women Business Loan Programs, Community Development Assistance Programs, and Block Grant Business Loan Programs.

State and local governments also create tax-increment financing (TIF) districts to encourage economic development: When an area is designated a TIF district, part of the property tax revenue allotted to each separate taxing body—a school or a library district, for instance—is kept constant for the long life of the TIF. And the Economic Development Administration (EDA), an arm of the U.S. Department of Commerce, supports business development with grants to state and local governments. (The National Association of State Development Agencies in Washington, D.C., is a good source of information on what any state offers.) In fact, the real action is at the federal level.

When an entrepreneur applies for a loan from a federal agency, he can expect his application to be scrutinized as a banker would scrutinize it. In both cases questions of collectability, collateral, and creditworthiness will be on the table. Where government loans differ from private loans is the political process that authorized them in the first place. Thus, the emphasis will be on the completeness of the loan application and not the character of the entrepreneur. Putting it another way, a bank's loan officer and loan committee are obliged to evaluate the people risk of every proposed loan; the government may be confined to a checklist review of the applicant's paperwork. And the paperwork is daunting, so time-consuming to prepare as to turn away more applicants than those who follow through to completion.

For the entrepreneur unwilling or unable to comply with the sometimes overwhelming documentation demands associated with SBA loans (see Small Business Administration later in this Chapter), the Low Doc loan, touted as the user-friendly SBA loan, only requires a two-page application—one page completed by the borrower and the other by the bank. Tax returns and personal financials complete the loan package. Low Doc is a great idea with a fatal flaw: It is only available for the tiniest of loans ($100,000 or less).

The political nature of government financing often subjects prospective projects to a "but for" test that is entirely foreign to the commercial lender. So, government funds might be made available to render a marginal project viable or to improve the rate or term of a bankable deal.

Politics enters into the calculation in another way, too. Shortfalls in appropriations and increasingly onerous regulations might turn the application process into an exercise in futility. Before going too far, the entrepreneur should be encouraged to test the sincerity of the government lender. If, for example, only a few loans were made under a given program the previous year when many applications were filed, then the entrepreneur might be well advised to invest his energies elsewhere.

There are seven broad categories of government financing programs. Following is a capsule description of each:

1. *Direct loans* are made to a business by a government agency that acts the way a commercial bank would. The agency's lending official considers whether the loan would meet the agency's eligibility and underwriting criteria and then invites the business owner to complete and submit a loan package for consideration by the agency's loan review committee. If funding is offered, the agency will set the terms of the loan. Direct loans are scarce and in time will probably disappear altogether. Even now they are limited to $150,000.

2. *Guaranteed* or *secured loans* are the most plentiful form of government-assisted financing. These are traditional bank loans, but with a government agency guaranteeing a portion of the debt should the borrower default. The applicant deals almost entirely with the bank, and the bank treats the applicant as it would treat any prospective borrower. Once the loan officer concludes that a loan can only be made if it is guaranteed, she will identify a government agency that might be willing to step forward, help the applicant meet the agency's requirements, and commit to a loan subject to the agency's agreement to guarantee. Guaranteed loans allow entrepreneurs to borrow money more easily than they might under a conventional banking relationship, and they allow banks to loan more to entrepreneurs than they otherwise could; for regulatory purposes, they need carry only the nonguaranteed portion of guaranteed loans on their books.

3. *Project grants* are monetary awards tied to specific projects that government agencies decide to support. In each case the grant

matches the entrepreneur's or others' investment in the project. Project grants are carefully monitored, requiring the venture to submit to audits and satisfy the conditions of the grant on a strict and continuing basis.

4. *Direct payments* are similar to project grants. They support conservation and other public-welfare projects and usually require the entrepreneur to "cost share," that is, invest a portion of the funds necessary to undertake the project.

5. *Export insurance* protects exporting companies against the peculiar risks that arise when a company sells goods to foreign buyers. The government encourages exports, and the insurance it makes available to entrepreneurs permits them to limit their economic exposure to foreign political and credit risks at an affordable cost.

6 *Equity participations* by federal agencies, relatively rare as they are, support innovation. As any private equity investor would, the agency will evaluate the quality of management and the viability of the venture before committing capital. Even then applicable regulations will probably limit government financing to a minority position.

7. *Enterprise zones* are defined neighborhoods in need of economic development where businesses are encouraged to locate. Inducements include tax abatements of various kinds, direct loans, interest-rate subsidies, and loan guarantees. In addition, participating businesses are eligible for earmarked local lending under the Community Reinvestment Act. Enterprise zone opportunities are administered by the U.S. Department of Housing and Urban Development. Several states have followed suit and offer investment capital under parallel programs; the entrepreneur should see what his state offers by contacting the state's economic development office.

Small Business Administration

The SBA is the principal source of government loans to entrepreneurs. Located within the U.S. Department of Commerce, the SBA was created in 1953 by the Small Business Act, which established the Congressional policy "that the Government should aid, counsel, assist and protect, insofar as possible, the interests of small-business concerns in order to preserve free competitive enterprise." In implementing that policy, the agency has identified three primary lending objectives:

1. To stimulate small business in depressed areas
2. To promote minority enterprise development
3. To promote the contribution of small business to economic growth and a competitive environment

For SBA purposes, a small business is an independently owned and operated enterprise that is not dominant in its field. The enterprise also needs to satisfy industry-specific size standards, generally tied to number of employees or annual receipts. In most cases, a business with 500 or more employees will not qualify as a small business eligible for SBA loans.

Even if a venture is a small business, it will not qualify for an SBA loan or loan guarantee if its purpose in borrowing money runs afoul of SBA rules. For a variety of obvious public-policy reasons, the SBA won't help fund any of the following transactions or activities, among others:

- Repaying shareholders' loans
- Paying off unsecured creditors
- Gambling or speculative enterprises, such as trading commodities futures
- Lending or investing
- Newspaper, magazine and book publishing
- Engaging in pyramid sales plans
- Pursuing a nonprofit mission
- Relocating a business to void a union labor contract

If the business is an SBA-defined small business and if the purpose of the loan it seeks doesn't violate public policy, a loan application will nevertheless be rejected if the business has assets that might reasonably be liquidated for additional capital; financing is available from a commercial lender; or collateral isn't adequate to meet the SBA's underwriting requirements.

The SBA tends to apply the same collateral and credit standards that banks use. The advantage of an SBA loan, then, is its ability to make a business loan available with more attractive terms or rates than a bank might, or to make a loan or loan guarantee when a cautious banker would not put the bank's capital at risk.

The entrepreneur, recognizing the SBA's unique view of this world, would be well advised to arm himself with the facts and figures of his business before his first meeting with the SBA or a banker likely to require an SBA loan guarantee. At a minimum, the following documentation should be carefully and fully prepared:

- A brief history of the business
- A one- or two-page summary of the business proposal, including a statement of sources and uses of funds
- A narrative description of the anticipated benefits of the loan
- A description of the collateral offered as security
- Personal financial statements for each 20 percent or more shareholder, partner, officer, member, or owner
- Résumés of the owners and key management personnel
- Balance sheets, income statements, and reconciliations of net worth for the past three years
- An aging schedule of accounts receivable and payable no more than ninety days old
- Monthly income statements and cash flow projections for at least one year
- A schedule of liabilities, setting forth for each liability the date it was incurred, its original amount, the current principal balance, its interest rate, the amount of the monthly payment due, its maturity date, and a description of any collateral that secures it

The SBA's largest loan program, almost entirely a loan guarantee program, is the "7(a) program," which takes its name from the section of the Small Business Act that established it. Under 7(a) direct loans are available only to disabled persons, veterans, and SSBICs. Otherwise, the program guarantees loans, after a borrower has been turned down by a commercial lender, for the purchase of borrower-occupied real estate and fixed assets, such as machinery and equipment, and for working capital the entrepreneur may require for expansion.

The SBA may guarantee up to 75 percent of a bank loan or as much as 80 percent of a small loan, one for $100,000 or less. The guarantee can be as much as $750,000. (Here, as elsewhere in *Advising Entrepreneurs*, the dollars and percentages are accurate when written but, of course, are subject to change.)

Subject to the applicable dollar and percentage tests, 7(a) loans can finance all the capital needs for expansions of existing businesses; start-ups can typically borrow up to 75 percent of the capital they need. SBA's 7(a) loans can be mixed and matched with other federal loans, but all told the SBA will not guarantee more than $750,000.

The interest rate applicable to 7(a) loans is tied to the prime or reference rate. By law, it may not exceed prime plus 2.75 percent, or prime plus 2.25 percent, for a loan whose term is less than seven years. The rate may be fixed or floating and, if floating, may be adjusted monthly, quarterly, semiannually, or annually. Repayments are usually monthly or quarterly over the life of the loan.

A 7(a) loan's term tracks the life of the asset whose purchase it is funding or the cash flow of the borrower. For example, fixed assets may be financed for their effective lives (usually 3 to 7 years), whereas real estate may be financed for up to 25 years. Working capital terms are usually 7 years.

It is tough to qualify for a 7(a) loan. Not only must the entrepreneur demonstrate the capacity to repay the loan, he must also offer enough collateral to make comfortable both the SBA and the bank whose loan the SBA is being asked to guarantee.

The collateral package is likely to include a general security agreement and a security interest or lien on all the assets of the business, which generally need to represent 125 percent of the amount of the loan. The entrepreneur will also be expected to guarantee the debt personally. And both the bank and the SBA will require the venture to carry enough life insurance on the entrepreneur's life, naming them as beneficiaries, to pay off the debt in full should the entrepreneur die during the term of the loan.

Whereas the 7(a) program helps entrepreneurs whose credit is at issue, the "504 program" is available to entrepreneurs who face problems relating to terms or collateral. It best fits established but expanding businesses that have strong credit and collateral but are seeking a more cost-effective strategy for fixed-asset financing.

A 504 loan requires the participation of four players: a private-sector lender who loans 50 percent of the project's costs out of nongovernment funds, a development company or the venture itself that funds a 10 percent equity stake, the SBA that commits the remaining 40 percent, and a Certified Development Corporation (CDC) that acts as agent for the loan. In the event of default, the private sector lender is a preferred creditor, entitled to acquire and liquidate all collateral assets until it is made whole. For that reason, private lenders are big boosters of the 504 program. The SBA stands behind the lender and by contract retains a claim against any remaining collateralized assets to satisfy the debtor's obligation to it as a consequence of its 40 percent share.

The 504 program is a valuable tool for the entrepreneur, but he needs to understand its unique features. For one thing, as a trade-off for investing or pledging his total net worth as collateral, the entrepreneur must demonstrate that the project to be financed will have a positive impact on the local economy; generally, at least one new job must be created for every $35,000 in debt secured by the government's 40 percent participation in the loan package. For another, 504 loans can bear two different interest rates: the private lender sets its own rate for its portion of the loan, and the SBA component carries an interest rate of 1 percent over the T-bill rate of similar maturity at the time the debentures securing the loan are sold.

Other Federal Opportunities

The federal government also makes financial support available to small businesses through other agencies. The Small Business Innovation Development Act, for example, is a cross between a loan program and a grant program. It requires that agencies including the Department of Defense, the Environmental Protection Agency, the Department of Health and Human Services, and the National Science Foundation set aside research and development funds for small businesses.

Small businesses with 500 or fewer employees can compete for Small Business Innovation Research (SBIR) contracts and grants. The process has three phases:

1. In Phase I, a participating agency will grant as much as $100,000 for a qualifying project to test its feasibility and demonstrate its scientific or technical merit.
2. In Phase II, up to $750,000 will be awarded over two years to develop the project that holds promise.
3. In Phase III, a private–public partnership will bring the innovation to market. The agency is then likely to sign a production agreement to support the research and development.

The entrepreneur who is motivated to engage in research and development (R&D) activities with government agencies might be hard-pressed to find such opportunities. There are two ways to identify them:

1. Request the SBA's office of Innovation, Research, and Technology to put the entrepreneur on its distribution list for semiannual presolicitation announcements. The SBA, not itself a participating

agency, oversees the Small Business Innovation Research Program. Through its announcements, it keeps interested parties aware of requests for proposals (RFPs) from all the agencies involved in the program.

2. Consider submitting an unsolicited R&D proposal to any participating agency. Before proceeding, the entrepreneur should be encouraged to assess the odds of a favorable reaction. The National Technical Information Service (NTIS), a government clearinghouse of technical information, is an excellent source to learn whether or not a given agency funds unsolicited proposals and, if so, of what kinds, whether or not current funding might be available, and whether or not the proposed research duplicates previously or currently authorized research.

R&D projects are also the subject of so-called Cooperative Research and Development Agreements (CRADAs), which allow businesses to work collaboratively with government labs. The public and private joint venturers share both funding and staffing obligations and the rights to any inventions or patents they develop. The typical CRADA, most often benefitting biotechs (but available for all kinds of R&D), has the government exclusively license the resulting intellectual property to the business venturer.

A final lead: The federal government can even be a source of equity capital. The vehicle is the SBIC, a private investor operating under the government's aegis.

Although a very new venture is unlikely to meet the tough underwriting criteria of SBICs, many small businesses do qualify. By law SBICs must invest only in companies whose net worth is less than $18 million and whose average after-tax earnings over the previous two years is less than $6 million. SBICs must be privately capitalized with at least $2.5 million to $5 million, and no more than 20 percent of their capital may be invested in any one small business.

What sets an SBIC apart from other VC firms is leverage. Once the SBIC has invested substantially all of its capital in small businesses, whether as an equity owner or a creditor, it is privileged to borrow money (up to three times its investments) from the U.S. Treasury at a very low interest rate and put it profitably to work in other small-business investments.

A specialized SBIC, or SSBIC, is also privately capitalized. It invests in small businesses located in economically depressed areas as well as

those owned by minorities and women. An SSBIC is eligible to participate in government-guaranteed loan programs. The qualifying entrepreneur who is on a fast track, already funded but in need of more capital,
might well consider approaching an SSBIC, but the entrepreneur should
be prepared to tell a compelling story: SSBICs expect to see their investments triple in three or four years. SBICs, SSBICs, and Minority Enterprise Small Business Investment Companies (MESBICs), which can
commit up to 30 percent of their capital to one small-business investment,
are all listed in the membership directory of the National Association of
Small Business Investment Companies.

Joint Ventures and Strategic Alliances

ne of the greatest and continuing challenges for the entrepreneur, for whom all the capital she really needs may remain just outside her grasp, is to leverage her strengths creatively, thereby gaining access to the most valuable of resources. Bigger, more established companies may see themselves as slow to react to new markets and new opportunities and may welcome alliances with nimbler entrepreneurs whose growth is hampered by financial disadvantage.

Strategic combinations can range from contractual R&D arrangements through outright acquisitions (see Chapter 16). This chapter focuses on the larger company's partial ownership of the entrepreneurial venture as a device to finance the latter's growth. Of course, money alone does not usually warrant such a concession; the business risks of a joint venture and the shared decision making it requires can rarely be justified unless both venturers are convinced that joining forces will inure to their long-term benefit and foster a shared and compelling vision.

Alliance Strategies

Many growing companies acquire or upgrade technology by forging partnerships with leading tech-based companies instead of paying cash or relying on credit, both of which are likely to be in short supply. Bartering goods or services for technology seems to work: In a recent five-year period, AT&T, to name one major company that plays the game, is said to have entered into more than 300 partnership agreements with ventures of various sizes.

A variation on the theme is *syndication*, which some believe is the ideal way to run an entrepreneurial business in a networked, information-intensive economy. The idea is to sell one's products to a large number of customers—really, co-venturers, who combine them with other compatible products and resell them. The business model is the virtual company, which assembles content or even commerce created by others and packages it for sale over the Internet.

Syndication works best with information goods and, for that reason, is perfectly compatible with the way many Internet businesses position themselves: Any number of consumers can see—and thus buy—the same information. Syndication makes sense for Internet entrepreneurs who are mixing and matching content on their sites so long as the whole has greater value to the consumer than the sum of its parts. And the number of websites that might be linked can create a vast independent distribution network for the information goods the entrepreneur markets.

A more formal relationship is a *joint venture*—simply a new entity, whether a corporation, a limited-liability company, or a partnership, created and owned by two or more unrelated businesses. Each contributes capital to the venture based on its own strengths. The more seasoned venturer may, for example, contribute cash, manufacturing processes, and a distribution network. The fledgling enterprise might contribute its patents and inventory. In such a case, the cash-strapped smaller company gains access to the money it needs to grow while the larger company provides the operational capacity both players know they need to exploit the opportunity they now share.

Such a venture holds promise when the larger company is especially interested in one specific and opportune profit center of the smaller company. The larger company is not interested in acquiring the smaller, nor is the smaller company interested in being acquired. Both see merit in effecting a joint venture around their common area of interest, and both recognize an advantage in maintaining a targeted ownership position that complements their other holdings.

Another fact pattern that invites consideration of a joint venture involves the entrepreneurial venture that has serendipitously developed a technology that can best be exploited outside its core business. Lacking the cash and marketing prowess to exploit the opportunity it now sees, the smaller venture turns to a cash-rich company whose proven distribution channels make it an attractive candidate with which the smaller venture might comfortably share both risks and rewards. Together, they launch a new company they will jointly own: The patent holder contributes its proprietary technology, and its more established co-venturer contributes cash, marketing savvy, and relationships, each as consideration for its respective equity stake.

An alternative to an operating joint venture is the larger company's minority equity investment in the smaller entrepreneurial company. Such a structure contemplates the bigger concern's ownership of less than half the common stock of the smaller concern, often coupled with convertible debentures, debentures with options or warrants, or convertible preferred stock (see Venture Capital Agreement in Chapter 6). Minority equity investments are popular when adolescent high-tech companies lack the capital they need to grow, but whose businesses as a whole are sufficiently attractive to larger companies that they are inclined to bet on management's capabilities to execute their business plans successfully.

The alliances that work best are those collaborations where the parties work together to create new value, rather that those less ambitious structures where each partner is merely looking to get something back for that which it contributes. Successful strategic-alliance partners value each other's skills. The most durable alliances tend to exhibit certain characteristics. They are:

- *Excellence.* Each partner is strong and joins forces with the other not to compensate for its shortcomings, but enthusiastically to pursue the opportunities before them.
- *Priority.* The parties are in their relationship for the long haul, and the alliance is an important component of the business strategy to which each is strongly committed.
- *Mutuality.* The parties know they need each other to meet their objectives, and each identifies in the other skill sets and assets complementary to its own.

- *Contributions.*   Each partner puts its reputation and future on the line. They share equity ownership, and are eager to invest whatever resources they can to make the venture the success they know it can be.
- *Openness.*   The partners readily exchange information and candidly resolve their inevitable conflicts, recognizing that enlightened communication is a value they need to embrace.
- *Integration.*   The partners discover innovative ways their cultures can coalesce and their people can work together more efficiently and effectively. They try to sublimate their egos for the common good.
- *Institutionalization.*   Over time the relationship is underpinned by both a formal legal status and an emotional dedication. It transcends bureaucracy, petty politics, and the personal preferences of individuals.
- *Honesty.*   The partners learn genuinely to trust one another and pull for one another. The advantage of each becomes the advantage of both.

Licensing

Sometimes the entrepreneur can avoid both the dilution of her equity ownership and the burdens of debt—yet still develop the positive cash flow she needs to grow her venture—through licensing. Under a licensing agreement, an entrepreneurial company grants to a licensee the right to manufacture its product, sell its service, or exploit its intellectual property such as a patent, trademark, or technology. The licensee pays the licensor (the entrepreneurial company) a royalty, a per-unit or percentage-of-sales cash payment or series of cash payments structured as the licensor and the licensee agree. Licenses can be exclusive, where the licensee is granted the sole right in a given territory over a stated term to manufacture the product, sell the service, or exploit the intellectual property; or they can be nonexclusive, where many licensees compete among themselves for rights they are all granted. And all licenses should restrict the licensee's use to designated purposes.

Licensing rights in one's product, service, or technology invites creativity. The licensor might request cash up front from her licensees to defray the costs of developing, prototyping, or patenting a product. Retaining the legal right to oversee production or marketing can be the key to preserving the full value of one's intellectual property and the good will it engenders. Skewing royalties toward the front end of a term can generate more cash flow when it can do the licensor more good. And the structure of a royalty stream from certain kinds of licenses warrants special attention; software licenses, for example, justify higher payments as the number of users increases.

Identifying a Strategic Partner

The first step in embarking on a strategic alliance is the entrepreneur's clear and cogent definition of her growth strategy. She should be on guard against the whims and preferences of potential co-venturers who seek to dictate the nature and scope of the relationship. The financial advisor should help the entrepreneur look at her company realistically and help her assess whether or not an alliance may help her cause, and, if so, just what kind of a combination is likely to yield the greatest net benefits for her. The entrepreneur should be encouraged to understand clearly which compromises of control, autonomy, and competition she simply ought not tolerate, and, no matter how attractive a possible alliance may appear, consistently stand by those core values. Understanding at the outset which features may reasonably be negotiated and which should remain nonnegotiable will cast the quest for the ideal co-venturer in a positive and constructive light.

Zeroing in on the right strategic partner is as much art as science. The financial advisor can be of considerable service to his client by developing categories of prospective co-venturers whose strengths may complement the venture's weaknesses. Manufacturers, suppliers, and distributors may come immediately to mind. So might competitors and even companies in ancillary businesses that might welcome the opportunity to cross-sell the client's product or service. Once the most productive categories have been identified, promising specific candidates in each category can be contacted and their general interest tested.

Concurrently, the logistics of the alliance—and the rights and obligations of its participants—should start to take shape. Early on, the financial advisor would be well advised to consider the financial and market implications of any relationship the entrepreneur entertains. Factors, including the following 15, deserve special attention before negotiations begin in earnest.

Preliminary Strategic Alliance Checklist

1. Preliminary due diligence of co-venturer
2. Financial status of co-venturer
3. Legal issues affecting co-venturer

4. Products and services of co-venturer
5. Co-venturer's markets and competition
6. Co-venturer's management
7. Co-venturer's R&D
8. Adequacy and environmental compliance of co-venturer's facilities
9. Co-venturer's manufacturing operations
10. Co-venturer's purchasing and traffic capabilities
11. Public relations issues
12. Legal form of new venture
13. Capitalization of new venture: cash, facilities, and technology
14. Products and services to be offered by new venture
15. Markets to be exploited by new venture

Working toward a Strategic Alliance Agreement

After one or more possible venture partners have been identified and vetted, the entrepreneur or her financial advisor will initiate the deliberate process of negotiating first a nonbinding letter of intent and later a definitive agreement, which successfully addresses all the relevant legal and business issues and positions of both parties for a harmonious collaboration. The shrewd negotiator will always remember that, at the end of the day, the parties will be partners in the truest sense of the word and, for that reason, each must always be considerate of the other's legitimate business interests. Those interests are likely to include the following:

- Who is to contribute what capital to the new venture, both initially and on an ongoing basis, and how is that capital to be valued? The parties may agree that their capital is contributed at fair market value (see Valuing Assets in Chapter 11), but technology and management know-how are not easily valued. Moreover, when technology whose value is greater than its tax basis is contributed, the transferor may thereby incur an income tax liability that equitably should be taken into account.
- What business plan is to be followed? Each party should perform its own financial analysis, and both together should sign off on a business plan that they can endorse. The development of the plan will require exchanges of information relating to financial and accounting matters, operations, personnel and other important issues—significant by evidencing the first substantive collaboration between the new co-venturers.

- Who is to control the venture? Managerial control need not track equity ownership. In fact, the most successful joint ventures, even those with two 50 percent owners, allow one owner the rights and responsibilities of management, generally through a management agreement. Shared control is usually impractical and in neither party's long-term best interest.

- How will the minority owner's rights be protected? The joint venture agreement will typically include blocking-rights provisions, requiring a supermajority or unanimous consent before the venture can implement the most important kinds of decisions. These may include selling the venture's major assets, incurring large capital expenses, borrowing more than the annual budget requires, or replacing key managers. The minority owner may also negotiate the right to participate in any decision about the distribution of profits.

- How will any transactions between the venture and its owners be engineered? If products are to be sold to the venture by an owner or to an owner by the venture, the co-venturers will need to establish a fair method for setting intercompany or transfer prices. They will need to agree about the allocation of overhead expenses and any other charges either of them will incur on the venture's behalf.

- How will disputes be resolved? A coordinating committee of senior managers from both companies might meet periodically, both to keep themselves informed about the progress of the venture and to work through any conflicts that might surface as the co-venturers' cultures seek to accommodate one another. Other techniques are arbitration, where an impartial third party serves as a judge and effects a binding resolution to any major dispute; and mediation, where a trusted third party facilitates a voluntary resolution that both co-venturers can comfortably accept.

- And, finally, should all else fail, how would the venture unwind? The truth is that most strategic alliances fail. That sad reality ought not dissuade an entrepreneur from pursuing a carefully conceived venture, but it does require the thoughtful financial advisor to anticipate how reverse business planning might mitigate the client's risk. The venturers will always agree that, however and whenever the relationship terminates, each should do her best to land on her feet. Damage control might require selling the venture or some of its equity to one or the other co-venturer or to an independent investor. Or, it might require liquidating the entity and selling its assets to more than one buyer. In all events, any methodology should find its way into the strategic alliance agreement when both parties are optimistic about the future and their goals are deemed entirely in synch.

The strategic alliance agreement is likely to include a clear resolution of all the following issues before the venture is launched and when the entrepreneur enjoys her greatest bargaining power.

Strategic Alliance Agreement Checklist

1. Preliminary data
   Identities of strategic alliance partners
   Business purpose and description
   Effective date of the agreement
2. Organization of the jointly owned company
   Name
   Place of business
   Location of business
   Legal form
   State of organization
3. Capitalization
   Cash initially to be contributed by each strategic alliance partner
   Additional cash to be contributed at future dates
   Equity and debt structure
   Debt to be obtained from third parties
   Guarantees to be provided by strategic alliance partners
   Transfers of technology
   Transferability of stock
4. Ownership interests
   Strategic alliance partners' respective ownership interests
   Consequences of failure to contribute capital
5. Term
   Duration of the venture
   Extensions and renewals
6. Rights and obligations
   Products to be provided by strategic alliance partners
   Facilities
   Specifications and warranties

License of technology
Confidentiality
Indemnification and hold-harmless agreement
Performance bonds
7. Management
   Authority of the stockholders
   Authority of the board of directors
   Meetings
   Retention of personnel
8. Books and records
   Inspection of record
   Annual budget
   Annual financial reports
   Selection of fiscal year
   Selection of independent accountants
   Tax returns
   Annual certification
   Reserves
9. Income and tax provisions
   Distributions
   Repayment of contribution loans
   Tax allocations
   Notices of tax audits
   Separate reporting
   Withholding
   Penalties
10. Blocking rights
   Additional capital
   Officers
   Litigation
   Commitments outside the ordinary course of business
   Disposition of major assets
   Declaration and payment of distributions
   Calls for additional capital
   Deadlock procedures
11. Restrictions on the disposition of stock
12. Adjustment of a strategic partner's equity
   By agreement
   Upon merger

13. Product liability
     Insurance
     Claims administration
14. *Force majeure*
15. Confidentiality
16. Closing
     Date, place, and deliverables
     Conditions precedent
     Certificates
     Opinions of counsel
     Necessary approvals
     Permitted delays
17. Representations
     Authority
     Standing
     No conflicts
     Lawful transfers
     Disclosures
     Survival
18. Termination
     Stated date
     By agreement
     By notice
     By bankruptcy or change in control of strategic partner
     Buyout terms
     Liquidation
     Survival of technology
     Reconveyances
     Releases
     Continuing obligations
19. Other
     Publicity
     Governing law
     Venue
     Arbitration
     Further assurances
     Legal fees and other expenses of each party borne by that party
     Integration
     Counterparts

20. Exhibits
    Definitions
    Articles of Incorporation
    Bylaws
    Identification of initial board of directors and initial management
        team
    License agreement
    Form of opinion of counsel

Part Three

Protecting the Entrepreneur and His or Her Assets

Risk Management

Every business relationship the entrepreneur enjoys and every business asset he owns will present its own special risks. Indeed, reward is a function of risk, or so it is said. But the prudent entrepreneur and his financial advisor know that risk is not to be accepted blindly or uncritically. Instead, the risks inherent in every transaction should be carefully identified and assessed. Only where the risk-reward calculus warrants should risks be assumed. Where it does not, risks should be systematically shifted to others.

Organizational and Operational Considerations

The very way in which the business is organized—and the way its entrepreneur-owner regards it—will enhance or mitigate the risks he personally takes on just by operating his business. There are several make-it-or-break-it decisions the financial advisor should police as she protects the interests of her entrepreneur client. They include the following:

- *The amount of capital contributed to the venture.* Not only is a thinly or inadequately capitalized venture likely to run into operational and financing problems, it puts its owner at greater personal risk and motivates business creditors to look behind the business entity for the satisfaction of their claims.

- *A respect for organizational formalities.*   A flimsy "corporate veil" can be pierced by a court, and the limited liability the shareholder thought was perfected can be sabotaged by neglect. If shareholder or member transactions are not adequately documented and the business is not treated as a separate legal entity, a corporation's or limited liability company's creditors can sue its shareholders or members and attack their personal assets.

- *The way documents are signed.*   Officers of corporations and managers of limited liability companies should not sign their names to letters or contracts without specifically stating the representative capacity in which they are signing. Mary Wilson, for example, should always sign as "Mary Wilson, President." Otherwise, an inference can be drawn that Mary intended to take on the burdens of the writing individually, and she may be personally saddled with its obligations.

- *The payment of withholding taxes.*   So-called responsible persons under IRS rules, usually company officers and those authorized to sign company checks, may be personally on the hook for at least the trust fund portion of Social Security (FICA) taxes. The government is disinclined to subsidize cash-strapped businesses who elect to use tax money to stay afloat.

- *The segregation of business assets.*   Commingling business funds and personal funds, even inadvertently, sets the stage for an argument that, no matter what an entity's organizational documents may read, the entity is really the owner's alter-ego, and he should be liable for its debts. The maintenance and preservation of segregated records for the business and its owners are essential to defend such a charge.

- *The signing of personal guarantees.*   A creditor's enforcement of a business owner's personal guarantee puts his nonbusiness assets— including his home and his savings—at risk. For that reason personal guarantees should be resisted. Where a creditor is not to be denied, the guarantee's term and amount should be limited.

No matter how well the entrepreneur protects himself and his venture, every business is exposed to obvious and not-so-obvious risks, risks that can cost big money and, at worst, can stymie future growth. The entrepreneur should be encouraged to guard against those bleak possibilities by taking a conservative approach to protecting himself and his business.

Developing a Risk Management Agenda

An affirmative risk-management program should be developed with the counsel of a competent insurance agent or broker, one familiar with the entrepreneur's needs and the peculiarities of the insurance marketplace. The entrepreneur should choose his agent carefully, as he would any professional, and count on her for the following services:

- A thorough insurance-oriented evaluation of the venture's present and proposed business operations
- A careful comparison of insurance alternatives
- Negotiation of contracts for coverage where the entrepreneur's needs justify a special word on his behalf
- Administrative help in the establishment of simplified procedures within the business to handle necessary insurance paperwork
- Sound advice on loss prevention
- Guidance in compliance with the Environmental Protection Act (EPA) and the Occupational Safety and Health Act (OSHA). The latter, a broad employee-protective federal statute, covers virtually all employers, except those whose health and safety standards are regulated by other laws. OSHA defines the employer's general duty to "furnish . . . a place of employment . . . free from recognized hazards that are causing or are likely to cause death or serious physical harm." A "recognized" hazard has judicially been interpreted as one that is preventable and generally known within an industry or to the public at large. While the hazard must be identifiable, it need not be obvious; airborne particles that can only be detected by delicate sensors are a recognized hazard.

  Beyond this general duty, the Occupational Safety and Health Administration, a part of the U.S. Department of Labor, has promulgated specific industry standards. These are derived from data gathered by the Bureau of Statistics and from the continuing research conducted by the National Institute of Occupational Safety and Health.
- Assistance in claims processing
- An annual review of the company's insurance program

Insurance Principles

Finding a good insurance agent is only the beginning of the entrepreneur's insurance planning. Granted, with its own jargon and its own legal rules, insurance is a bewildering concept for most laypersons, and the entrepreneur might prefer to leave insurance planning entirely to others. But sound business management demands his continuing control. With a firm grasp of a few basic principles outlined here and with appropriate financial advice, the entrepreneur's decisionmaking in insurance matters is bound to improve.

An insurance policy is simply a contract by which the insurance company or carrier undertakes the risk of paying out a dollar amount, or benefit, upon the occurrence of an unlikely event (usually a casualty). In exchange, the insured agrees to pay a fee, or premium, for the carrier's assumption of this risk. The policy describes what is covered, when, and to what extent, and the financial advisor should study it carefully. It may also set out all kinds of procedures: how to file a claim, how to cancel coverage, how to assign benefits, and even how to order more coverage.

The basic policy may be amended, or endorsed, at the outset or later on. Endorsements can be used to extend coverage to the particular risks of the business or locale. Or they can be used to exclude unnecessary or separately insured perils, thereby lowering the premium. Special policies (on boilers or plate glass, for example) allow the deletion of these risks from general coverage and thus reduce insurance costs.

Insurance policies can be specific or blanket. A specific policy identifies or schedules each item of insured property, locates it, and assigns a value to it. (Scheduling a valuable piece of equipment or an art object establishes its worth up front.) A blanket policy may offer greater flexibility in claims settlement by assigning value to insured property as a lot; a recovery limit is not set for any individual item, just for the aggregate.

A package policy insures multiple risks in a single, comprehensive contract. When similar risks are packaged and insured together, gapping and overlapping coverage can successfully be avoided, and so can disputes between carriers. On the other hand, the packaging of dissimilar risks might deprive the entrepreneur of the broader coverage individual policies would offer and will surely complicate the financial advisor's comparative analysis of competing policies.

If there are wide fluctuations in the value of the company's inventory or other insurable assets, reporting insurance may be more economical. Unlike other insurance premiums, which are usually based on the value of insured property when purchased, reporting insurance premiums and coverage can rise and fall with the venture's periodic reports of asset holdings.

The actual payout on a loss can be the actual cash value (the cost less true physical depreciation) or actual replacement cost. These standards differ dramatically, so the financial advisor should note which value the company elects in any policy she is reviewing. And she needs to spot whether an adjustment is made in instances where insured items have a far greater value than their replacement costs; blueprints, manuscripts, microfilm, and computer software are good examples.

The payout will be reduced if the entrepreneur fails to keep his part of the bargain described in a coinsurance clause (alias the average clause, the percentage-of-value clause, or the contribution clause). The coinsurance clause is used by carriers to keep insurance costs down by preventing selective underinsuring. It works like this: the insured agrees to buy coverage for, let's say, at least 80 percent of his property's value. The payout is limited by the percentage of any deficit in coverage. An insured who is obliged to maintain 80 percent (or $80,000 coverage on a $100,000 asset), but who carries only a $40,000 policy, will find his benefit cut in half at the time of loss. As property appreciates in value, the coinsurance clause calls for additional insurance purchases, so frequent reappraisals are a good idea.

A deductible—the first dollars of loss, those that become the company's expense and not the carrier's—is a big premium saver. With a deductible, the benefits the company buys can be limited to a percentage of a loss, can start at a specific dollar level, or can commence after the passage of a fixed loss-time period. A variation is the disappearing deductible, which gradually diminishes as a loss increases. For expected minilosses or really remote maxilosses, the entrepreneur might decide to opt for the largest deductible he can reasonably afford, and his insurance costs should plummet.

Insurance Strategy

The wide variety of insurance policies available to the entrepreneur attests to the staggering complexity of insurance-purchasing decisions. The financial advisor should assist her client in developing an organized method for evaluating his insurance needs, and he can successfully avoid both underinsurance and overinsurance. The following eight steps should help in the formulation of a cohesive strategy:

1. Pinpoint the company's legal liability on contracts, leases, deliveries, and all its transactions and consider covering each kind of exposure.

2. Assess nontransactional risks, too, such as any valuable artwork in the company's offices.

3. Evaluate the venture's overall susceptibility to business interruptions, whether from a fire, a machine breakdown, the loss of a key employee or supplier, or in the transportation network that supports the business.

4. Forecast the company's product liability to consumers, other users, and even nonusers. And remember that implied and express warranties (under the Uniform Commercial Code) may be ripe for insurance backup.

5. Once the financial advisor has translated all this vulnerability into a dollar projection, she should back off: only a tiny fraction of the risks a business faces is insurable. The financial advisor should help the entrepreneur sort out what he can insure from what he cannot, including the biggest risk of all, the risk of plain old mismanagement.

6. After the entrepreneur learns what is insurable, he should disregard all the inconsequential risks he really does not need to cover; insuring against predictable small losses is usually an expensive nuisance.

7. Finally, he should forget about insuring any risk he can deal with in some other way at less cost and effort. More on this cost-justification idea later, when self-insurance is considered (see Self-Insurance later in this chapter).

8. The financial advisor should not let the entrepreneur's purchase of all the coverage he needs and can afford conclude his insurance planning. Even for the insured, any loss is, at best, an inconvenience; at worst, a disaster. Loss prevention, with the guidance of a professional, is central to enlightened risk management.

Well-intentioned insurance planning will prove ineffective if the entrepreneur takes insurance at face value. Insurance companies exist to make money and, to that end, have earned a well-deserved reputation for "fine printing." With the financial advisor's guidance, an entrepreneur can guard against hearing bad news such as the following when it may be too late:

- *"You have no insurable interest."*   Unless the company would suffer a direct financial loss from the insured property's damage or destruction, the entrepreneur should not expect a payout. A few policies will even demand the company's sole and unconditional ownership before policy benefits attach. The entrepreneur should be certain to inform the carrier of his ownership interests at the time of the insurance purchase and of any changes as they occur.

- *"You breached your warranty (or representation)."* The company's application for coverage will elicit warranties, facts the applicant guarantees to be true, and representations, assertions the carrier has a right to rely on. Any warranty or material representation that proves false might result in having a policy voided retroactively. So, the entrepreneur should shun even a white lie.

- *"The policy was never formally assigned to you."* While accrued insurance proceeds are assignable without carrier permission, policies themselves cannot be assigned without the insurance company's consent. When buying insured property, the entrepreneur should make certain that contractual-assignment provisions are fully observed, or he should obtain new coverage.

- *"The insurance company is not bound."* Where a standard insurance contract and its endorsement conflict, the endorsement governs. A broker's opinion about a policy's true intent will not be binding on anybody, so if there is ambiguity, the entrepreneur should seek written clarification from the carrier. By the same token, the entrepreneur's letter to a broker, detailing changes in relevant facts or circumstances, will not constitute legal notice to the carrier unless the broker happens to be an agent of the carrier. The entrepreneur should insist on acknowledgment by the insurance company.

- *"You violated the policy."* The venture's violation of a policy term or condition will usually suspend coverage until the violation is corrected. In a few states, however, coverage will remain suspended until specifically reinstated by the insurance company. The entrepreneur should be safe; after any violation is remedied, he should ask for written confirmation that coverage has resumed.

- *"You have double coverage."* Buying a second policy on insured property requires the consent of the first carrier or endorsement for additional insurance on the first contract. Even if these requirements are met, the venture can never collect more than the insured property's value; the two carriers on the hook would each pay a pro rata share of the loss.

Property Insurance

Now let's look at the venture's property insurance needs. Property coverage insures business assets against all the risks the entrepreneur can think of, and probably then some.

The basic fire policy is usually extended to cover direct damage from smoke, wind, hail, riots, aircraft, and most explosions. But the entrepreneur should not feel too secure: only stated risks are insured. He should consider endorsements to protect against supplemental perils (such as sprinkler damage, vandalism, and malicious mischief) and climatic perils (such as earthquakes and tornadoes). And he should bear in mind that the loss of money and securities, and even the loss of business, are simply not considered in the standard fire policy.

Crime policies may be necessary to the survival of a business. Where the risk of loss by crime is exceptionally high, the entrepreneur may turn to subsidized Federal Crime Insurance. But whatever the source he should consider burglary coverage, affording protection against forced entries; theft coverage, for disappearances without evidence of forced entry; and robbery coverage, insuring against losses by force, threats, or trickery on or off company premises. The entrepreneur can supplement these external crime coverages with internal insurance protection against forgery, and fidelity bond protection against employee dishonesty. Or he can package his crime insurance in a comprehensive "dishonesty, disappearance, and destruction" policy, and he will be safeguarded against employee thefts, too.

Floater and *transit* policies cover personal property against fire and casualty. Whereas a floater insures goods wherever they may be, a transit policy covers them only from a specific point of departure to a specific point of arrival.

A word about floaters: "Salesmen's samples" are excluded from automobile insurance policies, so they should be insured separately. And goods held for others deserve bailee's customers insurance.

Remember the venture's transit insurance needs, too. Inland transit policies, including special parcel post insurance and rail transport insurance, can be limited or broad, and are often keyed to particular bill-of-lading forms. Marine transit coverage is usually sold on an all-risk, warehouse-to-warehouse basis and can be purchased at low cost by businesses complying with rigid packaging and shipping standards.

Property coverage will compensate the company only for the value of a damaged or destroyed asset. Indirect-and-consequential coverage, in all its forms, looks to the more far-reaching economic ramifications of property loss.

If the company's business property is damaged or destroyed, business interruption insurance can restore its lost profits and reimburse it for ongoing operational and recovery expenses, even for the expenses of moving to temporary quarters. And the policy can be endorsed to protect the company against so-called contingent interruptions, such as a power failure or a business interruption suffered by a major supplier.

Rent insurance covers the reduction or loss of income resulting from damage to rental property. Leasehold insurance covers the value of improvements to leased property when damage causes the cancellation of a lease.

Accounts receivable insurance covers the cost of reconstructing damaged or destroyed receivable ledgers and supporting documentation and is thus an alternative to maintaining duplicate records off-premises. It can even compensate the company for collections lost in the interim.

Credit insurance can protect the company against the contingency of customer bankruptcy. This coverage is designed to lessen the impact of an extraordinary insolvency. A high deductible would meet or exceed a reasonable allowance for usual bad debts. In the foreign marketplace, the company can buy an insolvency and political risk policy from the Foreign Credit Insurance Association or the Export-Import Bank.

Profits and commissions coverage protects the commission of a seller whose income depends on a manufacturer's ability to supply a product.

Liability Insurance

Liability insurance protects a business against the claims of others who sustain personal injury or property damage for which the company is legally responsible. Courts are continually enlarging the scope of one's legal liability to others, and damage awards relentlessly grow larger year by year. Apart from a comprehensive general liability policy, specialized policies may satisfy the company's liability needs.

Workers' compensation and occupational disease coverage, mandatory in some states, will discharge the company's liability to employees for job-related injuries or diseases, liability that is the company's even though it may not be negligent. Those employees who are permissively excluded from coverage can be protected under employer's liability insurance. Both workers' comp and employer's liability should be carefully integrated with disability insurance (to reimburse an employee's salary or part of it when workers' comp benefits do not apply) and with any disability provisions in the company's retirement plan.

No-fault auto insurance plans have redefined needs in the critical auto liability area. Such plans prescribe immediate payments to passengers in insured vehicles for lost wages and actual expenses, without regard to fault; pain-and-suffering damages are limited by statute. Where no-fault has not yet been enacted, auto liability coverage often is required by law and is always a necessity.

The company is protected if its vehicle causes an accident resulting in personal injury or property damage. Policy limits run from $10,000 to $100,000 or more for each person injured or killed, from $20,000 to $300,000 or more for the total of injuries and deaths sustained in the same accident, and $5,000 or more for property damage. Tort law may hold a business liable for auto accidents caused by its employees, even when they are driving their own vehicles, so the company should buy nonowned auto coverage and contractually bind its employees to maintain adequate coverage on their own cars.

Liability coverage is often packaged with other kinds of protection, such as (1) collision protection, which pays for damages to the company's vehicles (less a stated deductible) even if its employee is to blame; (2) comprehensive coverage, which guards against noncollision damage (including fire and theft, on a deductible or actual-cash-value basis); (3) medical payments for passengers of the company's vehicles (generally up to $10,000); and (4) uninsured motorist protection, which insures the passengers of the company's vehicles against injury caused by a driver without liability coverage.

Product liability coverage is costly, but it is indispensable to many businesses. Courts have uniformly declared that a company that manufactures or markets a product that is found to be unreasonably dangerous is responsible for injuries that result from the use of the product, even if there is no negligence involved. The manufacturer is deemed an expert, and the manufacturer, not the injured consumer, is thought to be in the position to bear the risk of accidental injury. The theory applies even to a wholesaler who sells a packaged product that passes through its warehouse unopened.

Umbrella liability coverage protects against excess claims, those over and above the limits of other liability policies, including the company's general liability policy. Intended to cover only extraordinary claims, umbrella coverage is usually written with a large deductible and may let the company purchase its other liability policies at lesser limits with smaller premiums.

Insurance Benefits for Employees

Just as some risks are conscientiously to be avoided, others are to be invited. These typically include paying some or all of the health, life, and disability insurance costs of the company's employees. Providing such employee benefits, although not generally required by law, economically enhances the company's ability to recruit and retain the workers whose continuing contributions will be indispensable to the entrepreneurial venture's success.

Health care coverage is the most common employee benefit. Except for employers in Hawaii who are obliged to pay for health insurance for virtually all their employees, and employers who are bound by union contracts, companies are not compelled to provide health care coverage for their workers, but most find it in their best interests to do so.

Health Insurance

Health care insurance policies are of several types. *Indemnity* or *reimbursement* plans pay the physician or hospital directly or reimburse the employee who fronts such costs. *Preferred provider organizations* (PPOs) are hospital-and-physician networks, often set up by the insurance companies that administer them: Although PPOs do not require employee participants to utilize network members, such members will have agreed to render medical services at a reduced fee and, for that reason, insurance companies provide incentives to employees to remain in the network. *Health maintenance organizations* (HMOs), on the other hand, require participating employees, except in emergency situations, to rely only on physicians and hospitals who have contracted to render specific services at agreed fees.

Employers who are cost-sensitive may be well advised to sign on to a program that includes managed care, one, for example that requires the employee to secure the insurance company's approval before going ahead with an expensive diagnostic procedure or that requires a second medical opinion before a nonemergency surgery is performed. A health care plan whose cost is shared by the employer and the employee and that bills the employee for a co-payment, a portion of each medical bill, will also help discourage overutilization by employees. Finally, PPO and HMO approaches are considerably less expensive than traditional indemnity policies.

The financial advisor can be of great assistance to the entrepreneur who recognizes a need to offer health coverage to his employees. Among the choices he faces are the following:

- Should the business pick up the full tab?
- If not, how should the business share premium expenses with its employees? An 80 percent–20 percent split is fairly typical.
- Should the employee's benefit start at the first dollar of medical expenses or should a deductible of, say, $500 be payable by the employee before the policy can be drawn on? Obviously, the greater the deductible, the lower the cost and, perhaps, the less the employee's reliance on the policy.
- Should the business or its employees pay the additional cost of covering employees' dependents?

Even if employees are asked to pay for the full cost of their health insurance, they will still benefit since group coverage costs less than individual coverage. However, employee perceptions should be considered as should competitive employment conditions. Given that coverage can be reasonably structured in a way that is sensitive to the company's budget, and since health insurance premiums are tax deductible for most employers, they will provide health coverage to their employees and help satisfy their legitimate concerns about available and affordable health care.

An alternative approach to fund employee health costs is the *Medical Savings Account* (MSA). Here, the employees get a tax break and, since the entrepreneur is also an employee, so does he. In fact, it works particularly well for entrepreneurs and their ventures.

MSAs are available only if employees are not covered by basic health insurance, but self-insuring for incidental doctor visits is permitted. MSAs are primarily concerned with the possibility of a medical catastrophe. The employer pays the premiums on a policy whose deductibles range from $1,500 to $2,250 for individuals and from $3,000 to $4,500 for families, and whose copayments do not exceed $3,000 for individuals and $5,500 for families. All amounts are indexed for inflation.

The employer makes a tax-deductible contribution each year for all eligible employees of up to 65 percent of the individual deductible, or 75 percent of the family deductible. The employee then uses the MSA to pay uncovered medical expenses. The difference grows tax-free for the employee until it is withdrawn, together with the earnings it has generated over the years, at retirement age.

Life Insurance

There is also a tax feature associated with employer-paid life insurance, another common employee benefit that effectively shifts an economic risk to the employer. It also does so inexpensively: Life insurance is the cheapest insurance an employer can offer employees. What's more, the employer can pay and deduct the premiums on up to $50,000 of group term or temporary life insurance for each employee. The employee receives the benefit tax-free. All that is required is that the plan not discriminate in favor of highly paid employees.

Disability Insurance

Disability insurance replaces some or all the income employees lose should they become sick or injured. This too is a reasonable way for the employer to help mitigate employees' risks and, in the bargain, earn and maintain their loyalty.

Again, a tax subsidy is available for the premium paid, but should the employee later claim a benefit, disability insurance proceeds will be taxable to him or her. Although other design choices may be considered, long-term disability insurance is most often made available to employees through a group policy.

Self-Insurance

With so much expense and sometimes so little to show for it, more and more businesses are deciding to bear the risk of certain kinds of loss internally. The concept is neither novel nor outlandish: deductibles and uninsured risks in named-peril policies always create self-insurance exposure for businesses.

Risk retention should never be a negligent default in planning. It can be a deliberate and positive way of reducing overall costs and enhancing cash flow when losses are predictable or when insurance costs are prohibitively high.

Self-insurance must be a rational program geared to the enterprise's fiscal condition, and not a simpleminded jump at front-end cost savings. Some businesses limit their self-insurance exposure to 5 percent or less of their net working capital; others set a maximum of 1 percent of average pretax earnings over the previous five years. The financial advisor can help develop a conservative risk profile for the enterprise.

In general, any good self-insurance program is a product of the kinds of risks that are retained. Small property-damage exposure, for instance, probably needs little or no formal structuring: as losses occur they are merely charged against an operating budget. If a business has the working capital and management orientation to retain major risks, it will ordinarily set up a loss reserve, either on paper or actually funded, with the premium that otherwise would be used to pay an insurer. If the retained risk is a deductible, the loss reserve amounts to the difference between the cost of coverage from the first dollar and the premium actually paid.

As a self-insurer, the company should eventually try to accumulate at least twice as much as it might lose in a single occurrence. In the meantime, it should prepare to finance its retained risk by making a one-time, start-up contribution, by slowly phasing into self-insurance until the fund can hold its own, or by arranging standby bank loans capable of a quick drawdown at current interest rates.

Although the company's reserve might be an expensive undertaking (especially since it may be ineligible for tax deductions except when losses are incurred), it can become a source of income through investment, rather than an insurance-premium drain. And loss control may well be improved: When each profit center bears the risk of its own losses, managers will diligently strengthen their safety and security precautions.

One way to start retaining risks is for the entrepreneur to opt for large-scale deductibles where straight-dollar amounts are excluded from each loss payment. The amount of retained loss can be fixed, and the balance can be insured with carriers offering claims management and loss control services.

Another way to combine self-insurance with classical policy purchases is retrospective rating. Retrospective rating is popular in general liability and in auto and workers' comp lines (where allowable by law) and is particularly useful where a business anticipates a marked improvement in its claims experience.

Retrospective rating works this way: The company pays its insurer a basic premium to approximate the cost of administering the program, including the adjustment of its claims. The company also pays an excess loss (catastrophe) premium to buy insurance on claims over a predetermined self-insurance limit. The total of actual losses for a one-year term is multiplied by a loss-conversion factor to establish the insurer's actual fee for handling claims.

Retrospective rating is one innovative way of fixing an income floor for the insurer and an expense ceiling for the insured. Risk retention, whether through retrospective rating or any of a stunning variety of other imaginative approaches, is surely not desirable for every business; legal, inspection, and administrative expenses alone will restrict some to traditional insuring. Yet, every entrepreneur should have an open mind to the dynamic opportunities of insurance. With the aid of his financial advisor, the entrepreneur should carefully relate his company's risk-management needs to the financial position and objectives of his business.

Director and Officer Liability

As the venture grows, the entrepreneur, now an officer, director, or manager of an enterprise larger than himself, is likely to become accountable to more and more stakeholders. Officers, directors, and managers are faced with ever greater duties and exposure to liability under federal and state laws and case decisions. Because of their close relationship with the venture and its decision making, such insiders increasingly find themselves named as defendants in suits alleging breach of statutory or common law duties. This may occur if the value of the company's stock declines, or if shareholders, rightly or wrongly, claim fraud or mismanagement.

Under state and federal statutes, administrative agency rules, and court decisions, corporate directors and officers must act diligently or be held responsible for their acts and omissions. In addition, dominant or controlling stockholders or groups of stockholders may occupy fiduciary relationships to the company and to the other stockholders; and their dealings with the company are also given rigorous scrutiny.

Liability may be imposed by statute on officers and directors for their failure to meet day-to-day operating requirements of the corporation. In addition to potential liability for misstatements and omissions in securities transactions under federal securities laws, legal exposure can arise from many sources:

- Laws dealing with tax withholding, minimum wages, and overtime
- Equal employment regulations
- Environmental protection laws
- Restrictions on declaring dividends
- Laws relating to improper purchase of stock in the company
- Laws concerning pension and other benefit plans
- Regulations regarding loans to company employees
- Special requirements of duties for regulated industries

This laundry list is by no means exhaustive, but it suggests the variety of responsibilities that a corporate board of directors in today's legal climate is expected to fulfill. A board is usually authorized to designate executive and other committees and to delegate powers to them, but any delegation will not transfer final responsibility away from the directors.

Although each director is responsible for learning about and reviewing major corporate actions and being sure that adequate disclosures are made, boards may meet infrequently; thus, the typical board may not effectively manage all of the business of a growing corporation. Directors may be held liable for something they did not know about if they had not personally ascertained that procedures were established to inform them of material events of the corporation, and if they had not utilized those procedures to be sure they were kept abreast of company matters.

Few executives, however well heeled, can easily face the prospect of paying vast sums out of their own pockets to disgruntled stockholders or others. For outside directors, those who are not employees of the company, the risk may be even more acute. Years ago such directors generally were paid a nominal sum for attending board meetings. Today they are expected to spend a substantial amount of time on the company's affairs (15 days a year is a common benchmark) and to prepare at length before each meeting. Their pay is correspondingly higher, but few, if any of them, would face the increased risks of personal liability for such compensation alone.

As a general statement, directors should develop at least a basic familiarity with the business of the company. If directors feel that they do not have adequate business experience to enable them to carry out their duties, they should consider resigning. When the duty to know is imposed, ignorance is considered neglect of duty on the part of the director and creates the same liability as actual knowledge and omission to act on that knowledge.

Although directors are required to investigate company affairs sufficiently so that they may competently supervise the activities of the officers to whom authority has been delegated, they are entitled to rely on the officers' expert advice unless the directors have notice or knowledge of any facts that would raise suspicion of misconduct. However, a director may be found responsible for the wrongdoing of agents of the company if the director fails to act with due diligence in their supervision.

The corporation's board is limited in practice to something less than total management. Under generally accepted interpretations, the board performs the following functions:

- It authorizes major company actions
- It determines that there are effective internal audit procedures so that the board is adequately informed of the company's financial condition
- It gives advice to management
- It reviews the performance of officers and managers, setting objectives and measuring company results against them
- It reviews the corporation's investments at regular intervals to insure that they comply with all applicable provisions of law

Directors are expected to maintain an awareness of major company affairs to consider any material adverse developments that may come to their notice, and to investigate when their knowledge and experience inform them that certain events or circumstances require further inquiry to be made. Although they are not expected to be insurers, directors are obligated to devote substantial time to the business of the corporation and must scrupulously comply with their fiduciary duties of care and loyalty to the company.

To help the client mitigate all the risks of serving as a director and officer, there are a number of actions the financial advisor may consider and then recommend, whether or not a crisis or urgent situation has arisen. These actions include:

- Determining if the state of incorporation has adopted a statute authorizing the limitation of certain types of director liability or defining the duties of a director without reference to a "duty of care" (as distinguished from his duty of loyalty, which is absolute) and if so, taking advantage of that statute.
- Reviewing existing insurance coverages and all available new or increased coverages, and weighing premium costs against expected benefits (see Insurance Strategy earlier in this chapter).
- Considering adding or strengthening indemnity (hold harmless) clauses in corporate bylaws to protect officers and directors adequately.
- Reviewing limitations on the tax deductibility of self-insured indemnity payments, remembering that insurance premiums for officer-director coverage are fully deductible.
- Reminding officers and directors that they are not allowed to profit personally from corporate business where conflicts of interest exist, to expropriate corporate opportunities, or to receive unreasonable compensation or other payments.

- Making sure officers and directors know their responsibility under federal securities laws regarding the use of inside information, the adequacy of disclosures, the offer or sale of securities, trading in the corporation's own securities, exercising due diligence, and offering to buy or sell control, and, if a securities offering is planned, analyzing closely Section 11 of the Securities Act of 1933, as well as other applicable laws, regulations, and court decisions.

Delaware's management-friendly statute allows businesses organized in that state to include a provision in their certificates of incorporation to eliminate or limit personal liability of directors to the corporation or stockholders for monetary damages caused by breach of fiduciary duty. The law provides, however, that no such charter provision can eliminate or limit a director's liability for breach of the director's duty of loyalty; for acts or omissions not in good faith or involving intentional misconduct or knowing violation of law; for willful or negligent conduct in paying dividends or repurchasing stock out of other than lawfully available funds; and for any transaction from which the director derives an improper personal benefit. In essence, the statute, and the laws of other states following Delaware's lead, permit a corporation, by a provision in its certificate of incorporation, to protect its directors from monetary liability for gross negligence.

Such statutes do not abolish the duty of care. Directors continue to owe a duty of care to their corporations when they make decisions and oversee corporate activities. This duty has special significance in remedial situations as opposed to actions for personal monetary damages. For instance, the duty of care may affect the outcome of injunction and rescission cases and of elections, proxy contest, resignations, and removal contexts.

Indemnity

Delaware and other states that have adopted Delaware's model also allow corporations to indemnify their officers and directors. The law applies to persons involved as plaintiffs or defendants in most actual or threatened litigation or an investigation by reason of their capacity as officer, director, employee, or agent of the corporation or of another corporation, trust, partnership, joint venture, or other enterprise they served at the request of the indemnifying corporation. The provision is intended to enable corporate officials to resist unjustified claims knowing that their reasonable expenses will be paid by the corporation if they prevail, and to facilitate service by competent people as corporate directors. Indemnity is not an alternative to insurance; insurance can protect directors and officers in situations to which indemnity does not extend, but indemnity can also apply more broadly than insurance in certain cases.

Delaware law and the laws of other states authorize a corporation to obtain insurance to cover the personal liability of officers, directors, employees, and agents, with the premiums to be paid by the corporation, stated, for example, in 8 Del. Code § 145(g), as follows:

> A corporation shall have power to purchase and maintain insurance on behalf of any person who is or was a director, officer, employee or agent of the corporation, or is or was serving at the request of the corporation as a director, officer, employee or agent of another corporation, partnership, joint venture, trust or other enterprise against any liability asserted against such person and incurred by such person in any such capacity, or arising out of such person's status as such, whether or not the corporation would have the power to indemnify such person against such liability under this section.

Such a provision permits a corporation to insure for potential liability regardless of whether or not the corporation might lawfully indemnify the particular indemnitee under the circumstances. Thus, judgments or amounts paid in settlement of a derivative suit can be insured, including expenses, even when a director has been held liable.

Even so, directors' and officers' policies normally exclude coverage for claims deemed undesirable under state law, deliberate wrongdoing or willful misconduct, and transactions in which the insured individual has derived a personal pecuniary benefit.

Corporations, even high-growth entrepreneurial ventures, can exercise vast powers, and focus for restricting those powers has settled on the board of directors, which is charged with the management of the inanimate corporate entity and is the primary target of major efforts to increase responsibility. Although tighter new laws do not yet require an independent audit by each director, all the members of the board, the entrepreneur surely among them, should regularly review financial statements and board proposals with a watchful idea for any potentially illegal or oppressive action.

Valuing the Entrepreneurial Venture

F ew challenges that face the entrepreneur and her financial advisor are as complex and difficult as the valuation of a business she buys or sells. And the same issues arise when a financial advisor establishes the value of a business for buy-sell (see Chapter 12) or estate planning (see Chapter 17) purposes. Various disciplines of law, economics, and accounting coalesce to yield a result that today may be the product of sophisticated computer modeling and advanced mathematics. In the end, *value* is a perception shared by buyer and seller, each of whom must make a difficult but informed business decision.

Ironically, it may not be today's value at all that attracts the parties' attention. Instead, the buyer may seek an income stream with potential for future growth. She may think it only fair to purchase the business at today's value; thus, any enhancement to that value will be due to the buyer's efforts, not the seller's. Conversely, the seller seeks to sell an opportunity and be rewarded not only for what it is, but for what it can become. Thus, the valuation method on which the purchase price is based must not only take into consideration those events that probably will occur, but also those events that may be unlikely to occur.

Several legitimate methods are available for appraising a business; yet, the value of a business to a buyer who intends to manage it as a going concern may be wholly different from its value to an individual whose interest is confined to passive investment.

The appraisal of a business is based on the facts and circumstances surrounding the particular transaction under review. The most reasonable technique to be employed with respect to one business may prove inappropriate to the acquisition of another, even though both appear to be of a similar nature. Even more frustrating to the financial advisor is the realization that the precise valuation of a business may be impossible since all the relevant facts pertaining to a specific business can seldom be secured.

Where an entrepreneurial business is to be acquired or sold, an accurate valuation is always a primary concern for both the buyer and seller. Although the financial advisor is not generally called on to determine the purchase price itself, he should be aware of the alternative valuation methods to advise a client competently as to the fairness of the purchase price.

Evaluation Methods

If it is necessary to assess the assets and liabilities of the business as a whole, or the market value of the assets to be acquired, the buyer should consider engaging the services of a professional appraiser. It should be noted that the fair market value of an asset and its income-producing capacity may not necessarily correlate. Nevertheless, where it is necessary to allocate the purchase price among the individual assets of the seller—as tax or other reasons may dictate—an appraisal of the assets, establishing the fair market value of each, may facilitate that process. The employment of a professional appraiser does not limit the financial advisor's responsibility; it remains critical that he have a basic knowledge of the techniques involved in order to advise a client effectively.

Initially, the appraiser should obtain all historical data available that are relevant to the business to be acquired, including, for example, prior years' income tax returns and balance sheets. The nature of the business will suggest the scope of written documentation the appraiser will seek to review; thus, where the business is a partnership, the appraiser should thoroughly analyze all partnership agreements. Beyond obtaining written data about the business, the appraiser may well contact some or all of the business's key personnel; they will assist in the interpretation of the written information that will have been made available.

The data obtained by the appraiser are then contrasted with data available for other businesses of similar size and nature. This enables the appraiser to evaluate the past and project the future profitability of the business. One way the appraiser can compare the data relating to the business to be acquired with other businesses of a similar size and nature is by formulating certain financial ratios (see Analyzing Financial Statements in Chapter 3). Such ratios, along with personal interviews with key personnel, are extremely helpful. Other persons dealing with the business, including customers and creditors, may also serve as valuable sources of information.

An analysis of historic income and an evaluation of business assets are the two primary ways an entrepreneurial business is valued. The historic income method is significant for purposes of ascertaining a base on which the future profitability of a business can be predicted. So, where the business to be acquired is a going concern, its income-producing capacity, rather than the value of its assets, is the key to its value. A company's historic income will not always represent its income-producing potential. Although a thorough analysis of historic income is required, certain adjustments need to be made to obtain an accurate reading on the future profitability of the company.

After the business's income-producing capacity is determined, its value is estimated by applying a multiple of the past or projected future profits of the business to be acquired. The multiplier will vary based on the character of the entity and its future potential. The multiplier is generally lower if the business is considered to be of high risk, and many entrepreneurial ventures, by their very nature, are; the multiplier is higher if a low-risk business is to be acquired. Since the character of the business will affect its income-producing capacity, projecting the future profitability of the business rests on the judgment of the individual making the evaluation.

To facilitate the valuation process, the written income history of the business should be obtained for at least five years prior to the date of the acquisition. Certain items not included in the historic income statements should also be taken into account, including the business's standing in relation to other businesses of similar size and nature. And, where sufficient evidence establishes that the profitability of the business will decrease in future years, the purchase price should be adjusted accordingly.

The historic income statements, as well as the balance sheets of the business, must be amended to reflect the true value of the entity. For example, intangible assets should be given separate consideration, so the balance sheet as adjusted will set forth a figure based on tangible net value. Further, income statements may need to be adjusted for such items as depreciation or amortization, to obtain a clearer perspective of the adjusted income of the business. Adjustments made to historic income statements and balance sheets permit a basis to be computed that will enable a comparison with the financial information available for other businesses of a similar size and nature.

As an alternative, a business may be evaluated on the adjusted book value of its assets, or their value as ascertained by an appraiser. Asset value is often used to evaluate a business that is primarily operated for investment purposes. In such a case, the operating assets of the business are evaluated independently of those assets that are not used in the operation of the business; only income derived from the operating assets is used in determining the value of the business assets.

Certain other factors must be taken into consideration when evaluating a business, including:

- The purchase price obtained on the sale of a business of a similar type and size
- The position of the business in relation to other comparable businesses
- Projections with respect to the future income potential of the business
- The form in which the acquisition is cast, with its attendant tax consequences to both the buyer and seller.

Finally, although the financial analysis of the business is an important element in determining its purchase price, the significance of negotiation should not be underestimated. If the seller desperately wants to dispose of a business, the buyer obviously has an opportunity to negotiate a lower purchase price. On the other hand, if the buyer is very eager to acquire the business, the seller gains the opportunity to obtain a higher purchase price.

Valuing Assets

Evaluation of a business that uses the asset or book value methods is usually implemented in cases where the business to be acquired is service-oriented or one that produces minimal or no income. Where determination of the purchase price is to be based on book value, certain adjustments have to be made to the figures in the books to assure accuracy.

The major drawback in adopting the book value method is that the book value of the assets will often depart from fair market value; book value is only a means for determining the cost at which the assets were acquired. Fair market value, or the income-earning potential of the assets, is rarely a function of cost.

Cash

An issue of primary concern arises where the purchaser acquires cash along with the business. A transfer of cash generally occurs in a stock acquisition. Where a large sum is involved, the purchaser should be cautioned that the business may need a significant amount of capital to maintain its operations or that it may be of a seasonal nature. In either event, the purchaser should not rely on the use of cash she acquires to effect a bootstrap acquisition, one in which the purchaser will use a portion of the business's working capital to underwrite the purchase price. Moreover, to the extent the purchaser must obtain a short-term loan to finance the acquisition, she will not be able to count on the accumulated cash to repay the loan if it constitutes working capital. If the buyer must borrow funds to obtain part of the purchase price, the accumulated cash may reduce the borrowing needs to operate the business when it is first acquired.

Where cash is included in a transaction, it is transferred at face value. If business assets include foreign currencies, the buyer should demand that such sum be converted, at applicable exchange rates, into U.S. dollars.

Receivables

Generally, a fairly precise valuation of the seller's receivables may be obtained. Receivables are usually evaluated by reference to their cash equivalent and may be acquired at their face value, which is probably the maximum price a seller can obtain. A buyer might seek to pay the lowest price that would be realized from the sale of the receivables in an arm's-length transaction to a third party—a distress sale.

Items such as customers' credits, allowances, and age of the accounts must be taken into consideration when evaluating the seller's receivables. Although historic financial data of the business will assist the purchaser in assessing such information, the seller is always in a superior position to adjust the value of the receivables. At closing, any amounts owed by the business's owners should be deducted from the total amount of receivables due.

In many cases, a purchaser would be well advised to buy the receivables of the business acquired. By owning and, consequently, collecting the receivables, she can maintain a relationship with those customers who have previously availed themselves of the business's products or services. If it is not in the purchaser's best interest to acquire the receivables (if, for example, she doubts their collectibility), the purchaser may contract to try to collect them on the seller's behalf, or the receivables may be sold to a bank or other financial institution prior to the closing. Such an approach safeguards the buyer against any unforeseen losses incurred in the collection of the receivables.

Inventory

Appraising inventory is often a complicated procedure. Taking a physical inventory is certainly the most cautious approach. Even though business operations may need to be suspended during the physical inventory, it is in the best interest of the purchaser and seller alike to know exactly what inventory is to be sold and acquired. A physical inventory will also educate the purchaser about any items not readily disposable in the ordinary course of trade or business that can then be excluded from the inventory to be acquired. In this way the purchaser can avoid investing in obsolete, obsolescent, or otherwise unmarketable goods.

The purchaser's blind acceptance of the seller's book value could prove expensive; should a physical inventory establish a value greater than book value (where no reconciliation is made through a physical inventory), the buyer is apt to end up with an inflated dollar profit. This possibility will only be avoided through the taking of an inventory. The buyer's eventual income tax bill will also be exaggerated if the figures are not accurate.

If the seller has used the last-in, first-out (LIFO) method of valuing inventory, the actual value of the inventory may exceed its book value. This would create a LIFO reserve—the difference between the LIFO and the first-in, first-out (FIFO) method of valuing inventory. It should likewise be noted that inflation or appreciation may increase the value of the seller's inventory, or the inventory may be undervalued because of the seller's failure to allocate direct overhead costs to inventory items.

If a retail business is to be acquired, the aging assumption to be adopted on the taking of a physical inventory should be determined in advance. It is important that the physical inventory be taken on an aging as well as a cost basis. Depending on the age of the inventory items, certain deductions may be credited to the purchaser—the greater the age, the greater the deductions.

If the business to be acquired has parts included in its inventory, the physical inventory should take into account surplus supply and outdated stock. A physical inventory of parts permits the buyer to exercise judgment about which parts are potentially salable and which are not; the latter need not be acquired. Where parts are to be purchased, current invoices should be thoroughly analyzed by the purchaser to insure against the acquisition of obsolete parts.

The valuation, or costing, of inventory items includes both finished and unfinished goods. In the costing of finished inventory items, where cost and market value are approximately the same, the buyer should be allotted a profit-margin deduction, or she will not realize a profit on the future sale of these items. Costing of finished inventory items should be at fair market value less a fair profit margin to determine the correct value of the inventory.

The Internal Revenue Service's Revenue Procedure 77–12 sets forth guidelines in making fair market value determinations where assets of a business, including inventory items, are purchased for a lump sum. The revenue procedure provides three basic methods that may be used to determine the fair market value of inventory: the cost of reproduction method; the comparative sales method; and the income method. All methods of valuation are based on one or a combination of these three methods.

Cost of Reproduction

The cost of reproduction method of valuing inventory generally provides a good indication of fair market value if inventory is readily replaceable in a wholesale or retail business, but generally should not be used in establishing the fair market value of the unfinished goods of a manufacturing concern. In appraising a particular inventory under this method, however, other factors may be relevant. For example, a well-balanced inventory, available to fill customers' orders in the ordinary course of business, may have a fair market value in excess of its cost of reproduction because it provides a continuity of business, whereas an inventory containing obsolete merchandise unsuitable for customers might have a fair market value less than the cost of reproduction.

Comparative Sales

The comparative sales method of valuing inventory uses actual or expected selling prices of finished goods to customers as a basis for determining their fair market values. When the expected selling price is used as a basis for valuing finished goods inventory, consideration should be given to the time required to dispose of this inventory, the expenses that would be incurred in such disposition (including any applicable discounts, sales commissions, and freight and shipping charges) and a profit commensurate with the amount of investment and the degree of risk. The inventory to be valued may represent a larger quantity than the normal trading volume; the expected selling price can be a valid starting point only if the customers' orders are filled in the ordinary course of business.

Income

When applied to fair market value determinations for finished goods, the income inventory valuing method recognizes that finished goods must generally be valued in a profit-motivated business. Since the amount of inventory may be large in relation to normal trading volume, the highest and best use of the inventory would be to provide for a continuity of the marketing operation of the going concern. The finished goods inventory will usually provide the only source of revenue of an acquired business during the period it is being used to fill customers' orders. The historic financial data of an acquired company can be used to determine the amount that could be attributed to finished goods in order to pay all the costs of disposition and provide a return on the buyer's investment during the period of disposition.

Revenue Procedure 77–12 suggests that the fair market value of work in process should be based on the same factors used to determine the fair market value of finished goods reduced by the expected costs of completion, including a reasonable profit allowance for the completion and selling effort of the buyer. In determining the fair market value of raw materials, the current cost of replacing the inventory in the quantities to be valued usually provides the most reliable standard. Because the valuation of inventory is an inherently factual determination, no rigid formulas can be applied. The revenue procedure does, however, present useful guidelines for determining the fair market value of inventories.

Machinery

The notion of buying and maintaining machinery is foreign to some entrepreneurs who view it as a vestige of the Old Economy. In reality, though, machinery continues to demand substantial capital from many entrepreneurs.

Once the buyer has determined what machinery needs to be acquired to maintain the operation of the business, such machinery should be evaluated. Although there is no difficulty in obtaining the book value of a piece of machinery, book value again may be radically different from market value. In addition, the book value attributed to a piece of machinery may not reflect installation charges related to its acquisition. The salability of a second-hand piece of equipment often depends on the state of the economy. Where heavy machinery is to be acquired, the expense of removing or installing the equipment is likely to be significant.

Regardless of whether there is a market for the seller's machinery or not, the purchaser should normally not acquire equipment that is unnecessary in the operation of the business. The acquisition of unneeded machinery usually proves detrimental to the buyer. So, before committing to purchase any machinery, the buyer should determine if it is being used for operational purposes.

Although a professional appraiser may be retained for the purpose of evaluating machinery, it is more common to appraise machinery on its book value minus depreciation, unless the facts and circumstances related to the individual situation dictate otherwise. Of course, the purchaser should inquire as to the method of depreciation used by the seller to be assured that the value attributed to the equipment is not excessive. Where a portion of the seller's equipment is leased, the terms of the lease should be reviewed as to termination rights and related issues.

Intangible Assets

In most cases, intangible as well as tangible assets must be evaluated upon the sale of a business. Intangible assets may include such items as patents, trademarks, Internet domain names, and franchises. The Internal Revenue Service's Revenue Ruling 68–609 presents a formula approach that may be useful in determining the fair market value of the intangible assets of a business. The formula reads as follows:

A percentage return on the average annual value of the tangible assets used in a business is determined, using a period of years (preferably not less than five) immediately prior to the valuation date. The amount of the percentage return on tangible assets, thus determined, is deducted from the average earnings of the business for such period and the remainder, if any, is considered to be the amount of the average annual earnings from the intangible assets of the business for the period. This amount (considered as the average annual earnings from intangibles), capitalized at a percentage rate of, say, 15 to 20 percent, is the value of the intangible assets of the business determined under the "formula" approach.

The percentage of a return on the average annual value of the tangible assets used would be the percentage applicable to the type of business involved on the valuation date; if such a percentage is not available, 8 percent to 10 percent may be used. The 8 percent rate of return and the 15 percent capitalization rate are applied to both tangible and intangible assets of low-risk businesses with stable or regular earnings. The 10 percent rate of return and 20 percent capitalization rate are generally applied to high-risk businesses. When using the formula approach, the average earnings period and capitalization rates depend on the facts involved in the particular situation.

The revenue ruling provides that past earnings to which the formula is applied should reflect probable future earnings. Ordinarily, past earnings should be analyzed for at least a five-year period, and abnormal years falling above or below average should be discarded. Where the business to be acquired is a sole proprietorship or partnership (or limited liability company taxed as a partnership), a reasonable amount of compensation for services performed by the owner or partners (or members) should be deducted from earnings. Only those tangible assets entering into net worth, including accounts and bills receivable in excess of accounts and bills payable, are used to determine earnings with respect to the tangible assets. The capitalization rate is influenced by the nature of the business, the risk involved, and the stability or irregularity of earnings.

Revenue Ruling 68–609 cautions that the formula approach should not be used if a better way to value intangible assets can be determined. Where assets of a going business are sold on the basis of a realistic capitalization rate, though not within the range of figures indicated in the revenue ruling, the same capitalization rate should be used to determine the value of the intangible assets. Consequently, the "formula" approach may be used for determining the fair market value of intangible assets of a business only if there is no better basis available for such a determination.

Treasury regulations provide guidelines for the valuation of stock attributed to a closely held corporation (or, by extension, other closely held enterprises) where actual sale prices and bona fide bid and asked prices are lacking. In such cases, fair market value is determined by taking the following facts into consideration:

- The company's net worth
- Prospective earning power
- Dividend-paying capacity
- "Other relevant factors"

"Other relevant factors" may include:

- The goodwill of the business
- The economic outlook in the industry
- The company's position in the industry and its management
- The degree of control represented by the block of stock (or other equity) to be valued
- The values of other companies engaged in the same or similar lines of business

Real Property

Where real property is to be acquired with the business, the purchaser should make sure that the title is not defective. A defective title could reduce the value of such real property. Frequently, the unrealized appreciation attributable to real property exceeds its depreciated value. Leaseholds or leasehold improvements are generally treated as liabilities.

The valuation of real property hinges primarily on its character. Each piece of real estate has its own unique characteristics, which must be taken into account. Some of the elements that may be analyzed when evaluating real estate include:

- Location
- Size
- Current and future use
- Improvements
- Environmental factors
- Zoning limitations
- Condemnation awards for property of a similar nature

Where improved real estate is to be acquired, it is generally appraised as a unit. This holds true even though, for purposes of computing depreciation, the land and improvements must be evaluated on an individual basis. Three methods are generally used to evaluate improved real property, sometimes in combination:

1. The income capitalization method. With this approach, value is determined by reference to the income-producing capacity of the property. Rental income derived from the property is a significant factor in the evaluation process. When employing the income capitalization method, income derived from the property is capitalized at an applicable rate of return. The income capitalization method is used when information from comparable sales is not readily obtainable, but sufficient data about the income-producing capacity of the property are available.

2. The replacement cost method. When using this method, the valuation of real property is based on its actual cost or on the cost of replacing the property, less any applicable depreciation. There must be a link, however, between replacement cost and the fair market value of the property. The replacement cost method is often used when the property in question is either "special purpose" or new.

3. The comparable sales method. Value is computed by reference to the purchase price actually obtained for property of a similar nature. This method is desirable only if prior sales of the other property were effected at arm's length. As a general rule, the comparable sales method is reliable only where there have been several recent sales of real property possessing characteristics similar or identical to the property to be acquired.

Valuing Liabilities

The purchaser may agree or be required to assume all or a portion of the seller's liabilities. As a result, the purchaser must determine what the liabilities are and the amount for which she will be held responsible. Unlike assets, liabilities are not always included in the financial records of the business. Following are some of the factors that should be taken into consideration when evaluating the seller's liabilities:

- *Employee Benefit Plans.* Pension plans should be reviewed to ascertain current and future liabilities the purchaser may be required to assume. Even where vested liabilities are covered by sufficient assets, nonvested liabilities may amount to a sizable sum of which the purchaser should be aware. Although funds may be available for current benefit payments, other benefits may extend into the future.

- *Product Liability Litigation.* The business's counsel should be interviewed by the purchaser to obtain all available information concerning pending product liability litigation. Warranty claims should be reviewed to determine the potential future liability of the purchaser; the amount of such future claims, however, is often difficult to predict. Current as well as past product lines should be considered when ascertaining potential future liabilities. The extent of such liabilities often depends on the type of business and nature of the product in question. In addition, the following factors should be analyzed: (1) the estimation of future liabilities; (2) the means to minimize current liabilities; and (3) the possibility of an agreement between buyer and seller that could cap the buyer's future product liability.

- *Potential Tax Liabilities.* The purchaser should learn the amount of potential liabilities, if any, arising from federal income tax and investigate any tax reserve, as well as the liabilities to which it applies. The buyer should also consider liabilities that may arise from the Federal Insurance Contributions Act (FICA), federal withholding, and state taxes.

- *Contingent Liabilities.* The purchaser should determine the likelihood that a contingent liability will occur, and the amount of liabilities she will be obligated to assume. Contingent liabilities may be handled in one of two ways: the buyer may agree to be held responsible for a prearranged dollar amount (with the seller being held responsible for any amount incurred over and above that figure), or the seller may agree to remain responsible for the full amount of any contingent liabilities.

- *Loans.* The purchaser should determine whether the seller has taken out any loans. The terms of the loans as well as the seller's ability to repay them in advance of their due dates should be verified.

- *Patent Agreements.* The seller may hold one or more patent agreements. If this is the case, the purchaser should investigate any potential liabilities that may arise from such agreements (for instance, where a patent agreement violates the rights attached to patents held by others).

Other factors may also have to be considered when evaluating the seller's liabilities. There is no one method that may be used in all cases.

The nature of the seller's business will ultimately determine the liabilities to be investigated.

Determining the Purchase Price

A determination of the value of the seller's assets, taking into account deductions allowed to the purchaser for assets not used in the operation of the business, establishes a basis for ascertaining the purchase price. In most cases, this base price is affected by the earnings potential of the business to be acquired. A multiple of earnings may be used to establish to what extent the purchase price will exceed the value of the assets.

In many instances, the financial statements used to compute a purchase price are those generated at or near the date of the closing. Thus, the multiple of earnings on which the purchase price is based may include that period of time up to the date of closing. If the final purchase price hinges on financial information that is to be compiled later, the purchaser and buyer should have an agreement as to the preparation of such information.

Where the purchase price is based on earnings that have been increasing on a steady basis, the earnings to be taken into account may be those for a period ending on or after the date of closing. Because of the steady increase in earnings, the seller may demand that the business be sold at a multiple of those earnings in order to retain a right to a percentage of the business's future earnings. However, the buyer may not be willing to comply with this demand unless there is confidence that the previous earnings rate will continue. This problem may be resolved by having a portion of the consideration tendered to the seller upon closing; the remainder would then be paid only if the future earnings of the business warrant.

Financial statements must be scrutinized to determine whether prior earnings of the business have been properly reflected and if a determination of anticipated earnings may be accurately projected from these earlier results. The purchaser should be aware, however, that the financial data have been prepared by the seller's accountants or internal personnel. Even where the statements have been audited by independent auditors, their assurance only means that the statements conform to standard accounting conventions. For this reason, the purchaser or her accountants should investigate the seller's methods of preparing financial statements. The seller may have attempted to present current income in a more favorable light by selecting from among several alternative accounting methods which would not misrepresent the seller's financial information.

However, the use of certain methods, while not inappropriate for a business that continues its previous operations, may distort results for a business about to be sold.

If the purchaser is knowledgeable in the area of financial analysis, she may wish to conduct the investigation. If she is not, her accountant should be instructed to undertake the investigation. If the purchaser does not have an accountant, one should be retained expressly for this purpose. Some of the issues that should be noted by the purchaser or her accountant include the following:

- Material changes in returns or warranty claims
- Changes in the method of setting reserves
- Changes in depreciation methods
- Inclusion of future shipments in current sales figures
- Specific sales reported currently that are larger than past sales of a similar nature
- A material difference in the amount of current sales, as a whole, in relation to past sales
- Variations or changes of accounting conventions among the items of financial information reviewed
- Variations in interest charges over a number of accounting periods
- Fluctuations in repair and maintenance expenses

Of course, other issues may also prove to be relevant when analyzing the seller's financial statements. Such other issues may depend on the nature of the information made available by the seller to the purchaser.

Projecting Business Earnings

The historic income of the business to be acquired may be fairly easy to chart; yet, historic income is only of significance to the purchaser as a basis for determining potential future income. If it appears likely that future earnings will be lower than past earnings, a reduction in the purchase price may be negotiated.

In most cases, multiplying historic earnings to compute the purchase price is a simplistic and inadequate measure. The income produced by the business in the seller's hands is of little interest to the purchaser. The purchaser is instead interested in the potential income of the business in her hands. As a result, the purchaser should attempt to obtain a projection of the business's future earnings. The seller may argue, however, that such a projection is not an accurate forecast of the income potential of the business. Consequently, the purchaser must also gather other pertinent information to facilitate making an accurate and persuasive projection (for example, cash requirements and cash flow, the competition, and related market considerations). Such an investigation will serve the further purpose of informing the purchaser of the likelihood of obtaining a reasonable return on her investment.

To obtain a realistic income projection, the purchaser should decide whether it will be possible to expand the operations of the business in a cost-effective manner. If such a possibility exists, it will contribute to the determination of the final purchase price. So will the conclusion that machinery or equipment will need to be replaced sooner rather than later. The effects of existing competition, as well as the probable consequences resulting from new competition in the market, must be analyzed. This analysis should include a study of the pricing methods used by the competition for products of the same or similar nature as those produced or sold by the business to be acquired. The likelihood of competitors expanding their businesses should also be explored. In addition, the product produced or sold by the business to be acquired should be analyzed to see whether it might become obsolete.

An assessment should be made of the seller's most important suppliers and customers to determine whether the purchaser can depend on them in the future. The future availability of raw materials used in the seller's business should be evaluated, as well as the potential for an increase in their price. In a case where the purchaser is to acquire a business of a similar nature to one she already owns, the purchaser may already have the answers to many of these questions. Otherwise, the purchaser may have to explore these and other pertinent questions on an individual basis to secure the information required to help make an accurate projection of the business's earnings.

The Character of the Business

A multiple of earnings may be used to establish the purchase price of the business. For such a valuation, the character of the business to be acquired must be taken into consideration. Generally, the multiple of earnings is higher where the business is operating on its own merits rather than the merits of the seller (for instance, in the case of a production or manufacturing business). Alternatively, the price-earnings ratio is generally lower where a personal service business is to be acquired, because the income from the business and the seller's own services are directly related; the purchase price will usually not significantly exceed the value attributed to the seller's assets.

Where there is a likelihood that the business will continue to grow, the purchase price that may be demanded by the seller may conceivably arrest the business's development and growth potential for a number of years. As a result, the purchaser may be forced to pay a relatively high price for the business in relation to its current income. Prevailing interest rates often correlate to the percentage to be attributed to the price-earnings ratio, the ratio between earnings of the business and its purchase price or its value as determined in the market. As a general rule, the higher the interest rates, the lower the price-earnings ratio.

The price-earnings ratio must be lowered accordingly if some or all of the following factors will affect the operations and future earning power of the business:

- Existing or new competition
- Larger facilities or possible expansion of operations by competitors
- Technological developments of new products that may make current products obsolete or obsolescent
- Production capacity
- Contractual commitments

When stock, rather than cash, is used as consideration, the purchase price will often be higher. Consequently, a discounting with respect to the stock consideration will result, causing a higher price-earnings multiple to be used. Where a small business is acquired for cash, the price-earnings multiple typically will not be subject to any significant increase.

In theory, the price-earnings multiplier may be ascertained by contrasting such multiples with the prices commanded for shares of stock sold over a national stock exchange for businesses of a same or similar nature as the business to be acquired. As a general rule, however, where a closely held corporation is to be acquired, the price-earnings ratio will be somewhat decreased.

However, the ratio is an arbitrary figure that may be decided only after an extensive analysis has been made of the industry in question. This includes the evaluation of other similar businesses, and the cost of stock of other similar corporations and their earnings, if the acquisition is to be of a corporation.

Multiples will usually range up to 5 times before-tax earnings or 10 times after-tax earnings. Privately owned, high-growth companies will not command the stratospheric multiples that their NASDAQ-traded brethren may see, but even their multiples may reach 20 times or so after-tax earnings.

Dilution of Earnings

Where a currently existing and operating business is to acquire another business, the purchaser needs to predict the earnings of both businesses. The purchase price of the seller's business must not be so great as to dilute the combined earnings per share for the indefinite future. In the case of a closely held corporation, the cash flow consequences may be of primary concern.

A dilution of earnings may similarly occur in a case where the purchase price is to be paid with cash. If the income from the acquired business will not cover the cost of charges resulting from the imposition of real or imputed interest on the money used or borrowed to finance the acquisition, the second business probably should not be acquired. The purchaser, may, however decide to suffer such a consequence, assuming the aggregate earnings projections justify the investment.

If the purchase price will be paid in cash, a positive contribution to earnings per share will result because any cost attributed to capital that is considered to be a payment of interest may be deducted by the purchaser for income tax purposes. Nevertheless, to obtain the necessary cash, the purchaser may be dedicating an inappropriate percentage of her borrowing power to the acquisition. For that reason, other investment alternatives should be considered: Would it be of greater benefit to the purchaser to acquire other capital assets and not the seller's business?

In the final analysis, whether such an investment is worthwhile must result from the buyer's educated judgment that a reasonable rate of return will be generated on the capital deployed to make the acquisition.

Methods of Projection

With financial information supplied by the seller, certain financial ratios may be considered by the purchaser as the inner workings of the business are explored. Such ratios can help compare and contrast the financial facts of the business under review with information available from other businesses of similar size and nature. This comparison may allow the purchaser to develop statistical conclusions that will aid in calculating a fair purchase price for the business. Ratio analysis is useful for most business valuations; only where capital expenditure is not an issue or where the seller's assets are merely being acquired for the purchaser's own business is it to be forsaken.

The current ratio is commonly used in the evaluation of the business. It is ascertained by dividing current assets by current liabilities.

$$\text{Current Ratio} = \frac{\text{Current Assets}}{\text{Current Liabilities}}$$

This ratio permits the purchaser to determine the business's capability of satisfying current debts. A company is more likely to satisfy its current debts if its current ratio is high. It follows, therefore, that a business with a high current ratio generally will be of interest to the purchaser.

Other ratios that may be used to obtain pertinent information about the seller's business are the operating ratio, in which net profits are divided by total sales

$$\text{Operating Ratio} = \frac{\text{Net Profits}}{\text{Total Sales}}$$

and the turnover ratio, in which the cost of goods sold is divided by average inventory

$$\text{Turnover Ratio} = \frac{\text{Cost of Goods}}{\text{Average Inventory}}$$

The net profit-on-sales ratio and the net profit or net worth ratio indicate the income-producing capacity of the business. The fixed assets-to-net-worth ratio, the debt-to-net-worth ratio, and the purchases-to-trade-payables ratio may also be of use to the purchaser with respect to the evaluation. Of course, these examples only provide a sampling of the ratios available to the purchaser for use in an evaluation. After the ratios have been computed, the results should be compared with the average figures available for the industry as a whole.

The evaluation of a business necessitates understanding financial ratios and their respective applications. Nevertheless, the mere comparison of the ratios with those of other similar businesses is only one first step in the appraisal of a company. The importance of statistical information obtained by the purchaser is that it permits the formulation of pertinent questions that should be addressed to the seller or the seller's employees. In addition, the implementation of cash flow and cash requirements projections must be initiated by the purchaser. Only with a full understanding of the proposed purchase's cash flow implications will the purchaser be certain there is enough cash to maintain business operations. It follows that any estimated projections be developed as accurately as possible to avoid future negative surprises to the purchaser.

Many larger corporations have been disposing of subsidiaries or divisions in recent years. The purchase price for these acquisitions has frequently been obtained in whole or in part through loans. Such loans may be the result of a deferral of all or a portion of the purchase price by the seller or may be obtained from a third-party lender, or both.

Where such a leveraged buyout is to be accomplished, special factors must be taken into consideration to evaluate the business, including the business's cash flow, which is often a primary factor in the evaluation; and below-market interest financing (an additional value intrinsic to the transaction), whether offered by the seller or assumed by the purchaser. Most important, the purchaser should compute the amount of debt the cash flow can service, providing a reasonable level of amortization.

Discounting Value

The sophisticated buyer and the IRS both understand the difference between owning shares in a public company, which can easily be sold through a stockbroker or even online, and owning an interest in a closely held, private concern for which there is no easily identifiable market. For that reason, the buyer is justified in claiming discounts when valuing a privately held business.

There is also good reason to discount a minority interest in a private business, one representing less than 50 percent of the ownership. After all, owners of minority interests are not assured of employment in the business, let alone dividends or a meaningful role in determining policy. The flip side is that owners of a majority interest may find the value of their holdings inflated by a control premium.

The Financial Advisor's Role

The valuation of a business for purposes of determining purchase price may not be the function of the financial advisor. Nevertheless, he should have a basic understanding of the valuation methods used competently in order to advise the entrepreneur whether the purchase price is realistic.

The purchaser's financial advisor should ascertain the seller's motivations for selling the business. Especially in a case where a small business is to be acquired, the purchaser must be satisfied that the business is not being sold because of some subtle defect that could negatively impact its future operations or profitability. It is essential that the seller disclose to the purchaser the extent of any problems or risks involved in the operation of the business. Where such a disclosure is initially made, subsequent indemnification by the seller may be limited or, in fact, may prove unnecessary. The buyer's financial advisor must also determine his client's ability to defray the amount of the purchase price, within a reasonable period of time, out of the future earnings of the business. The advisor should explore the future prospects of the business to determine that the buyer's goals in entering into the acquisition are likely to be satisfied. Such factors as production, competition, market, and other items that may be pertinent to the type of business being acquired should be evaluated. In brief, the purchaser's financial advisor must establish that his client is likely to realize the benefit of her bargain in the business to be acquired.

12

Buy-Sell Designs

The entrepreneur may make a significant financial investment in the successful venture, but he also invests his time, his sweat, and his tears. With proper planning, the business may continue to provide a return on his investment even after his death.

A buy-sell agreement can secure a number of very tangible benefits for the owner of a business and his family. Among other things, a properly drafted buy-sell agreement:

- Guarantees that the business will survive an owner's death
- Ensures continuity of management
- Keeps outsiders out of ownership
- Provides a deceased owner's estate a fair return on his investment when his business interest is transferred
- Sets a fair valuation of the business interest for federal estate tax purposes
- Provides a market for the interest of a departing, retiring, or deceased owner
- May preserve the business's favored tax status

This chapter explores the buy-sell agreement in the corporate context. Although these designs are, in many respects, applicable to other entities, tax consequences may vary. For the financial advisor who is interested in reading primary source material, statutory, regulatory, and case law citations are included.

Buy-Sell Agreement

The buy-sell agreement allows or requires the purchase and sale of a shareholder's interest when a triggering event occurs. Three kinds of buy-sell agreements are *stock redemption*, in which the corporation agrees to buy the departing shareholder's interest in the business; *cross-purchase*, in which the surviving or remaining shareholders agree to buy the interest pro rata; and *wait-and-see* buy-sell, which is a hybrid that allows the corporation and its shareholders to postpone a purchase decision until the time of the buyout. Whatever its form, the agreement establishes the terms of a purchase, including the events that trigger it, the method of valuation, and a workable funding mechanism.

Triggering Events

The buyout is usually triggered by the happening of an event that, by its very nature, interrupts the business's continuity of management and ownership. Events commonly triggering a buyout include:

- *Death.* The death of a shareholder is the most obvious event about which the financial advisor should be concerned in structuring buy-sell agreements. Mandatory buyout provisions allow the decedent-shareholder's estate to create liquidity through the sale of an otherwise illiquid asset—shares in a closely held corporation—while securing certainty of succession for the surviving shareholders. This chapter focuses on a shareholder's death as the triggering event.
- *Lifetime Transfers.* Inter vivos transfer restrictions make sure the terms of the buy-sell won't be subverted by a shareholder's transactions during his lifetime. The business or its owners may secure a "right of first refusal," either on the same terms as a third-party offer or on those set out in the buy-sell agreement.
- *Bankruptcy.* In the event a shareholder is adjudicated a bankrupt, makes an assignment for the benefit of creditors, or effects or permits some other involuntary transfer of ownership interest, the company and its other shareholders may hold an option to purchase the shareholder's stock.
- *Retirement.* The retirement, voluntary withdrawal, or termination of employment of a shareholder may trigger the purchase of his interest. This trigger not only contemplates a shareholder's reaching normal

retirement age, but also the possibility of a clash among co-owners, which cannot be successfully resolved and reasonably requires the exit of one or more of them.

- *Disability.*   The physical or mental incapacity of a shareholder, rendering him unable to carry out the regular duties of his office, may trigger a buyout. The disability buyout generates liquidity for the disabled shareholder's support, and prevents a spouse or other family member from gaining control of his shares. The agreement should provide the means for determining when a triggering disability has occurred.

Funding the Buyout

Life insurance is the ideal source of buyout funding. Premium payments guarantee that policy proceeds will be available to complete the buyout at a shareholder's death. Since these premiums are paid over time, the total amount necessary to fund the buyout is discounted for time-value. Further, life insurance proceeds are generally received free of federal income tax and, in carefully drafted plans, free of estate tax. Finally, tax-deferred accumulation inside the policy may provide a source of cash for funding certain living buyouts. Disability buyout insurance is commonly used as a complement to life insurance funding.

When insurance is unavailable or unaffordable, the buy-sell agreement can establish a "sinking fund," no more than a savings plan to fund the obligations it creates. To the extent the business or its owners are to fund buyouts independent of insurance, the agreement may contemplate the seller's extension of credit to them. In that event, it is of the utmost importance that the agreement specify the terms of credit, including:

- The applicable interest rate
- The length of amortization of the payout term
- Any security arrangements to back up the payment obligations. These may include personal guarantees, security interests in identified collateral, or an escrow agreement establishing a segregated pool of funds available to the seller should the buyer fail to meet its obligations.
- Any restriction on the buyer while the obligation remains unpaid. These might limit salaries, perks, and loans paid to insiders, and capital expenditures. They also might restrict other borrowing or any activity that is outside the ordinary course of the buyer's business.

Stock Redemption or Entity Agreement

Under a stock redemption or entity agreement, the shareholders enter into a binding agreement with the corporation for the purchase of the shareholders' stock. The agreement requires the shareholders and their estates to sell, and the corporation to buy, the shares of a departing shareholder at an agreed or determinable price. In most cases, the corporation then obtains life insurance on each shareholder's life equal to the value of that shareholder's interest, naming itself both owner and beneficiary of the policy. Corporate premium payments under this scenario are nondeductible expenses (Internal Revenue Code (IRC) § 264(a)(1)). Upon a shareholder's death, the corporation receives the policy proceeds. Pursuant to the buy-sell agreement, his estate then sells the decedent-shareholder's entire stock interest to the corporation in return for a cash payment. Buyouts triggered by events other than death may be funded by the life insurance policy cash values. In any event, the stock redemption increases the surviving shareholders' proportional interest in the corporation.

The stock redemption approach offers many advantages, including the following:

- A stock redemption plan is usually easy to put into place.
- The plan requires only one policy for each shareholder.
- The corporation pays the premiums, sparing the shareholders any direct financial burden.
- The cash value of the insurance is carried as an asset on the corporation's balance sheet without concerns of excess "accumulated earnings," so long as the cash value does not exceed the reasonable needs of the business.
- Policies can be transferred to the insured shareholders without creating a "transfer for value" (see Combining the Life Insurance Retirement Plan and the Buy-Sell later in this chapter).

But a stock redemption agreement also presents some problems. They include the following:

- The surviving shareholders' basis in the corporation's stock remains the same, although the value of their business interests increases. When they later sell their shares, they will incur a bigger taxable capital gain than they would have if the redemption had never occurred.

- Corporate creditors can make claims against policy cash values of corporate-owned life insurance, possibly jeopardizing or even depleting buy-sell funding.
- Insurance cash value and death proceeds may result in the imposition of a corporate alternative minimum tax (see Alternative Minimum Tax later in this chapter).
- Nondeductible premium payments are more costly than they would be under a cross-purchase approach if the corporation is in a higher income tax bracket than its shareholders.

Avoiding Dividend Treatment

Generally, corporate distributions to shareholders with respect to its stock will be treated as dividends to the extent that the corporation has "accumulated earnings and profits" (AEP) (IRC § 316(a)). Dividend distributions are taxed as ordinary income (IRC § 301(c)(1)). Distributions in excess of AEP are treated as a return of basis to the shareholder. Nondividend distributions in excess of basis are treated as capital gains (IRC § 301(c)). And, in a corporation where AEP are high, the entire redemption payment could be subject to dividend treatment.

But certain corporate distributions made to repurchase stock will be treated as distributions in *exchange* for the stock redeemed and taxed at favorable tax rates (IRC §§ 302–304). Capital gains treatment allows a shareholder to use his basis in the stock to offset the distribution, thus protecting a portion of the cash received as a tax-free return of capital (IRC §§ 302(a), 1001). And, with redemptions at death, where the shareholder's basis is stepped up to its fair market value, the entire distribution may be deemed a tax-free return of capital (IRC § 1014(a)(1)).

Shareholders may ensure that the corporate distribution is treated as capital gain rather than ordinary income by satisfying one of four safe harbors provided in IRC Section 302. Satisfaction of any one of them will except the redemption from the general rule that corporate distributions to shareholders with respect to its stock are dividends.

The safe harbor rules hold that a corporation's distribution as payment for its stock will be treated as a sale or exchange if (1) it is not essentially equivalent to a dividend; (2) it is substantially disproportionate with respect to the shareholder's interest; (3) it effects a complete termination of the shareholder's interest; or (4) it is in partial liquidation of the redeeming corporation. If the redemption does not satisfy one of these safe harbor exemptions, the distribution will be taxed as a dividend to the shareholder to the extent of AEP.

The following paragraphs describe how to qualify for each of the four safe harbor tests.

Dividend Equivalence Test

The redemption will qualify as a sale or exchange if it is not "essentially equivalent" to a dividend (IRC § 302(b)(1)). A pro rata redemption from all shareholders will be deemed essentially equivalent to a dividend, as no effective change in the shareholders' pro rata interests in the corporation results. (*United States v. Davis*, 397 U.S. 301 (1970); Treas. Reg. § 1.302-2(b); Rev. Rul. 81-289). The effect on both the shareholders and the corporation is the same as if a dividend had been paid. However, redemptions of one particular shareholder's stock reduce that shareholder's interest in the corporation's business relative to the other shareholders.

To avoid a finding of equivalence, the transaction must result in a significant or meaningful reduction in the shareholder's proportionate interest in the corporation (*Davis*, 397 U.S. at 313). Determining whether a redemption results in a meaningful reduction is fact-based, so the dividend equivalence test is the least reliable of the safe harbors. The Internal Revenue Service (IRS) has considered the effect of the redemption on the shareholder's interest in the business, including the shareholder's right to control the corporation, to participate in earnings, and to share in assets on liquidation (Rev. Rul. 75-502). Redemptions that reduce a shareholder's interest from majority to minority will likely be deemed meaningful (see, e.g., Rev. Rul. 75-502). A partial redemption in which one shareholder directly or constructively owns all of the corporation's stock results in no meaningful reduction in the shareholder's proportional interest in the business. Such redemptions are considered essentially equivalent to a dividend, irrespective of the business purpose of the redemption (*Davis*, 397 U.S. at 312).

As with each of the safe harbor tests, the IRC Section 318 attribution rules (see Stock Attribution Rules later in this chapter) apply in determining whether a redemption has resulted in a meaningful reduction. This may prevent exchange treatment for buyout redemptions in family corporations.

Substantially Disproportionate Tests

The redemption will qualify as a sale or exchange if the redemption is substantially disproportionate to the shareholder's interest (IRC § 302(b)(2)). A redemption will be treated as substantially disproportionate where the shareholder after the redemption, owns less than 80 percent of the percentage of total voting stock of the corporation owned immediately prior to the redemption; less than 80 percent of the percentage of total value of the corporation's voting or nonvoting common stock owned immediately prior to the redemption; and less than 50 percent of the corporation's total voting power.

Tests for these reductions will be strictly applied by the IRS. The minimum number of shares that must be redeemed to satisfy the 80 percent tests may be calculated by the following formula:

$$N = [PT/(5T-4P)]+1$$

where

N equals the minimum number of shares that must be redeemed

P equals the number of shares owned by seller prior to redemption

T equals the total number of shares outstanding prior to redemption

Family attribution rules apply in determining whether such reduction has been achieved and cannot be waived for purposes of this test (IRC § 318). Achieving the mathematical reductions required by this exception may be increasingly difficult where the shareholder is construed to own the interests held by certain family members (see Stock Attribution Rules later in this chapter).

Complete Termination Test

The redemption will qualify as an exchange if the corporation redeems all of the shareholder's interests in the corporation, thereby terminating his interest (IRC § 302(b)(3)). A shareholder may accomplish a complete redemption in steps, if each step is a clearly integrated part of a firm and fixed plan (see *in re Estate of Lukens*, 246 F.2d 403 (3d Cir. 1957); *Bleily & Collishaw, Inc. v. Commissioner*, 72 T.C. 751 (1979)). For example, the agreement may call for a redemption followed by a cross-purchase of the remaining shares. Both steps qualify for capital gains treatment as part of a termination plan. The IRS will consider a redemption complete irrespective of the sequence of events (see, e.g., *Zenz v. Quinlivan*, 213

F.2d 914 (6th Cir. 1954)). Again, family attribution rules apply in determining whether such a termination has been achieved.

Partial Liquidation Test

The redemption will qualify as an exchange where the redemption is part of a partial liquidation of the corporation (IRC § 302(b)(4)). A redemption under this scenario is an unlikely strategy in most estate planning redemptions.

Stock Attribution Rules

Stock attribution rules complicate the application of the Section 302(b) safe harbor exceptions. These rules effectively impute to one shareholder the ownership of stock by another and often impose more onerous redemption requirements in satisfying the safe harbor exceptions. The attribution rules discourage shareholders from structuring buyouts where a "withdrawing" shareholder maintains a substantially unchanged, but indirect, interest in the corporation. A shareholder may waive these rules only for purposes of the complete termination test.

The IRS will treat a stockholder as owning stock owned by family members and related entities for purposes of determining whether a redemption is essentially equivalent to a dividend, substantially disproportionate, or a complete termination of the stockholder's interest in a corporation (IRC §§ 302(c), 318). These attribution rules include the following:

- *Majority Shareholder Attribution.* A shareholder owning 50 percent or more in value of a corporation's stock is considered to own a proportionate share of the value of any stock owned by the corporation (IRC § 318(a)(2)(C)). Likewise, any stock owned by such shareholder will be attributed to the corporation (IRC § 318(a)(3)(C)).
- *Option Attribution.* Owners of stock options are considered owners of the underlying stock (IRC § 318(a)(4)).
- *Partnership Attribution.* A partner is treated as the owner of a pro rata share of the stock owned by his partnership (IRC § 318(a)(2)(A)).
- *Beneficiary Attribution.* The beneficiary of an estate is considered the pro rata owner of stock owned by the estate (IRC § 318(a)(2)(A)). The beneficiary of a trust is considered the owner of stock owned by the trust in proportion to the beneficiary's interest in the trust (IRC § 318(a)(2)(B)(i)).

**Table 12.1   Amount of Stock Owned by Entities that Will
Be Attributed to a Related Individual**

Entity	Related Individuals	Attributions
Corporation	Majority shareholder	In proportion to ownership
Partnership	Partners	Pro rata
Trust (other than Grantor Trust)	Beneficiaries	In proportion to actual interest
Estate	Beneficiaries	In proportion to actual interest
Grantor Trust	Grantor	100%

Table 12.1 summarizes the entity attribution rules.

- *Family Attribution.*   An individual is deemed to own stock owned by his spouse, children, grandchildren, and parents (IRC § 318(a)(1)). Stock constructively owned by an individual pursuant to the attribution rules will generally be deemed owned by that individual for reattribution purposes. However, stock constructively owned by one family member cannot be reattributed to a third family member (IRC § 318(a)(5)(A), (B)). This prevents, among other things, sibling attribution (a son's stock, for example, attributed to his father, and reattributed to his sister) and attribution to grandchildren of stock owned by grandparents (grandfather's stock, for example, attributed to his son, and reattributed to his grandson).

These family and entity attribution rules present additional challenges to the financial advisor when calculating safe harbor satisfaction. For example, assume that a husband and wife each owns 25 percent of a company. The other 50 percent is owned by the wife's revocable trust, of which she is the grantor. The husband will be deemed to own not only his shares but the shares owned by his wife, plus, through spousal attribution, the shares held in the wife's grantor trust. Accordingly, even after a complete redemption of the husband's interest, he is still in constructive control of 100 percent of the business.

Table 12.2 summarizes the family attribution rules.

Because many buy-sell agreements relate to corporations in which family members are stockholders, most of the attribution problems in planning and drafting buy-sell agreements involve the family attribution rules, and they may be waived only to effectuate a complete termination

Table 12.2   Percentage of Stock Owned by Family Members
that Will Be Attributed to an Individual

	Spouse %	*Child* %	*Grandchild* %	*Parent* %	*Grandparent* %	*Sibling* %
Individual	100	100	100	100	0	0

of interest (IRC § 302(c)(2)). To do so, the redeeming shareholder must
meet the following three requirements:

1. Immediately after the redemption, the shareholder must have no
   interest in the corporation (other than as a creditor), including any
   interest as an officer, director, or employee.
2. The shareholder must not acquire any interest in the corporation
   (other than as a creditor, or through bequest or inheritance) during
   the 10 years following the redemption.
3. The shareholder must agree to notify the IRS of any acquisition of
   an interest in the corporation within 10 years after the distribution
   (IRC § 302(c)(2); Treas. Reg. § 1.302-4(a)).

Even so complying, the client should know that a waiver of the family
attribution rules is invalid if either of the following apply, unless federal
income tax avoidance was not one of the principal purposes of the
redemption: (1) any of the redeemed stock was acquired in the 10 years
prior to the redemption from a family member; or (2) any family member
owns stock acquired from the redeeming shareholder within the 10 years
prior to the redemption (IRC § 302(c)(2)(B)). Only the family attribution
rules may be waived, and only when applying the complete termination
safe harbor of IRC Section 302(b)(3).

Redemptions to Pay Death Taxes

Whether or not the redemption is protected under one of the Section 302
safe harbor provisions, a redemption at death will be considered a sale or
exchange, thereby qualifying for capital gain, rather than dividend, treatment, up to the amount of a decedent-shareholder's federal and state
estate taxes and interest, plus funeral and administration expenses (IRC §
303). An IRC Section 303 redemption may be used independently or as
a supplement to a cross-purchase. In the family business context, such

redemptions allow the family to retain control of the corporation while providing the decedent's estate with cash to pay estate taxes. Attribution rules are not applicable to redemptions made pursuant to Section 303.

Redemptions at death will be treated as a sale or exchange to the extent of death taxes if two requirements are met:

1. The value of the stock in the estate must exceed 35 percent of the decedent's gross estate, after funeral and administration expenses, claims, and losses deductible for estate tax purposes under IRC §§ 2053–2054 (IRC § 303(b)(2)(A)). If the stock included in the decedent's gross estate equals 20 percent or more of the value of the outstanding stock of each of two or more corporations, they may be combined in order to meet the 35 percent requirement (IRC § 303(b)(2)(B)).
2. The seller must be obligated to pay death taxes and expenses, whether or not the proceeds are actually used for that purpose (IRC § 303(b)(3)).

To qualify for Section 303 treatment, the redemption must occur within three years and 90 days after filing the federal estate tax return (IRC §§ 303(b)(1)(A), 6501(a)). The shareholder may extend the Section 303 redemption over 14 years where the estate defers estate tax payments pursuant to Section 6166 (see Tax Deferral Opportunities in Chapter 17).

To secure the benefits of IRC Section 303, the shareholder should not own any insurance policies on his life that would make the proceeds of a policy part of his gross estate. See IRC § 2042(1). The inclusion of insurance proceeds could so alter the relative proportions of assets in the estate that it would be impossible to meet the percentage requirements of Section 303. By avoiding any "incidents of ownership," including rights to access the policy's cash value, the shareholder may preserve the Section 303 election.

Alternative Minimum Tax

The alternative minimum tax (AMT) prevents profitable C corporations from avoiding income tax through the use of deductions and exclusions. Calculation of AMT requires adding back to the corporation's taxable income certain deductions and exclusions known as "preference items." Normally, life insurance policy cash value accumulations and death proceeds are not included in taxable income, but they are preference items for purposes of the AMT calculation (IRC §§ 72(e)(5), 101(a), 56(g)(4)(B)(ii)). As a result, corporate-owned life insurance policies held to fund buy-sell agreements have the potential to increase the corporation's tax burden.

In the calculation of AMT, only 75 percent of life insurance cash value buildup and proceeds are subject to tax at the 20 percent AMT rate (IRC §§ 55(b), 56(g)(1)). The effective tax rate on life insurance proceeds and cash buildup is thus 15 percent (75 percent of the increase in cash value or the proceeds multiplied by the 20 percent rate). The corporation may deduct from alternative minimum taxable income that portion of the premium allocated to death protection (IRC § 56(g)(4)(B)(ii)). The corporation must pay the excess of AMT over its ordinary tax liability. Any amounts paid pursuant to AMT liability may be carried forward—and recovered—in subsequent years to satisfy any ordinary income tax liability, but not future AMT (IRC § 53).

Cash value increases alone will rarely trigger an AMT liability because of the allowable premium deduction. Typically, the AMT will only recognize such increases where the corporation has a current AMT liability from other sources or where the policy is extraordinarily cash-rich. The receipt of a death benefit is relatively more likely to trigger an AMT liability.

A Subchapter C corporation may plan for the AMT by purchasing a death benefit large enough to fund both the buyout and its AMT obligation. This amounts to a corporate purchase of 118 percent of its stock redemption obligation under the buy-sell agreement. As an alternative, the purchase price may be revised downward to reflect the corporate AMT liability.

Accumulated Earnings Tax

Once a corporation has accumulated earnings beyond its reasonable needs, the IRS will presume any accumulation was intended to avoid income tax and will impose the accumulated earnings tax.

The corporation may accumulate earnings as long as the accumulation does not exceed the "reasonable needs of the business" (IRC §§ 531, 537). Once the corporation accumulates earnings in excess of its reasonable business needs, an additional tax of 39.6 percent will be imposed on the accumulated taxable income (IRC § 531). Corporations are allowed an accumulated earnings credit equal to the greater of (1) the reasonable retention need of the business, and (2) the amount by which $250,000 (or

$150,000, in the case of personal service corporations) exceeds the accumulated earnings and profits of the corporation at the close of the preceding tax year (IRC § 535(c)). This tax applies only to earnings accumulated for the purpose of avoiding income tax to shareholders (IRC § 532(a)).

Accumulations to fund corporate obligations under a stock redemption may be deemed a reasonable need of the business if the redemption is to benefit the corporation, and not the surviving shareholders. Courts have generally viewed the following to be reasonable business needs:

- Avoidance of potential shareholder disputes
- Elimination of dissension
- Desire for continuity of management
- Accumulation of earnings to satisfy a buyout obligation after that obligation has been triggered

See, for example, *Mountain State Steel Foundries, Inc. v. Commissioner*, 284 F.2d 737 (4th Cir. 1960), where it was held that an accumulation to fund a redemption in order to eliminate shareholder conflict serves a valid business purpose.

Redemption agreements funded through retained earnings should document these business reasons to ensure accumulated earnings tax avoidance. But accumulation of income merely to fund a buy-sell agreement is not a sufficient business reason. See, for example, *John B. Lambert & Associates v. United States*, 76-2 U.S.T.C. ¶ 9776 (Ct. Cl. 1976). Accumulations to fund a buy-out of a majority of stockholders will be especially scrutinized as offering its primary benefit to the shareholders. See, for example, *Pelton Steel Casting Co. v. Commissioner*, 28 T.C. 153 (1957), *aff'd*, 251 F.2d 278 (7th Cir. 1958).

Following the same logic, accumulated earnings tax will not be imposed on income retained for the purchase of life insurance if the insurance serves a valid business need and is generally related to that need. See *General Smelting Co. v. Commissioner*, 4 T.C. 313 (1944). Life insurance policy cash value accumulations to fund a redemption obligation will be considered reasonable only when the redemption has a corporate purpose. Again, the reason for the accumulation will determine whether the accumulated earnings tax is applicable.

The code specifically exempts from the accumulated earnings tax amounts accumulated to fund the business's Section 303 redemption obligations (IRC § 537(a)(2)). However, this exemption is limited to the sum of death taxes and funeral and administration expenses (IRC § 303(a)). The shelter applies only to amounts accumulated in the year of, and those subsequent to, the shareholder's death (IRC § 537(b)(1)).

Split-Dollar Redemption

Under a stock redemption plan, the corporation buys and owns a life insurance policy on the life of each shareholder. It names itself the beneficiary of the policy, and uses the death proceeds to fund the redemption triggered by a shareholder's death. Should the buy-sell agreement terminate before the death of the shareholder, the corporation remains the owner of the policy, giving the insured no personal life insurance benefit. Use of the "reverse split-dollar" method offers a solution to this problem.

With reverse split dollar, each shareholder purchases and owns a life insurance policy on his own life. The shareholder pays the premiums and retains a portion of the death benefit equal to the lesser of the policy cash value or cumulative premiums paid. He then assigns or endorses the remaining death benefit to the corporation. The corporation pays premiums equal to its imputed economic benefit (generally, the so-called PS-58 cost in lieu of the insurer's annual renewable term costs). This arrangement secures death proceeds for the corporation to fund a buyout at the shareholder's death while allowing the shareholder to own the policy for his own personal benefit. Should the agreement be terminated before the death of the shareholder, the endorsement may be released by the corporation, and the shareholder may take advantage of the policy's cash value to supplement his retirement income.

Disadvantages of Redemption

Although the stock redemption arrangement does provide for the succession of the business after death of an owner, various tax issues and risks compromise its efficacy. Issues of the AMT, the retained earnings tax, dividend treatment, and stock attribution attach only when the corporation is the purchaser.

Other adverse consequences may discourage a corporate redemption. Corporate creditors may attach the cash value of any corporate-owned life insurance policy. Additionally, where the corporation distributes property (including a corporate-owned life insurance policy) in redemption of stock, the corporation may realize a taxable gain to the extent that the property's fair market value exceeds its basis (IRC § 311(b)). Further, a stock redemption generally does not step up the surviving shareholders' basis in the corporation, while the value of their interests increases. Finally, any corporate-owned life insurance will be considered a corporate asset, and may increase the value of the stock for estate tax purposes (Treas. Reg. §§ 20. 2031-2(f), 20. 2042-1(c) (6)). For these reasons the stock redemption buy-sell arrangement may not be the design of choice.

Cross-Purchase Agreement

A cross-purchase agreement requires each shareholder to buy, pro rata, the interest of a departing shareholder on the happening of a triggering event. Cross-purchase agreements obligate only the owners, allowing the corporation to remain a bystander. A cross-purchase is often favored over a stock redemption plan because it: (1) avoids the AMT and accumulated earnings tax on C corporations; (2) allows each succeeding shareholder to receive his stock from decedent's estate at a stepped-up basis—that is, at its fair market value at the time of the decedent's death; and (3) altogether avoids issues of dividend treatment and the attribution rules.

Under a cross-purchase approach, the shareholders enter into a binding agreement for the purchase and sale of their interests in the corporation. This agreement requires the surviving shareholders to buy, and the deceased shareholder's estate to sell, the decedent's stock at an agreed or determinable price. To fund the purchase, each shareholder buys life insurance on the other shareholders equal to their pro rata share of the insured's stock interest. Each shareholder is the owner and beneficiary of policies on the lives of the other shareholders. Death places the stock in the decedent's estate. At the same time, the surviving shareholders receive insurance proceeds with which they purchase their share of the stock from the estate. The decedent's estate receives a new, fair market valuation—a step up in basis—for the stock owned at death (IRC § 1014). As such, the decedent typically recognizes no capital gain pursuant to the sale.

A cross-purchase arrangement offers several advantages:

- The surviving shareholders receive an increase in their basis in the corporation's stock equal to the purchase price of the shares they acquire.
- Corporate creditors have no rights against the life insurance proceeds or policy cash values held by the shareholders.

- Life insurance proceeds received by the shareholders will not increase the corporate AMT liability.
- Cross-purchases do not give rise to dividend questions or attribution rules.
- Policies can be transferred to the insureds without creating a transfer for value.

But problems can arise, including the following:

- The plan becomes increasingly difficult to administer with each additional shareholder.
- The shareholders may have difficulty paying premiums.
- The cash value of policies owned on other shareholders' lives are includible in the decedent shareholder's estate.
- The shareholders will violate the transfer-for-value rule where, to provide additional funds for a later buyout, the deceased's estate transfers policies to shareholders other than the respective insureds.
- Careful consideration must be given prior to electing the cross-purchase method as agreements with mandatory purchase provisions may restrict the shareholders' flexibility in choosing to execute a stock redemption later. A corporate purchase that relieves the shareholders of a "primary and unconditional obligation" to purchase stock may result in a constructive dividend, taxable to the shareholders (Rev. Rul. 69-608; see, e.g., *Sullivan v. United States*, 363 F.2d 724 (8th Cir. 1966); *Jacobs v. Commissioner*, 41 T.C.M. 951 (1981)). To avoid this pitfall, the buy-sell may be structured in a wait-and-see format, giving the corporation the first right to purchase shares and shareholders the second right to purchase shares. Any shares that remain unpurchased must then be purchased by the corporation (see Wait-and-See Buy-Sell Agreement later in this chapter).

Trusteed Cross-Purchase

The financial advisor may well recommend a trust to administer a cross-purchase agreement. Trusts reduce the number of policies required in multiple shareholder cross-purchase arrangements. They also offer comfort to the shareholders that the policies will be used for their intended purpose, while delegating to others all the administrative details, such as maintaining insurance policies and eventually transferring stock. However, the use of a trust may create transfer-for-value problems avoidable only through the use of a partnership.

In a trusteed cross-purchase, a selected trustee is made both the owner and the beneficiary of the policies subject to the buy-sell agreement. The trustee takes physical custody of the agreement, the insurance policies, and the stock. At the death of an insured, the trustee receives the policy proceeds and turns them over to the decedent-shareholder's estate in payment of the decedent's business interest. In turn, the estate relinquishes its business interest to the trustee, who then delivers it to the surviving shareholders.

However, the very use of a trustee presents a tax trap. Transfers of interests in life insurance for valuable consideration will convert insurance proceeds into taxable income (IRC § 101(a)). Under a trusteed agreement, the decedent-shareholder's beneficial interest in the remaining trust-owned policies on the life of each other shareholder must be transferred so as not to subject the decedent's estate to the terms of the buy-sell. Simply removing the decedent-shareholder from the mix gives the surviving shareholders increased beneficial interests in the policies held by the trustee on the lives of the remaining shareholders. The IRS will likely deem this a transfer of interests in consideration of the reciprocal promises to permit this shift and as such, a transfer for value, subjecting at least a portion of the proceeds received on the death of a subsequent shareholder to ordinary income tax. To avoid this problem, the shareholders should also be partners in a bona fide partnership (see Partnership in Chapter 4).

A policy transfer in which an insured retains "incidents of ownership" will result in inclusion of that policy's proceeds in the insured's estate (IRC § 2042). In a pure cross-purchase, policy proceeds are generally not included because the shareholders possess no incidents of ownership in the policies on their lives. With a trusteed plan, however, estate inclusion will depend on the trust's terms and administration.

A carefully structured trusteed plan may provide some protection against estate inclusion. Where the trusteed buy-sell gives the trustee all of the rights in the policy, and the trustee is obligated to exercise those rights in accordance with the terms of the buy-sell agreement, the shareholders will be deemed contractually to have surrendered all rights in the policy (*First National Bank of Birmingham v. United States*, 358 F.2d 625 (5th Cir. 1966)). Where no incidents of ownership are retained by the shareholders, policy proceeds will not be included in the insured's estate (*Estate of Infante v. Commissioner*, 29 T.C.M. 903 (1970)).

Conversely, a decedent who retains a reversionary interest in a life insurance policy along with a right to control incidents of ownership with others after transferring the policy to a trust will have the policy's proceeds included in his estate (Tech. Adv. Mem. 93-49-002). Where the buy-sell trustee acts more as an agent for the shareholders than as an independent trustee, the decedent may be found to have held incidents of ownership in the policy.

Partnership Cross-Purchase

Replacing the trust with a partnership takes advantage of a built-in exception to the transfer-for-value problem raised in the trusteed agreement. Here, the partnership operates just as the trust, in that the partnership is both the owner and beneficiary of the policies. The partnership functions to complete the buyout on the death of a shareholder. However, unlike the trust situation, the death of a shareholder does not create a transfer for value. Although the shareholder's death terminates his interest in the partnership, the transfer of the decedent's beneficial interest in the remaining life insurance policies to the survivors is excepted from the transfer-for-value rules (IRC § 101(a)(2)(B)). In addition, this exception allows in-force policies to be transferred to the partnership to fund the buyout. Proceeds from policies transferred within three years of the insured's death are includible in the decedent's estate (IRC § 2035). Even if the insured dies after a three-year period, proceeds will be includible in the insured's estate to the extent that he holds incidents of ownership in the policy, which would be equal to his partnership interest.

The partnership should be a bona fide partnership for federal income tax purposes in order to avoid the transfer-for-value rule. Transfers to partnerships that do not qualify as partnerships for federal income tax purposes will not be granted exception under the transfer-for-value rule. However, the regulations state that, for tax purposes, the term *partnership* "is broader in scope than the common law meaning of partnership, and may include groups not commonly called partnerships" (Treas. Reg. § 1.761-1(a)). Some commentators have construed a Private Letter Ruling to suggest that a valid partnership exists where its only activity is to hold and manage a portfolio of life insurance policies (Priv. Ltr. Rul. 93-09-021). This reading, however, may be too broad. Accordingly, prudence dictates transfers to partnerships that are previously established and in a business conducted for profit.

Split-Dollar Cross-Purchase

In a simple cross-purchase, each shareholder is required to purchase insurance on the lives of the other shareholders. Premium payments may impose a financial hardship on the shareholders. So, corporations may choose to bonus out premium dollars to its shareholders for the purpose of paying premiums. However, the corporation may be unable or unwilling to fund the purchase. Split-dollar life insurance may provide a solution to this problem.

As in the typical cross-purchase plan, each shareholder purchases policies on the lives of the other shareholders. At the same time, each shareholder enters into a split-dollar agreement with the corporation, providing for the employee-shareholder to pay that portion of the premium equal to the economic benefit of the coverage received in that year. The economic benefit is equal to the lesser of the PS-58 rate or the insurer's annual renewable term rate (Rev. Rul. 66-110). With a nonemployee shareholder the economic benefit will be taxed as a dividend to the extent there are undistributed earnings and profits (Rev. Rul. 79-50). The corporation pays the remaining portion of the premiums, and takes back from the shareholder a collateral assignment of the policy to secure reimbursement of its premium payments.

On death, the corporation is reimbursed for its cumulative premiums paid under the plan through policy proceeds. The remaining proceeds are then paid to the surviving shareholder who uses the funds to purchase the decedent's stock under the cross-purchase agreement. Under this type of split-dollar arrangement, known commonly as the equity split-dollar arrangement, the client should be aware that the IRS has ruled that, where the employer's investment element is limited to total premiums paid by the employer, income will be reportable to the extent the cash surrender value of the policy exceeds the premiums paid by the employer (see Technical Advisory Memorandum [TAM] 96-04-001). Although the TAM is not law and has been widely criticized by the tax-planning community, it is an indication of current IRS thinking. Until further clarification, taxpayers who implement equity split-dollar arrangements should be advised of the planning implications of this TAM.

If the cross-purchase agreement is terminated before the buyout, the shareholder may reimburse the corporation and terminate the split-dollar agreement. Or, in the case of an employee-shareholder, the corporation may choose to relinquish its assignment without reimbursement, creating a taxable bonus to the employee equal to its interest. Termination of a split-dollar cross-purchase will, however, result in each shareholder owning policies on the lives of other shareholders. The shareholders may resolve this problem by transferring the policies to the respective insureds, subject to possible gift and income taxes. Some commentators view the release or repayment of a collateral assignment on cross-owned insurance as a transfer for value. In the typical split-dollar situation, the release of a collateral assignment will not create a transfer for value because the policy owner is also the insured. As such, the release is a "transfer to the insured," and excepted from the transfer-for-value rule (IRC § 101(a)(2)(B)). However, in the cross-purchase context, this exception is not available since the policy owner will be a shareholder other than the insured. But the very release or reimbursement may create a transfer for value, subjecting the transferred portion of policy proceeds to ordinary income tax. To avoid this problem, the shareholders may be advised to become partners in a bona fide partnership to ensure that the transfer falls within the "transfer to a partner of the insured" exception (IRC § 101(a)(2)(B); Treas. Reg. § 1.101-1(b)(1)).

The transfer-for-value issue also arises with the use of an endorsement split-dollar strategy in a cross-purchase agreement. With endorsement split dollar, the corporation owns a life insurance policy on the life of a shareholder. The corporation retains an interest in the policy equal to the greater of its cash value or premiums paid. The remaining death benefit is endorsed to the noninsured shareholder. When the buy-sell agreement is terminated, the corporation will regain full control over the policy, which then can be used for other business purposes—such as funding a nonqualified deferred-compensation or "death benefit only" plan. However, the execution of the endorsement in favor of a noninsured shareholder effects a transfer of a beneficial interest in the policy to a noninsured. Because a binding and enforceable buy-sell agreement constitutes valuable consideration, this may be considered a transfer for value. Without application of one of the exceptions enumerated at IRC Section 101(a)(2)(B), death proceeds will be subject to ordinary income tax.

Split-dollar cross-purchase arrangements are further complicated by controlling shareholder issues. Typically, with cross-owned life insurance, the estate of any shareholder will not be increased at his death by the amount of death benefit because the decedent holds no incidents of ownership over the policy on his life (IRC § 2042). Nevertheless, a controlling shareholder—any shareholder owning more than 50 percent of the voting power of the corporation—will be attributed with those incidents of ownership held by the corporation over split-dollar proceeds paid to third parties (Treas. Reg. § 20.2042-1(c)(6)). So, even though a controlling shareholder holds no direct incidents of ownership over a policy on his life, ownership will be imputed to him through his controlling interest in the corporation. Accordingly, the entire portion of the death benefit owned by the other shareholders on the life of the controlling shareholder in a split-dollar arrangement will be included in the controlling shareholder's estate (Rev. Rul. 82-145). This rule prevents insurance proceeds ultimately under the control of a majority shareholder from escaping estate inclusion through payment to third party beneficiaries.

To keep the proceeds out of the insured's taxable estate, the corporation must not hold any incidents of ownership in the policy. The restricted collateral assignment approach attempts to comply with Revenue Ruling 82-145 by eliminating all corporate rights in the policy except the right to reimbursement of premium outlays. This can be accomplished through an appropriately drafted split-dollar agreement coupled with a restricted collateral assignment form. The IRS, however, has cast some doubt on the effectiveness of this arrangement. In Private Letter Ruling 90-37-012, a split-dollar plan was structured to grant a corporation an interest in the insurance proceeds equal to its premiums paid. To this end, the corporation was designated as the owner of the policies to the extent of their cash surrender value and possessed a security interest in them. The IRS found that the corporation's "right to the cash surrender value and its security interest in the policies" did indeed amount to incidents of ownership. This analysis suggests that only a complete elimination of corporate policy rights will be effective in removing incidents of ownership.

An alternative to the restricted collateral agreement approach is the sole ownership (or "undocumented") split-dollar plan. With the sole ownership approach, the shareholder enters into a split-dollar agreement with the corporation. However, no assignments or other such forms are filed with the insurance company that would grant the corporation an interest in the policy. The split-dollar agreement alone evidences the plan's existence for income tax purposes. Under the agreement, the shareholder is bound to reimburse the corporation for its premium outlays, but not necessarily from policy values. While both the restricted collateral assignment and the sole ownership methods are used extensively in practice, sole ownership seems to be the less risky of the two. Still, sole ownership holds some amount of uncertainty. The IRS may ultimately choose to characterize this arrangement not as split dollar at all, but as a loan requiring compliance with the below-market loan rules of IRC Section 7872. Nevertheless, even this worst case construction would not subject policy proceeds to estate tax inclusion.

If a shareholder is not a controlling shareholder at the time that a buy-sell agreement is executed, he may become one through the attrition of other shareholders or the purchase of additional stock. Therefore, it is critical that buy-sell agreements using split dollar be periodically reviewed to ensure that the controlling shareholder problem has not come into play. The financial advisor should consider removing any incidents of ownership for any shareholder under such a cross-purchase because any one of them might become a majority shareholder.

Wait-and-See Buy-Sell Agreement

A wait-and-see buy-sell agreement allows shareholders to postpone the choice between a stock redemption and a cross-purchase buy-sell until the death of a shareholder. The approach requires that both the corporation and the shareholders agree to purchase the stock of a departing shareholder as the buy-sell agreement prescribes.

The shareholders may choose to fund the wait-and-see buy-sell as a stock redemption. Here, the corporation owns policies on each of the shareholders and holds the first option to purchase any or all of the decedent's interest. The shareholders hold the second option and may purchase pro rata, any shares not redeemed by the corporation. The corporation is then obligated to redeem the remaining shares. Although this structure offers flexibility, stock redemption funding with corporate-owned life insurance provides no cash for the shareholder purchase. Accordingly, cross-purchase funding should be utilized.

Wait-and-see cross-purchase funding requires shareholder-owned policies. The buy-sell agreement secures a right of first refusal for the corporation and the second option for the shareholders. Any shares not purchased through the exercise of these options must be redeemed by the business. On a shareholder's death, the surviving shareholders receive the proceeds of his policy. The corporation may exercise its option to purchase the decedent's interest. The surviving shareholders may then purchase pro rata any shares not redeemed by the corporation. The corporation must then redeem any remaining shares. This mandatory corporate redemption is usually funded with capital contributed by the shareholders from the insurance proceeds. Accordingly, buyout pursuant to this funding mechanism offers a step up in basis to the surviving shareholders irrespective of the purchasing entity.

The shareholders may wish to utilize a trust to administer the terms of the wait-and-see buy-sell. However, the same transfer-for-value issues attach as in a trusteed cross-purchase, satisfactorily addressed through a bona fide partnership. Much as in the typical trusteed cross-purchase, the trust acquires life insurance on the lives of the shareholders. On the death of an insured shareholder, the trust distributes life insurance proceeds to the surviving shareholders. The survivors then make a capital contribution to the corporation to fund the redemption. The shareholders' contributions increase their respective bases in the corporation. Alternatively, the shareholders may elect to proceed with a cross-purchase that will also produce a stepped-up basis.

In the family context, a corporate redemption may result in a taxable dividend to the deceased shareholder to the extent that the purchase price exceeds the Section 303 exempted amounts. The wait-and-see agreement may be structured to require that the corporation redeem only that portion of the shareholder's interest that qualifies for Section 303 treatment and that the surviving shareholders purchase the balance.

Employee Stock Ownership Plan

An ESOP is a qualified retirement plan designed to purchase the sponsoring employer's stock. It has been suggested that ESOPs are capable of providing tax-deductible premiums for life insurance to purchase the stock of a retiring or deceased owner. To effect that intent, the ESOP receives cash through corporate tax-deductible contributions (subject to certain limits). See IRC §§ 404(a)(9), 415(c)(6). The ESOP then uses these funds to purchase life insurance on the lives of shareholders. On an insured shareholder's death, the ESOP receives death proceeds with which it may negotiate the purchase of the decedent's stock. The ESOP will have converted otherwise nondeductible corporate premiums to tax deductions.

The use of an ESOP for buy-sell purposes has great appeal. Its advantages include the following:

- Employer contributions of stock or cash are tax deductible, subject to certain limitations, while not currently includible in the participant's income.
- Employees receive the additional benefit of stock ownership, thereby connecting them more closely with the corporation.
- The employee or beneficiary who receives a distribution of closely held stock from the ESOP also receives a "put option"—that is, the right to demand that the company repurchase the stock at its fair market value.

On balance, though, its disadvantages, including the following, probably outweigh its advantages:

- An ESOP may not enter into a binding agreement that obligates it to purchase a shareholder's interest at death (Treas. Reg. § 54.4975-11(a)(7)(i)). Accordingly, an ESOP may not be a purchaser in a traditional buy-sell.
- The IRS will not approve an ESOP that is a party to a buy-sell agreement, in that, as a qualified plan, it must operate mainly for the exclusive benefit of the employees, rather than for the benefit of the shareholders.
- Proceeds from the sale are generally received by the shareholder as dividends.
- The amount of life insurance that the ESOP may purchase to facilitate a buyout is limited in that it must invest primarily in qualifying employer securities (Treas. Reg. § 1.401-1(b)(1)). Life insurance coverage must be incidental to the plan's retirement benefits. Life insurance will be considered incidental if less than 50 percent of the company's contribution to the plan on behalf of the participant is used to purchase whole life insurance, or no more than 25 percent is used to purchase term insurance (Rev. Rul. 54-51; Rev. Rul. 61-164; Priv. Ltr. Rul. 87-25-088).
- The original shareholders will typically lose control over shares sold to ESOPs in that the ESOP must eventually distribute these shares to its participants.
- The ESOP must purchase employer stock at a price not in excess of its fair market value. Purchases in excess of fair market value are considered prohibited transactions, to which stiff penalties attach (IRC § 4975). The ESOP trustee would be required to retain an independent appraiser to establish the stock's fair market value at the time of sale (IRC §§ 401(a)(28)(C), 4975(d)(13); ERISA § 408(e)).

Despite these deficiencies, the corporate tax savings through ESOP contributions may be indirectly used to fund a redemption agreement or ESOP buyout. First, the corporation would contribute treasury stock to the ESOP equal to the corporation's projected premium payments. Stock contributions are tax deductible at their fair market value and result in income tax savings to the corporation without a cash outlay. The corporation would then use this cash to purchase the life insurance necessary to fund its redemption obligations. The corporation may also purchase insurance on key ESOP-participating employees to fund a corporate repurchase at the participant's death. At death, the corporation would receive insurance proceeds with which it could redeem all of the deceased's stock, either pursuant to a redemption agreement or through the insured's participation in the ESOP.

The corporation also can contribute its insurance proceeds to the ESOP, providing funds with which the ESOP may redeem the deceased's shares. Here, policy proceeds become income tax deductible.

Estate Tax Deferrals

If the value of a closely held business exceeds 35 percent of the decedent's adjusted gross estate, estate tax may be deferred for up to 14 years. The estate need only make annual interest payments for years 1 through 4, and 10 annual payments of principal and interest thereafter (IRC § 6166(a)). Various closely held business interests may be aggregated for the purpose of meeting the percentage requirement, provided that the decedent owned at least 20 percent of the total value of each entity (IRC § 6166(c)). To qualify as a closely held business, the interest may be in a sole proprietorship, a partnership, a corporation, or by extension, a LLC (IRC § 6166(b)). A partnership interest will qualify if 20 percent or more of the total capital interest in the partnership is included in the gross estate, or if the partnership has 15 or fewer partners. Stock in a corporation qualifies if 20 percent or more in value of the voting stock is included in determining the gross estate of the decedent, or the corporation has 15 or fewer shareholders.

Purchases pursuant to a buy-sell agreement could terminate the Section 6166 deferral election. Estate tax liability will be due immediately upon the sale of 50 percent or more of the value of the closely held business (IRC § 6166(g)). Stock redemptions to pay death taxes under Section 303 are excepted from this rule (IRC § 6166(g)(1)(B)). Deferral may be preserved under a buy-sell agreement through a series of sales, each in an amount equal to the next estate tax installment due. The final installment will include that portion of the purchase price that exceeds the deferred estate taxes. See Priv. Ltr. Rul. 92-02-020 (periodic redemptions made pursuant to Section 303 to pay estate taxes did not terminate taxpayer's Section 6166 deferral election). Nevertheless, the agreement must provide a fixed or determinable value for the decedent's stock if that valuation is to be accepted for estate tax purposes.

Premium Allocation

Premium payment is always a critical component in structuring a buy-sell agreement. In corporate redemptions, shareholders bear premium burdens in relation to their respective interests in the corporation. In cross-purchases, shareholders bear premium burdens in relation to the risk of the life they are insuring and the amount of stock held by that shareholder. This usually results in relatively higher premium payments for younger and minority shareholders.

Unrelated shareholders may choose to allocate premium payments to equalize the premium burden. One possibility would be for each stockholder to pay a share of the total premiums necessary equal to their proportionate interest in the company. Related shareholders who assume a larger portion of the premium payment must be careful to avoid a deemed gift.

Another choice is to have the corporation assist each shareholder in funding his cross-purchase obligation through: (1) a deductible bonus of premium dollars equal to his premium obligation, upon which the employee is responsible for payment of the taxes (IRC § 162); (2) a "double bonus" through which the corporation pays to the employee as compensation an equal amount to his premium obligation, plus the income tax the bonus incurs; or (3) a split dollar arrangement (see Split-Dollar Cross-Purchase earlier in this chapter).

Valuation

Setting a valuation of the business interest performs three functions. First, and most obviously, it fixes the amount to be received by the selling shareholder at buyout. Second, it preempts disputes among shareholders as to the business's fair value at a time when the shareholders do not know whether they will be purchasers or sellers and are thus likely to be most fair and objective. Third, the buy-sell agreement should set the estate tax value of each shareholder's business interest.

The buy-sell agreement must contain four elements to ensure that the IRS will respect the agreed valuation for estate taxes purposes:

1. The price must be either fixed or determinable by a formula (see Rev. Rul. 157, 1953–2 C.B. 255.)
2. The estate must be obligated to sell at the agreed price. Generally, an option to purchase at a predetermined price will fix the estate tax value. See *Estate of Carpenter v. Commissioner*, 64 T.C.M. 1274 (1992).
3. The obligation to sell at the agreed price must be binding during lifetime (Treas. Reg. § 20.2031-2(g); Rev. Rul. 59-60). This requirement is satisfied where the shareholder is required to offer stock first to the other shareholders in contemplation of a third-party sale. See, for example, *May v. McGowan*, 194 F.2d 396 (2nd Cir. 1952). The lifetime price may not exceed the price applicable at death at which the estate tax value is to be fixed. See *Brodrick v. Gore*, 224 F.2d 892 (10th Cir. 1995).
4. The agreement must constitute a "*bona fide* business arrangement and not a device to pass shares to natural objects of decedent's bounty for less than full and adequate consideration" (Treas. Reg. § 20.2031-2(h)). This requirement prevents a shareholder from de-valuing the business just to suppress the value of his estate, while passing the business interest at death.

The IRS will determine the value of a family business interest if an agreement sets a value at less than fair market value (IRC § 2703(a); Treas. Reg. § 25.2703-1(b)(3)). This rule allows the IRS to ignore valuations designed to avoid estate taxes. However, the IRS will consider below-market valuations that meet three requirements:

1. The agreement is in fact a bona fide business agreement
2. The agreement is not a device to transfer the business interest to members of the decedent's family for less than full and adequate consideration
3. The terms of the agreement are comparable to similar arrangements entered into by persons in an arm's-length transaction (IRC § 2703(b)).

If these three conditions are met, the IRS will consider the buy-sell agreement when determining valuation of the business interest for estate tax purposes. Businesses of which less than 50 percent is owned by the decedent-shareholder's family are excepted from this rule (Treas. Reg. § 25.2703-1(b)(3)).

A buy-sell agreement must provide either a specific or fixed price at which a business interest will be purchased or a specific method by which a purchase price will be established. Determination of the agreed price depends on the type of business conducted, the number of employees, the value of its assets, its size, and whether the business is publicly or privately held. Although using a fixed value for the business interest offers a simple solution to valuation questions, a fixed value cannot for long accurately reflect the true value of the business. A fixed purchase price usually necessitates periodic reevaluation, which may be automatic and mathematical. However, fixed-dollar valuations are not recommended for family businesses that might well fail to meet the comparability test.

In addition to fixed valuations, a variety of formulas may be used in valuing a business interest (see Chapter 11). The objective of any formula is to arrive at the fair market value for the business interest (see Treas. (Reg. § 20.2031-3). Most buy-sell formulas are based on one or more of the following factors:

- The nature of the business and its operating history
- The general economic outlook and industry prospects
- The book value of the interests and financial condition of the business
- The business's earning capacity
- The business's ability to distribute earnings
- The existence of good will or other intangible assets
- Comparable sales of interests in the business
- The market price of stocks of publicly traded corporations engaged in the same, or similar, lines of business (Rev. Rul. 59–60; see also Rev. Rul. 68-609, applying corporate stock valuation criteria to partnership interests).

Several common valuation methods have gained popularity in recent years. The most common valuation formulas are earnings-based, utilizing the present worth of the expected net income to be received over the life of the business. Many buy-sell agreements incorporate the business's book value, which is simply the value of business assets, less liabilities, as both are shown on the company books. Or, the owners may feel that an independent appraisal is the best measure of the company's value. In any case, the owners must remain sensitive to the company's basic operation when choosing the valuation method.

If the buy-sell agreement is not effective in fixing the value for estate tax purposes, the business interest will be valued at its fair market value on the date of the shareholder's death (Treas. Reg. § 20.2031-1(b)). In a corporate redemption, the value will be inflated because of the inclusion of the insurance proceeds paid out to the corporation. This increase may be offset by the loss of a key person.

Transfers for Value

Buy-sell agreements frequently contain transfer-for-value traps sabotaging the otherwise favored tax treatment of life insurance. Any transfer or potential transfer of a life insurance policy pursuant to a buy-sell agreement must be scrutinized to ensure that it will not run afoul of these rules. Proper planning will secure income tax exclusion of the policy proceeds when collected by the transferee.

Life insurance policies transferred for valuable consideration are generally income taxable to the extent that policy proceeds exceed the policy owner's basis (IRC § 101(a)). There are several exceptions to this general rule, including transfers to the insured, to a partner of the insured, to a partnership in which the insured is a partner, and to a corporation in which the insured is an officer or shareholder (IRC § 101(a)(2)(B)). Additionally, transfers of policies for which no valuable consideration is given—that is, bona fide gifts—will be excepted from the transfer-for-value rules (IRC § 101(a)(2)(A)).

Although consideration is clearly present in the payment of money for a policy, a more subtle consideration may exist in the buy-sell arena. Usually, the mutual promises contained in a buy-sell agreement are themselves considered sufficient consideration. In *Monroe v. Patterson*, 197 F. Supp. 146 (N.D. Ala. 1961), consideration was found to exist in a transfer of a corporate-owned policy to a trust established to administer a cross-purchase buy-sell agreement. The surviving shareholders argued that, because no money was paid for the policy, no consideration was given for the transfer and, therefore, no transfer for value had occurred. The district court disagreed, holding that the shareholders' mutual promises to purchase the insured's stock at death and the agreement to make premium payments constituted consideration. It follows that the putative gift of a loaned-against policy would be treated as a release of liability to the donor. Such a release would be deemed consideration for transfer-for-value purposes.

The IRS has additionally found that reciprocal transfers of zero-cash-value policies constitute adequate consideration to trigger the transfer-for-value rule. In Private Letter Ruling 77-34-048, two shareholders each owned a policy on their own lives. The shareholders simultaneously transferred these policies to each other to fund a cross-purchase agreement. Because each of the policies was in its first year, they had no cash surrender value. The IRS held that the transfer-for-value rule applied even though no sale of the policy was effected. The IRS found consideration in the reciprocal exchange of the policies between shareholders. The fact that the policies had no value at the time of transfer was irrelevant for purposes of applying the rule.

Under some business circumstances, a corporation may wish to abandon its life insurance-funded stock redemption plan in favor of a cross-purchase. Care should be taken as such a transaction could give rise to transfer-for-value problems. The corporation may simply cross-transfer its policies to the shareholders to effectuate the switch. Here, the corporation transfers to shareholder A its policy on the life of shareholder B, and transfers to shareholder B its policy on the life of shareholder A. This clearly creates a transfer for value. To avoid this problem, the corporation may either surrender its existing policies or retain them to provide key person insurance. New policies purchased and owned by the shareholders would be necessary to fund the cross-purchase. Alternatively, if the shareholders are also partners in a bona fide partnership, the policies may be transferred in reliance on the transfer-to-a-partner exception.

In a cross-purchase arrangement, a transfer-for-value problem may arise at the death of a shareholder who owns policies on more than one other coshareholder. The representative of the decedent's estate may wish to sell the policies owned on the lives of the other shareholders to either the corporation or the shareholders. If the policies are sold to the corporation, it may then establish a stock redemption plan to work in conjunction with the existing cross-purchase. Such a transfer to the corporation, in which the insured is a shareholder, is exempted from the transfer-for-value rule (IRC 101(a)(2)(B)). Or the shareholders may wish to use the life insurance to fund a future buy-sell through the cross-ownership of existing policies. This transfer creates a transfer-for-value problem.

Terminating a buy-sell agreement may also give rise to a transfer-for-value problem. On the termination of a corporate redemption agreement, the corporation may wish to "roll out" the corporate policies to the respective insureds. A rollout falls into the exception of a transfer to the insured, but exposes policy proceeds to estate taxation. The shareholder may seek to avoid estate inclusion through a rollout to the insured's spouse. Such rollouts are not exceptions to the transfer-for-value rule, and will subject policy proceeds to income taxation. The IRS will not recast the transaction—even if the insured might have received the policy from the corporation and then subsequently gifted it to his spouse without a transfer for value. See, for example, *Estate of Rath v. United States*, 608 F.2d 254 (6th Cir. 1979).

A wrinkle worth considering: The shareholder may avoid both estate inclusion and the transfer-for-value rule through a rollout to the insured's grantor trust. Trusts are generally taxed as separate entities. Accordingly, rollouts from the corporation to a shareholder's trust will typically constitute a transfer for value. However, a policy transfer to an insured's grantor trust will be deemed a transfer to the insured himself, an exemption from the transfer-for-value rule. See *Swanson v. Commissioner*, 518 F.2d 59 (8th Cir. 1975).

A grantor trust is established where the grantor retains control over trust assets. As such, the grantor is deemed to own those assets for income tax purposes (IRC § 671). Policy proceeds will be received by the grantor trust tax free. Indeed, if the transfer is the last in a series of transactions, the transfer will remove the taint of any previous transfers for value (Treas. Reg. § 1.101-(b)(3)(ii)).

Accordingly, when a buy-sell is terminated, a policy may be rolled out to the insured's grantor trust as an exception to the transfer-for-value rule. This transfer avoids income taxation on the policy proceeds and it removes the policy from the insured's estate. Of course, care should be taken in establishing the grantor trust to ensure that it meets the statutory requirements of IRC Sections 671-677.

Finally, trusteed buy-sell agreements may lead to transfers for value at the death of a shareholder. In a trusteed buy-sell, a trust for the benefit of the shareholders is the owner and beneficiary of insurance policies on the lives of the shareholders. At the first shareholder's death, the decedent's interest in the trust assets terminates, and the surviving shareholders receive a commensurate increase in their beneficial interests.

The survivors receive increased interests in the policies held by the trust, which the IRS may likely deem a transfer for value. Although no physical transfer takes place, each shareholder death results in a shift of beneficial interest in the policies to the survivors. The shareholders' reciprocal promises to transfer such interests complete the transfer for value that renders the proceeds taxable. Accordingly, the trust document must not allow for the automatic transfer of the decedent's interest in the polices to the surviving shareholders.

The decedent's estate has only two options in disposing of its interests in the remaining policies without creating a transfer for value. The estate may transfer its interest in each policy to the policy insured—subjecting a portion of the insured's policy to estate tax inclusion. Or the estate may transfer its interest in all of the remaining policies to the corporation. Shareholders should consider using a bona fide partnership as an alternative to, or in conjunction with, a trust.

Combining the Life Insurance Retirement Plan and the Buy-Sell

Life insurance policies that accumulate cash values are frequently used to provide a source of retirement income for valuable employees, including shareholder-employees. The use of cash-accumulating policies in the buy-sell context may serve double duty, providing a source of cash to fund a buyout as well as a stream of income during retirement.

In a redemption arrangement, the corporation may purchase policies of sufficient face amounts to provide funds for both purposes. When the buy-sell agreement is terminated, the corporation may use the policy's cash value—through a series of withdrawals and loans—to provide retirement income to the executive, irrespective of whether that employee is the policy insured.

In a cross-purchase, the pattern is somewhat trickier. In the typical arrangement, the shareholders own policies on the lives of other shareholders. At the termination of the buy-sell agreement, the shareholder would like to access policy cash values for retirement. However, each still owns the policies on the lives of the others. Shareholders are often reluctant to hold polices on the lives of others and instead, through reciprocal transfers, want to own the policies on their own lives. Transfers of policies to their insureds may be accomplished without subjecting the proceeds to ordinary income tax. Yet, such transfers place the policies in the hands of the insured, requiring that, absent a subsequent policy transfer, the proceeds will be included in the insured's taxable estate.

S Corporation Buy-Sell Issues

The earnings of C corporations are twice taxed—once to the corporation as income, and then to its shareholders as dividends. An S corporation is only taxed once, at the shareholder level (IRC § 1366). This favorable pass-through tax treatment makes the S election a profitable one, allowing shareholders to use S corporation losses (to the extent of their basis) to offset personal income. Additionally, S corporations are subject to neither the accumulated earnings nor AMT issues of C corporations (see Alternative Minimum Tax and Accumulated Earnings Tax earlier in this chapter).

To protect the S election, an S corporation's buy-sell agreement must be carefully designed. First, it should evidence the shareholders' intent to maintain the S corporation status absent an explicit agreement to terminate the election. Such a recital makes concrete the shareholders' desire to continue the S election, and works against the IRS in construing an inadvertent termination as deliberate. The agreement should also include provisions for the termination of the S status as an explicit limitation on terminating events. In addition, the agreement should restrict inter vivos transfers of shares to protect against any automatic termination of the S election. Such restrictions should limit transfers to nonqualified shareholders, or to shareholders in excess of the 75-shareholder restriction.

Although AMT and accumulated earnings issues do not arise with S corporations, S redemptions are subject to many disadvantages. The surviving shareholders receive only a partial step up in basis at the buyout (except with a terminated tax year, as explained later), and corporate premiums are paid with nondeductible dollars. In addition, premiums paid by an S corporation are currently taxable to its shareholders on a pro rata basis, rather than according to the insured's risk. Shareholders are taxed on corporate dollars used to pay the premiums as if they had been given bonuses in that amount, and had purchased the policies on their own. However, they do not personally own either the policy or its cash value. As such, a cross-purchase is often recommended for S corporations. With a cross-purchase funded by a double bonus, the corporation would give a bonus to its shareholders sufficient to pay both the premium payments and the income tax liability incurred in conjunction with the bonus.

Nevertheless, an S corporation redemption may provide the surviving shareholders with a full step up in basis when coupled with an election to terminate the tax year. Electing a short year also ensures that a redemption will not be underfunded. Typically, policy proceeds received by a corporation on the death of a shareholder are treated as shareholder contributions, increasing proportionately each shareholder's basis in the company. This increase also inflates the value of the decedent's stock, leaving policy proceeds inadequate to complete the buyout. Because the surviving shareholders must share this increase with the decedent, they receive only a partial step up in basis.

By electing a short year, the surviving shareholders may receive the full benefit of the proceeds. An S corporation may terminate its tax year on the unanimous election of its shareholders where any shareholder terminates his interest in the corporation (IRC § 1377(a)(2)). The election breaks the tax year (usually, for S corporations, the calendar year) into two short years, allocating all items of income and deduction as if each short year were a full year. In the redemption context, the election terminates the decedent's right to allocation of the death proceeds. Thus, death proceeds are fully allotted to the surviving shareholders, increasing their basis by the entire amount received.

It is important to note that this method works only with cash-basis S corporations. Accrual-basis taxpayers are deemed to receive income when the right to receive it attaches, not when they actually receive it. The right to receive insurance proceeds presumably attaches at the death of the insured. As such, a short-year election made by an accrual-basis S corporation will likely not accomplish a full step up for the surviving shareholders.

The buy-sell, with all its versatility, offers the entrepreneur and his financial advisor a complex range of choices. Each should be carefully explored in light of the client's and his co-owners' personal and business objectives and the tax rules that militate for or against the strategies available to them.

Asset Protection Strategies

Entrepreneurship may require the taking of risks, but the successful entrepreneur will not throw caution to the wind. She will seek to mitigate risk and is likely to call on her financial advisor to help her do so.

Ethical Obligations

The financial advisor, however, may be subject to competing demands. On the one hand, attorneys—and, by extension, other professionals— may have an affirmative obligation to advise clients of the techniques available to them to preserve their assets. Such a duty results from the twin principles that (1) lawyers who practice in specialized areas must possess the degree of skill and knowledge possessed by other lawyers who practice in the same area, and (2) lawyers must defend their clients' interests vigorously and with undivided loyalty to them.

On the other hand, a financial advisor should assiduously avoid aiding a client who seeks to defraud a creditor. If a lawyer concludes that the advice he gives might be employed by his client to transfer assets in a way that would defraud known creditors, the lawyer is ethically obliged to cease representing her. Presumably, similar proscriptions may be applied to other professionals, too.

Both state and federal bankruptcy and fraudulent transfer rules prohibit transferring a person's assets to defeat the claims of known creditors. The Uniform Fraudulent Transfer Act identifies a fraudulent transfer as a transfer of assets made by a debtor (1) with actual intent to hinder, delay, or defraud any creditor, or (2) without receiving reasonably equivalent value in exchange, when the debtor (a) was engaged or was about to engage in a business or transaction for which the debtor's remaining assets would be unreasonably small or (b) intended to incur, or believed or reasonably should have believed that she would incur, debts beyond her ability to pay as they became due.

In determining whether a debtor had "actual intent" to hinder, delay, or defraud a creditor at the time she made a transfer, the following factors (sometimes known as *badges of fraud*) may be taken into consideration:

1. The transfer was to an insider.
2. The debtor retained possession or control of the property transferred.
3. The transfer was concealed.
4. The debtor had been sued or threatened with suit before the transfer.
5. The transfer was of substantially all the debtor's assets.
6. The debtor absconded.
7. The debtor removed or concealed assets.
8. The value of the consideration received for the transfer was inadequate compared to the value of the asset transferred.
9. The debtor was insolvent or became insolvent shortly after the transfer.
10. The transfer occurred shortly before or shortly after a substantial debt was incurred.
11. The debtor transferred the essential assets of her business to a lienor who transferred the assets to an insider of the debtor.

As you read the strategies described in this chapter bear in mind the overriding caveat that the advisor should never assist the client in perpetrating a fraud against a known creditor. At the same time, the advisor should understand that it is fair game, and indeed it may be his duty, to assist clients in protecting their assets from the claims of potential future or unknown creditors.

Exempt Assets

Certain assets enjoy special status and may be statutorily exempt from the claims of creditors. The entrepreneur and her financial advisor would be wise to make the most of the following exempt assets.

Benefits from Qualified Retirement Plans

The U.S. Supreme Court has held that, except for claims of a spouse or the IRS, assets held in qualified retirement plans cannot be alienated to satisfy the claims of creditors nor are they includible within a bankruptcy estate.

IRAs, however, are not afforded the same protection under federal law. Instead, state law will determine whether or not IRAs are insulated from creditors' claims.

Life Insurance Cash Values and Proceeds

The Bankruptcy Code exempts only $8,000 of a life insurance policy's cash value, but state laws may be much more generous, many of them exempting all of a life insurance or endowment policy's or an annuity contract's cash value and proceeds. The shield can be enhanced if a policy is owned by an irrevocable insurance trust, a family limited partnership, or an LLC, but only if the insured maintains no ownership interest in the entity and no "incidents of ownership" in the policy it owns.

Place of Residence

Florida and Texas are well known for their unlimited "homestead" exemptions. If the entrepreneur lives in a state with a substantial homeowner's exemption, she might consider increasing the protected equity in her home by carrying little or no mortgage indebtedness on it.

If state law permits, the entrepreneur might also consider holding title to her principal residence with her spouse as "tenants by the entirety." Unlike the more typical joint tenancy form of home ownership, tenancy by the entirety insulates each spouse's interest from the claims of the other's creditors (except the IRS, any state, or a mortgage lender). Further protection may be gained from the fact that neither spouse can unilaterally sever a tenancy by the entirety, which can only be terminated by the agreement of both husband and wife.

A family residence can also be protected by holding title in a Qualified Personal Residence Trust (QPRT) or, perhaps even better, a one-half undivided title interest in separate QPRTs held by the entrepreneur and her spouse. The strategy is ordinarily recommended for estate tax savings, which are lost if the entrepreneur dies before the interests he retains in the trust expires, but the trust shields the residence from the claims of creditors no matter when the entrepreneur dies. (Other split-interest trusts, such as charitable split-interest trusts, Grantor Retained Annuity Trusts (GRATs) and Grantor Retained Unitrusts (GRUTs), share the same characteristic, and private annuities, installment notes, and other split-interest transfers can also help shelter assets from creditors' claims.)

Gifting Strategies

The most obvious way to avoid a creditor's claim against an asset is for the entrepreneur simply to give it away. But two impediments may preclude outright gifting. For one thing, she may be disinclined to part with the asset or to shrink her net worth. For another, she may resist effecting any transaction that triggers a tax; here, a gift tax. But techniques are available that sidestep either or both problems.

Assets can be controlled by the entrepreneur, at least to a considerable degree, even after she gives them away. Depositing an asset in a trust, for example, may allow the grantor-entrepreneur to retain a "limited power of appointment" that, although the asset would remain in the grantor's eventual estate for estate tax purposes, may nevertheless insulate the asset from the claims of creditors. (The law is unkind to grantors who remain a beneficiary of such a trust while seeking to shelter its assets from creditors' claims, so caution is advised.) It is self-evident that acquiring title to assets in the name of one's spouse (unless financing conditions require the entrepreneur to take title) will forestall creditors' action against them. But, if the entrepreneur already owns assets that she fears may be placed at risk, she can consider transferring title to her spouse.

Gifts to spouses are not subject to tax under either the federal estate or gift tax laws. A marital deduction is available to all interspousal gifts during one's life or at death. Yet, one spouse is usually not responsible for the debts of the other, nor can her assets be seized to satisfy them. Consequently, gifts from one spouse to the other may be both effective and tax-efficient when one seeks to protect an entrepreneur's assets.

If the entrepreneur is disinclined to make an outright gift to her spouse, she can consider using an inter vivos (lifetime) Qualified Terminable Interest Property (QTIP) trust to receive assets on the spouse's behalf. QTIP trusts offer significant estate tax savings by preserving the spouse's "exclusion" for federal estate tax purposes (see Federal Tax Rules in Chapter 17), but they also facilitate interspousal gifts with "strings attached."

Making gifts to others without a tax cost may be more challenging. However, the selection of an asset to be gifted might help reduce or eliminate any gift tax. If, for example, common stock in one's closely held business is gifted, the IRS will recognize "discounts" in value because of its lack of marketability or control. Similarly, other gifted assets are entitled to offsets when calculating value if they are subject to "built-in capital gain" tax liabilities.

Whenever gifts are made, the financial advisor should caution his client that they may not be effective to safeguard assets against the claims of government agencies, especially for Medicaid reimbursement. Outright gifts are subject to a 36-month look-back period; any gifts made within 36 months will be relied on as a resource that can delay or deny assistance. Gifts made to trusts are subject to a 60-month look-back period.

Choice-of-Entity Implications

Holding business interests in a vehicle that segregates them from the entrepreneur's other assets can benefit her asset protection planning. Corporations, LLCs, limited partnerships, and especially trusts are particularly useful in shielding assets from the claims of creditors.

The Corporation

The corporation enjoys the longest history of success in defeating the claims of business creditors who seek to reach beyond corporate assets. A body of judicial opinion allows a creditor to "pierce the corporate veil" where a shareholder treats her corporation as her alter-ego and fails to respect the separateness of the entity. However, with care and planning, the corporation can be relied on as a safe and effective vehicle to limit the personal liability of its shareholders. Of greater concern is the possibility that a personal creditor of a shareholder succeeds to her interest in the corporation. Under such circumstances both the debtor and the corporation's other shareholders can be seriously disadvantaged. For that reason and others, the shareholders should be encouraged to enter into a buy-sell agreement whose provisions would be likely to deter creditors from levying against a shareholder's stock (see Chapter 12).

The Limited Liability Company

An LLC offers great flexibility to the entrepreneur in protecting her business assets from the claims of creditors. Almost all states even permit single-member LLCs, which shield a sole owner's business assets from the claims of creditors while treating the entity essentially as a sole proprietorship for income tax purposes.

The Limited Partnership

A limited partnership shields a limited partner from obligations incurred at the partnership level; only her capital is ever at risk. In addition, the personal creditors of the limited partner are precluded from attaching the partnership or the partnership's assets. Their only remedy is a "charging order," the receipt of income as it accrues or is distributed. Ironically, a charging order may well force a creditor to pick up taxable income even though cash distributions may not be made. Such "phantom income" will render the creditor's remedy an imperfect one at best and may leave him without any practical resource.

The Trust

The trust is clearly the most effective tool for protecting the entrepreneur's assets, as well as the assets of her children and any other intended beneficiaries, from the claims of creditors. A trust is an ancient, common-law mechanism for holding property where one person, a "grantor," transfers assets to a "trustee" to hold, manage, and distribute them to or for the benefit of one or more "beneficiaries." The financial advisor is limited only by his creativity in designing the specific trust that will best meet his client's asset protection, tax, and dispositive objectives. Trust approaches include the following.

Revocable (or Living) Trusts

Revocable or living trusts have gained enormous popularity because of one heavily promoted feature: they avoid the costs, delays, and publicity associated with probate, the court-supervised process by which claims against a decedent's estate can be asserted and assets transferred to heirs in an orderly fashion. Holding assets in a revocable trust, however, will do little to protect them from the claims of creditors.

An exception exists where a claim is asserted by a spouse. In that case, the entrepreneur who has funded her own revocable trust with nonmarital assets—generally, those assets acquired before marriage or by gift or inheritance and not subject to the claims of a spouse—may successfully avoid inadvertently commingling them with marital assets and thereby converting them into marital assets. Such segregation may be particularly useful when coupled with premarital or postmarital agreements, which limit the spouse's interest in the entrepreneur's property should the latter die or should the couple divorce.

Spendthrift Trusts

Spendthrift trusts are defined by the protection they afford beneficiaries against the claims of creditors. Most states recognize spendthrift trusts, but state laws interpret them more or less broadly. As a general proposition, they serve to bar creditors' claims (except those for support obligations), but they do nothing to protect a grantor even though she may also be a beneficiary.

The financial advisor should be judicious in relying on a client's spendthrift trust and curb any unrealistic expectations. Once assets are distributed to a beneficiary, they become fair game for creditors. Moreover, even though some states presume that all irrevocable trusts are spendthrift trusts, failing to recite clearly the grantor's intent about a trust's spendthrift character may allow a court to draw an inference to the contrary.

Supplemental Needs Trusts

Supplemental needs trusts are sanctioned by state law to provide for certain distributions benefitting a disabled beneficiary without compromising his or her eligibility for public aid reimbursement or other government assistance. Usually, a supplemental needs trust cannot benefit its grantor. Caution should be exercised by the financial advisor who gives counsel to his client about supplemental needs trusts since the federal Medicaid statute, companion state laws, and the regulations interpreting them establish strict guidelines.

Discretionary Trusts

Discretionary trusts empower a trustee to distribute income or principal to one or more beneficiaries either in her sole discretion or based on some ascertainable standard, such as a beneficiary's support in reasonable comfort. So long as the trustee avoids a consistent distribution pattern, a beneficiary's creditor would probably be hard-pressed to argue that distributions are contractual and that the creditor should, as a matter of right, succeed to the beneficiary's interest in them.

Asset Protection Trusts

Asset protection trusts, particularly those authorized by Alaska and Delaware law, are notable in that they permit a grantor to set up a spendthrift trust for her own benefit. Unless funding the trust renders the grantor insolvent or is undertaken to defraud creditors, the trust's assets will generally not be subject to the claims of the grantor's creditors.

In evaluating the efficacy of an asset protection trust, the financial advisor should be aware of the gift tax consequences of funding such a trust. A gift to the trust will become complete when the property the donor contributes becomes exempt from the claims of the creditor. At that time, the gift will be taxable and, for purposes of computing the gift tax, special valuation rules (found in Sections 2701 through 2704 of the IRC) will apply.

To avoid current taxability, the trust agreement can reserve for the grantor a "limited power of appointment," the authority to rewrite the trust as circumstances and tax laws change. Doing so will render the gift "incomplete" and will subject the trust's assets to inclusion in the donor's eventual taxable estate. In addition, any trust distributions to beneficiaries other than the grantor will themselves be completed gifts, taxable for gift tax purposes (unless an exclusion applies; see Federal Tax Rules in Chapter 17).

Establishing an asset protection trust offshore—outside the territorial jurisdiction of the United States—provides essentially the same substantial benefits a domestic trust offers along with the further advantage of procedural impediments a creditor would encounter in enforcing a judgment in an inhospitable court. Jurisdictions that are commonly selected for asset protection purposes include the Bahamas, Belize, Bermuda, the Cayman Islands, Cook Islands, Gibraltar, Jersey, the Isle of Man, and the Turks and Caicos Islands. In all of these jurisdictions can be found institutional trustees that, to a lesser or greater degree, are well established, licensed, bonded, and regulated. The financial advisor should satisfy himself as to the experience, competency, financial strength, and integrity of any trustee which might be appointed. The grantor should be aware that pursuing a claim against an offshore trustee might be equally problematic for her and, for that reason, should identify within the trust agreement a local "trust protector" who would look out for her interests.

Offshore trusts pose unique tax issues, too. IRC Section 684 subjects foreign trusts to onerous tax rules that are avoidable if the trust agreement is drafted as a "defective" grantor trust, one whose income is taxed to the grantor and not the entity. The transfer tax consequences of creating offshore trusts can also be severe; as in the case of domestic asset protection trusts, the grantor should be encouraged to retain a limited power of attorney and thereby avoid the imposition of the tax.

Offshore trusts are recommended as much for the procedural hurdles they force creditors to overcome as for their legal substance. Other techniques offer practical protection to the entrepreneur merely by her disciplined segregation of assets and layering of entities one upon another.

Keeping liability-prone assets, such as high-risk business interests or environmentally contaminated real estate, in separate legal entities will help to ensure that any claim asserted against the owner of one will not affect other commonly owned entities and their assets. The segregation of assets will also make it easier for the entrepreneur to carve up her assets for gifting purposes or the pursuit of other tax planning strategies.

Finally, the financial advisor might suggest using a combination of entities to keep creditors at bay. A limited partnership's general partner might be an LLC, whose sole member might be an irrevocable trust. An offshore corporation might be wholly owned by a trust in another offshore jurisdiction. The more layers between creditors and the assets they target, the more time-consuming, expensive, and uncertain become their quest.

Part Four

Compensation Planning for the Entrepreneur and His or Her Employees

Cash and Deferred Compensation

Management is leadership, and the entrepreneur's ability to attract and develop top-notch people may have a greater bearing on his success in business than anything else.

How well the entrepreneur organizes, runs and compensates the management team can set him apart from his peers. He should start at the beginning with a formal, contractual relationship with every team player who's got it in him or her to help make him a success. The substance of the contract will vary from business to business, but here are a few important topics that the entrepreneur and his financial advisor should consider in drafting any executive employment agreement:

- *Duties and Responsibilities.*   Try to avoid duplication of effort, and agree right from the start about how much authority each executive is to have. But remember: the world turns, so reserve the right to make changes.
- *Best Efforts.*   Demand a full day's effort for a full day's pay.
- *Noncompetition.*   The contract should include a restrictive covenant, limiting competition for a reasonable time after employment ends. Federal or state law will strike down any clause held unreasonable in

time or geography—or one that effectively deprives the employee of his or her right to earn a livelihood, so the entrepreneur should work with his lawyer in defining the minimum he needs to be safe.

- *Trade Secrets.* These are the venture's property, as are its customer lists. All key people should acknowledge the venture's ownership of these items and grant the venture the right to injunctive relief, restraining any actual or threatened infringement.

- *Term.* In most cases, the company should choose a short, fixed term to start; it can always renew. The company should also retain the right to end the relationship for misconduct, nonperformance, disability, or other common-sense reasons such as the sale, merger, or discontinuance of the business.

- *Compensation.* The agreement should set out in great detail the base salary, any automatic adjustments, payment frequency, bonuses, deferred compensation, fringes, and forfeiture provisions. When privately held stock is part of the package, the corporation should be given a right of first refusal on its employee's shares should he or she die, resign, retire, go bankrupt, or simply want to sell them. And he or she should be bound to join in the sale of stock in the event the corporation's controlling owners elect to sell out.

  The financial advisor should help the entrepreneur design a compensation package that will give high-level employees the financial security and self-esteem they need to do a good job, and he should have no trouble recruiting and retaining all the talent he needs. The executives who help him run the show will become highly motivated and will contribute to increased productivity and increased profits for all to share.

Bonuses and Deferred Compensation

After a realistic base salary, many businesses pay their executives "current cash bonuses" that are tied to company profits or the achievements of stated employee-specific or companywide milestones. The employee is thus given a genuine incentive, and the employer can deduct it all in the year it is paid. One disadvantage is that executives can claim current bonuses that aren't contingent on future service and then move on to graze elsewhere.

One often proposed solution is the deferred bonus, one that is paid over a period of years after it is earned, even after retirement. A deferred bonus or other deferred compensation can be made expressly subject to forfeiture by an executive who engages in competition with the business or otherwise exposes it to loss. At first blush, deferral may appear especially desirable, since the employee may net more of his bonus dollars after retirement, when he might be in a lower tax bracket. But the entrepreneur should abandon that widely held belief. The likelihood is that a deferred bonus will be taxable at the same rate as a current bonus is, particularly if the retired executive will receive qualified retirement plan benefits and income from outside investments along with his or her deferred bonus.

In weighing the relative merits of a deferred bonus plan, the financial advisor should look at these pitfalls, too:

- The whole point of a plan—retaining truly exceptional executives— can be undercut by a hungry competitor who is willing to match the deferred payout.
- The company's top executives may resent being padlocked.
- Employees may question the company's ability to pay up when their time comes.
- Employees may gripe about the company's eventual payment in discounted (read inflated) dollars. One answer: In the interim, the company can invest the deferred funds for the employees.
- A forfeiture clause can backfire, forcing marginal employees to stay when they might otherwise leave.

Constructive Dividends

A nondeductible expense costs substantially more than a deductible one, so tax deductibility can maximize the output of every dollar the company budgets for the upper echelon—including the entrepreneur himself. The IRC allows an employer to deduct "expenses paid or incurred during the taxable year in carrying on any trade or business, including a reasonable allowance for personal services actually rendered."

What is "reasonable" and when compensation is "for personal services actually rendered" are issues the IRS frequently raises in claiming that a corporate shareholder-employee's paycheck is really a disguised, nondeductible dividend. Special tax rules on "golden parachutes" illustrate the general problem in this area, namely, what is "excess" beyond a "reasonable" amount?

A *golden parachute* is an arrangement that provides excessive severance payments to one or more executives at the time of a change in ownership or control of the corporation. A 20 percent excise tax applies to the recipient of excess parachute payments, and the corporate employer cannot deduct the excess amount. Payments are excessive to the extent that they exceed three times a base amount. The base amount is the average of compensation paid to the individual in question during the five taxable years prior to the change in ownership or control.

In the interest of safeguarding the tax deductibility of the compensation paid to the company's executives, the company should take these five steps:

1. At least annually, adopt a compensation package by a resolution of the directors (one of whom might well be independent). Define its elements, and cite its underlying philosophy.
2. Record any special factors justifying big salaries: long hours of work, unique abilities, experience and qualifications, and any other employee pluses. The IRS will consider these, along with industry comparisons and economic conditions, in judging reasonableness.
3. Establish a clear dividend policy; that way, salaries will less likely be viewed as hiding a return on one's business investment. Many small corporations pay a token dividend every year just to help counter such a challenge.
4. The directors should authorize any bonuses, and employment contracts should support any contingent payments to employees, especially shareholder-employees.
5. Finally, the corporation should enter into reimbursement agreements with all shareholder-employees such as the following:

> Compensation payments or reimbursements made to the employee that are disallowed, in whole or in part, as a deductible expense by the Internal Revenue Service shall be reimbursed by him to the full extent of the disallowance. It shall be the duty of the Board of Directors to enforce the repayment of each such amount disallowed. A payment shall be deemed to be disallowed only when the time has lapsed for an appeal from or review of the adverse decision of the last tribunal or agency to consider the issue.

If compensation is deemed nondeductible by the corporation, it is returned and made available for redistribution at another time, and perhaps in another way.

Company Retirement Plans

The bedrock of any compensation package is usually the company retirement program. The prominence of retirement planning as a high-level compensation tool derives from the qualification of certain formalized retirement programs. Qualified retirement plans are those that meet rigid IRS standards and the sweeping tax and labor principles of ERISA. Corporate employer contributions to a qualified plan are currently deductible; the earnings of such contributions grow tax free; benefitting employees by deferring personal taxation on their allocable shares of both contributions and earnings until later in life; and funds are made available at a time when their need may be greatest.

For a retirement plan to qualify for tax-favored status, it must be under a permanent, written program established by the employer. It must also be funded, which means that, when contributions are made, there is an independent entity, usually a trust, to receive and invest them until benefits are paid out to participants. In addition, a qualified plan must not discriminate as to contributions or benefits in favor of highly compensated employees. Many other requirements contained in the IRC and ERISA must also be met, both in design of the plan and in its administration.

Discrimination Testing

Qualified retirement plans are subject to testing procedures designed to eliminate discrimination in favor of highly compensated employees. A highly compensated employee is one who is a 5 percent or greater owner at any time during the plan year or the preceding year, or an employee who had compensation from the employer in excess of $80,000 for the preceding year. The employer may narrow the category of employees earning over $80,000 by making an election to include only those whose earnings place them in the top 20 percent of compensation. Once all eligible employees have been categorized as either highly compensated or nonhighly compensated, the qualified plan must then pass a coverage test to demonstrate that coverage is not discriminatory.

Types of Plans

Under a defined-benefit plan, an employer contributes to the plan an amount actuarially calculated to pay a set benefit at the participant's retirement. Under a defined-contribution plan, an employer makes contributions to each participant's individual account of either a certain fixed percentage of the participant's salary or any substantial and recurring amount. The participant's retirement benefit is generally based on the performance of the participant's account over time. Typical defined-contribution plans include money purchase plans, target benefit pension plans, traditional profit-sharing plans, age-weighted profit-sharing plans, stock bonus plans, employee stock ownership plans, and 401(k) plans. A brief general description of each of these types of defined-contribution plans follows.

Money Purchase Pension Plans

Under traditional money purchase pension plans, contributions are made to each participant's individual account. The employer's contributions are based on a fixed percentage of the participant's compensation. At least annually, the participant's account balance is determined by calculating employer (and any participant) contributions, and adjustments are made for earnings and losses of the plan trust.

Target Benefit Plans

The target benefit plan is another type of money purchase pension plan. At first glance it looks more like a defined-benefit plan than a defined-contribution plan. The target benefit plan starts with a target benefit calculated like a defined-benefit formula. For example, the target retirement benefit might be 25 percent of the participant's compensation. Once a target benefit is set, separate accounts are established for each participant, and employer contributions are made to each account based on the level premium funding method. This method works much like an annuity contract where the same premiums are paid each year to provide a target annuity benefit at retirement age. Participants may select assets for their accounts under target benefit plans, but participant contributions are not permitted. Unlike a defined-benefit plan, a target benefit plan's earnings may not necessarily reach the targeted benefit. Depending on the returns generated by plan assets, a participant could end up with a benefit different from the target benefit.

Traditional Profit-Sharing Plans

Like a money purchase pension plan, a profit-sharing plan requires that a separate account be set up for each participant. An employer's contributions may be discretionary or based on a fixed percentage of the company's profits. Participants may be given the right to choose (but may not have possession and control of) the assets in their account, or the accounts of several participants may be pooled by the plan trustees. Under either approach, a company need not necessarily have profits to contribute to a profit-sharing plan.

Age-Weighted Profit-Sharing Plans

Age-weighted profit-sharing plans work much the same way as traditional profit-sharing plans except that age-weighted plans consider both age and compensation in allocating contributions to participants. Although the amount of employer contributions is discretionary for participants with fewer years remaining until retirement, plan contributions usually will be greater to provide an equal retirement benefit at retirement age. An age-weighted profit-sharing plan works best for older participants because they will receive a substantially greater allocation of an employer's contribution than they would under a traditional profit-sharing plan.

Stock Bonus Plans

Stock bonus plans are also similar to traditional profit-sharing plans. Contributions, which may be made in the employer's stock or in cash, are not necessarily preset; are not required to be made every year; and need not be tied to a company's profits. When stock contributions are made to the plan, the deductible amount of the contribution is based on the fair market value of the stock at the time it is contributed. When the employer contributes cash to the plan, the cash may be used to purchase employer stock in the open market. Distributions from the plan are generally made in the form of employer securities.

The plan may or may not allow participant contributions. If participant contributions are part of the plan, they are usually maintained in a separate account.

Employee Stock Ownership Plans

An ESOP is a stock bonus plan, or a stock bonus plan combined with a money purchase pension plan. The primary asset of the ESOP is the employer's common stock, and the participant has the right to require the employer to make all distributions in employer stock. The plan must also give the participant the right to demand that the employer purchase any distribution of employer stock if it is not readily tradable on an established market.

ESOPs are unique in that they are permitted to borrow money to buy the employer's stock. An ESOP of this type is commonly referred to as a *leveraged* ESOP. Having adopted a leveraged ESOP, an employer may make contributions to the plan to pay off any loans the plan has taken on to buy employer stock. Special deduction rules apply to leveraged ESOPs.

401(k) Cash or Deferred Arrangements

The qualified pension plan that enjoys the greatest popularity is the 401(k) cash or deferred arrangement (CODA). A CODA may take the form of a traditional profit-sharing plan or a stock bonus plan. CODAs allow participants to defer their own compensation in addition to any employer contributions, usually expressed as a matching percentage of the participant's contribution. The plan is completely voluntary, and employer-matching contributions are not required, but are very common.

The plan may allow for a reduction of the participant's salary in exchange for a corresponding contribution to the plan's trust. The amount contributed by the employer under this arrangement is capped by law and adjusted annually. In addition to participant elective deferrals and employer-matching contributions, the plan may permit employer nonelective contributions. Unlike employer matching contributions, employer nonelective contributions are not dependent on the participant's elective deferral.

Limits on Benefits

Generally, limits on defined-benefit plans are expressed as a limit on the annual benefits as projected for retirement. Specifically, a participant may not accrue a benefit in excess of the lesser of a dollar amount established by statute and adjusted annually, or 100 percent of the participant's average annual compensation for his or her highest paid three years. The annual addition limits on defined-contribution plans are expressed as the lesser of 25 percent of the participant's compensation for the limitation year, or $30,000, again adjusted for inflation.

Deduction Limits

Qualified pension plans restrict the amount of compensation that may be considered for purposes of determining an employer's deduction for contributions. In computing the deduction limits, employers may consider only the first $150,000 of a participant's compensation, as indexed for inflation. In general, for profit-sharing plans and stock bonus plans, the employer may take a deduction for as much as 15 percent of the compensation paid or accrued (within the allowable limit) during the employer's taxable year.

The deductibility of contributions to defined-benefit plans and money purchase pension plans, however, are different. Defined benefit-plans and money purchase pension plan contribution deductions are based on the plan's reasonable funding method and actuarial assumptions.

Special deduction limitation rules apply to leveraged ESOPs. The amount of the deduction under a leveraged ESOP depends on whether the plan's contributions are used to pay off the loan principal. If so, then the employer may deduct up to 25 percent of compensation paid or accrued to participants. Subject to an excise tax for excess contributions, contributions over the 25 percent limit may be carried forward to following years and deducted, provided the 25 percent limit is not exceeded in any given year.

Excess contributions to a qualified pension plan may result in a nondeductible 10 percent excise tax. However, the tax does not apply to nondeductible defined-contribution plan contributions as long as they do not exceed the sum of the employer's matching contributions and the amount of any elective deferral contributions to a 401(k) plan.

A 401(k) plan has its own limits. While the goal of a 401(k) plan should be to permit all eligible employees to save up to the limit on tax-deferred savings, an "actual deferred percentage" test and an "actual contribution" test limit the amount that highly compensated employees may contribute to their 401(k) plans based on what nonhighly compensated employees defer. One strategy to deal with this problem is a plan design feature that deems all eligible employees to have automatically elected to participate in the plan at a plan-specified savings level.

The Simplified Employee Pension

The Simplified Employee Pension (SEP) presents a special opportunity for the self-employed entrepreneur. He can contribute up to 15 percent of his earned income or $30,000, whichever is less, as long as he provides the benefit for all his employees who are at least 21 years old and have worked for him three of the last five years. Once funds are deposited they cannot be withdrawn before age $59\frac{1}{2}$ without a 10 percent penalty and, unlike a 401(k) plan, a SEP does not allow for borrowing. SEPs are easy to live with in that no prior IRS approval is required, contributions can be made some years and not others, and banks and brokers can set them up without any hassle.

Nonqualified Plans

As attractive as qualified plans can be, they are limited in their ability to reward key executives, including the entrepreneur himself. As an alternative, so-called nonqualified plans have been adopted by many entrepreneurial concerns, both to overcome the limits placed on qualified plan contributions and benefits and to avoid the imposition of the most onerous of ERISA's provisions.

ERISA Compliance

ERISA was enacted in 1974 to regulate the operation and administration of employee benefit plans. The law is comprised of four parts or "titles," each having distinct areas of application. Title I: *Protection of Employee Benefit Rights* is enforced by the Department of Labor (DOL) and contains the provisions relating to employee benefit plans. Title II: *Amendments to the Internal Revenue Code Relating to Retirement Plans* contains the pertinent IRC provisions that apply to qualified plans and is enforced by the Department of the Treasury. Title III: *Jurisdiction, Administration, Enforcement* pertains to coordination between the DOL and the Treasury Department and establishes the responsibility of both agencies. Title IV: *Plan Termination Insurance* covers the creation and administration of the Pension Benefit Guarantee Corporation (PBGC).

ERISA: Title I

Subtitle B of Title I of ERISA contains provisions enforced by DOL. It was originally divided into five parts: Reporting and Disclosure (Part 1), Participation and Vesting (Part 2), Funding (Part 3), Fiduciary Responsibility (Part 4), and Administration and Enforcement (Part 5). (Provisions relating to continuation coverage under Group Health Plans [Part 6] and Group Health Plan Requirements [Part 7] were added later.) The following five types of plans are exempt from Title I:

1. Governmental plans
2. Church plans

3. Plans maintained to comply with workers' compensation, unemployment, or disability laws
4. Plans maintained outside the United States primarily for nonresident aliens
5. Unfunded excess benefit plans.

Qualified plans, and nonqualified plans that are not exempt, must comply with all five parts of Title I. Full Title I compliance for a nonqualified pension plan would require that the plan be established, operated, and administered in virtually the same manner as a qualified plan. This would defeat many of the advantages of establishing a nonqualified plan such as selective participation, lack of funding requirements, and flexibility of vesting schedules.

Perhaps the most serious consequence were nonqualified plans subject to full ERISA compliance would be the possible loss of the employee-participant's ability to defer income tax on plan benefits. Since a nonqualified plan that must comply with ERISA would be required to be "funded," it would be subject to immediate taxation of plan benefits unless there is a "substantial risk of forfeiture." In a voluntary deferral plan, where salary deferrals are fully vested, the only opportunity for loss exists if the plan is unfunded. In a funded plan where there is still a risk of forfeiture (that is, the employee is not vested), the employee would not be taxed until the risk of forfeiture is removed. Take, for example, a supplemental executive retirement plan (SERP) that is not vested until age 65. In a plan where there is periodic vesting, the amount that vests each year would be taxable to the executive. The vesting provisions of Title I would also apply, requiring that vesting occur over a short period of time (either five-year, "cliff" vesting or seven-year, "graded" vesting). The combined ERISA requirements of funding and vesting, if applicable, would effectively deny the executive any meaningful ability to defer income.

Reporting and Disclosure

Under ERISA employee benefit plans must provide detailed financial and other information to various government agencies as well as plan participants and their beneficiaries. Depending on the required level of compliance, reporting and disclosure can be as simple as a one-page notice, or an extremely complex process requiring several government forms and schedules together with a summary plan description and summary annual reports. The purpose of the reporting and disclosure element of ERISA is to ensure that participants receive a clear explanation of their rights and benefits, and that the appropriate governmental agencies are given the information needed to enforce ERISA's provisions.

Form 5500. The reporting aspect of ERISA is satisfied through an annual report called Form 5500, which provides detailed financial, actuarial, and plan information to the IRS, DOL, and PBGC. To eliminate duplicate reporting, Form 5500 is filed with the DOL only; the DOL then provides the IRS and PBGC with copies of the report. Form 5500 comes in two variations and a series of schedules.

Disclosure Requirements. In addition to the annual reporting requirement, disclosure documents must be provided to plan participants and beneficiaries. Disclosure under Part 1 takes three forms:

1. The plan administrator must furnish certain information to participants in the plan and beneficiaries receiving benefits under a plan.
2. The plan administrator must furnish certain other material to plan participants and beneficiaries on their request.
3. The plan administrator still must make other materials available for inspection, at reasonable times and places, to participants and beneficiaries.

The documents required to be furnished to participants and beneficiaries are: (1) Summary Plan Description; (2) Summary Annual Report; (3) Summary of Material Modification; (4) Statement of Benefits to Terminated Vested Employees; and (5) Notice of Failure to Meet Minimum Funding Standards. These documents must be distributed by methods that are "reasonably calculated to ensure actual receipt of the material by plan participants and beneficiaries."

Summary Plan Description. The Summary Plan Description (SPD) must be furnished to each participant or to a beneficiary receiving benefits under a pension plan within 90 days of a participant's becoming eligible or within 120 days of the plan becoming subject to the provisions of Part 1 of Title I of ERISA. Also, an updated SPD generally must be furnished every 5 years and a revised SPD furnished every 10 years.

The SPD must be written "in a manner calculated to be understood by the average plan participant, and shall be sufficiently accurate and comprehensive to reasonably apprise such participants and beneficiaries of their rights and obligations under the plan." ERISA § 102(a). When preparing the SPD, the level of education and comprehension of the typical participant must be taken into account. In addition, technical jargon and complex sentences should be eliminated and, whenever possible, examples and illustrations should be used. The SPD must not mislead or misinform, and benefits should not be exaggerated. Any exceptions, limitations, reductions, or restrictions cannot be hidden in small print and must be displayed as prominently as the description of benefits.

The SPD must contain the specific information described in the Labor Regulations. Information such as the name of the plan, the name and address of the employer, the type of plan, the name and address of the plan administrator, conditions to eligibility, circumstances for denial or forfeiture of benefits, the participant's rights under ERISA, and the procedures for presenting a claim for benefits must be contained in the SPD.

Summary Annual Report. Participants and beneficiaries must be provided a summary of the latest annual report (Form 5500) on an annual basis. The Summary Annual Report (SAR) contains a narrative summary of the information contained in Form 5500. The DOL has created a model SAR that must be used; variations are not allowed. Additional information that is not included in Form 5500, but is needed to summarize the annual report fairly, must be included under the heading, Additional Explanation. In general, the SAR must be furnished to each participant covered within nine months of the close of the plan year.

Summary of Material Modifications. When a material modification is made to a benefit plan, a summary of the modifications must be furnished to each participant and beneficiary receiving benefits within 210 days of the end of the plan year in which the modification is adopted. The summary must be written in the same nontechnical manner as the SPD.

Summary of Benefits to Terminated Vested Employees. The administrator of a plan must furnish each participant who has separated from service during the plan year and has a vested deferred benefit with an individual statement outlining his or her benefits. The information in the statement explains the nature, form, and amount of the employee's deferred benefit as well as other information, as contained in Schedule SSA of Form 5500. The plan administrator must also provide the separated participant with a statement of benefits on request.

Notice of Failure to Meet Minimum Funding Standards. If an employer fails to make a contribution required to meet ERISA's minimum funding standard, each participant and beneficiary must be notified.

In addition to the reports discussed previously, the plan administrator must make available, either at the principal office of the administrator or by mail at the request of the participant, copies of the relevant plan and trust documents as well as the latest annual report.

Participation and Vesting

Unless exempted, the participation and vesting provisions of Part 2 of ERISA apply to an employee benefit plan. Though employee welfare benefit plans and excess benefit plans are exempt from Part 2, retirement plans must comply. In order for Part 2 to be applicable, the plan must be an employee benefit plan under ERISA § 3(3), the employee benefit plan must be subject to Title I, and the plan must not fall under any exemption from Part 2. Mandated compliance by a nonqualified plan will defeat many of the objectives of implementing a nonqualified plan, such as discriminatory participation and stringent forfeiture provisions.

Participation.   If coverage under Part 2 is required, an employee must be entitled to participate on the later of the date the employee attains age 21 or completes one year of service. If an employee is entitled to 100 percent vesting after two years, completion of two years of service can be substituted for one year of service requirement. A "year of service" is defined as a 12-month period in which the employee has at least 1,000 hours of service. The computation of the 12-month period is made by reference to the date on which the employee commenced his employment, or the first day of the plan year for an employee who does not complete 1,000 hours of service during the first 12-month period of employment.

Vesting.   Vesting is directly related to an employee's length of service with the employer. Every retirement plan must provide that an employee's right to his or her normal retirement benefit is nonforfeitable on the attainment of retirement age. In addition, the plan must provide that an employee's own contributions are nonforfeitable and that employer contributions comply with the vesting schedules prescribed under ERISA,

With certain exceptions, a plan satisfies the requirements of ERISA if an employee who has at least five years of service has a nonforfeitable right to 100 percent of the employee's accrued benefit derived from employer contributions. As an alternative, an employee's nonforfeitable right to benefits can be accrued using the schedule in Table 14.1.

If the employer prefers, a less stringent vesting schedule can be used. The plan can designate any 12-consecutive-month period as the vesting

Table 14.1   Schedule of Employee Nonforfeitable
Right of Benefits

Years of Service	Nonforfeitable Percentage
3	20
4	40
5	60
6	80
7	100

computation period as long as the period applies equally to all participants and the period chosen does not artificially postpone the vesting of benefits. The definition of a year of service is the same as for participation purposes. When determining years of service, the following four criteria can be disregarded:

1. Years of service prior to employee reaching age 18
2. Years of service in which the employee declined to make required contributions
3. Years of service before the plan went into effect
4. Years of service before a one-year break in service, if the number of consecutive one-year breaks exceeds the greater of five or the number of prebreak years of service, and the participant's accrued benefit was forfeitable. A break in service is a 12-month period in which the employee does not complete more than 500 hours.

In addition to participation and vesting standards, Part 2 provides for changes in benefit accruals, and the method of timing of benefit payments. In general, the accrued benefit of a participant cannot be decreased by an amendment to the plan. Benefits must be provided in the form of a qualified joint and survivor annuity, and in the case of a married participant, a qualified preretirement survivor annuity. The payment of benefits must begin no later than 60 days after the latest of the close of the plan year in which (1) the participant attains the earlier of age 65 or the plan's normal retirement age; (2) the participant completes 10 years of participation in the plan; or (3) the participant terminates from service. Part 2 also provides that benefits provided under the plan cannot be assigned or alienated other than for purposes of a qualified domestic relations order (QDRO).

Funding

ERISA requires minimum funding standards to ensure that the funds needed to pay the promised benefits will be available when they are required. There are several important exemptions from the minimum funding standards: welfare plans, plans that fall under the "top hat exemption" (see ERISA for Deferred-Compensation Plans later in this chapter), plans without employer contributions (that is, voluntary deferral plans), insurance contract plans, excess benefit plans, and individual account plans. Examples of individual account plans would be profit-sharing or stock bonus plans. The minimum funding standards would apply to any type of defined-benefit plan (including SERPs that use a defined-benefit formula) or a money purchase plan.

If funding is required, an actuarial funding method must be used to determine the minimum funding standard each year. The value of the plan's assets must be based on any reasonable actuarial method of valuation that is permitted under applicable Treasury regulations. And all normal plan costs, accrued liabilities, past service liabilities, and experience gains and losses must be determined under the funding method used to determine the costs under the plan.

Each plan subject to the minimum funding standards must establish and maintain a funding standard account. The funding standard account balances the costs of the plan against the contributions and must maintain either a zero or positive balance. For instance, the total contributions (credits) should equal or exceed the total costs (charges). Charges include the normal cost for the current plan year, any unfunded past service liability, and experience losses. Credits include actual contributions to the plan and experience gains.

If the total charges exceed the total credits, an accumulated funding deficiency has occurred. A penalty tax of 10 percent is levied on any accumulated funding deficiency as of the end of the plan year. If the accumulated funding deficiency is not corrected, a 100 percent excise tax is levied. The employer has 90 days from the date a notice of deficiency is mailed by the IRS to eliminate the deficiency and avoid the 100 percent tax.

The IRS can grant a temporary waiver of the minimum funding standards if the employer were to incur a "temporary substantial hardship" by meeting the standards, and application of the standards would be adverse to the interests of the participants. The definition of a hardship includes the following:

- The employer is operating at an economic loss
- There is substantial unemployment or underemployment in the trade or business and in the industry concerned

- The sales and profits of the industry are depressed or declining
- It is reasonable to expect that the plan will be continued only if the waiver is granted

The waiver does not eliminate the funding requirement, but allows it to be amortized over a five-year period.

Fiduciary Responsibilities

Part 4 contains provisions for the compulsory establishment of a plan document, the establishment of a trust, fiduciary duties, and prohibited transactions. Unfunded plans maintained primarily for providing deferred compensation for a select group of management or highly compensated employees are exempt from Part 4 (see ERISA for Deferred-Compensation Plans later in this chapter).

Written Instrument.   Under Part 4, every employee benefit plan must be established and maintained pursuant to a written instrument. The instrument must provide for one or more fiduciaries who, either jointly or severally, have the authority to control and manage the operation and administration of the plan. A "named fiduciary" is defined as someone named in the instrument, or through procedures specified in the plan is identified as a fiduciary by the employer. The named fiduciary can employ others to render advice regarding the duties of the fiduciary and can appoint an investment manager to manage the investments of the plan.

Every employee benefit plan subject to Part 4 must:

- Provide a procedure for establishing and carrying out a funding policy and method consistent with the objectives of the plan and the requirements of Title I
- Describe any procedure under the plan for the allocation of responsibilities for the operation and administration of the plan
- Provide a procedure for amending the plan, and identifying the persons who have authority to amend the plan
- Specify the basis on which payments are made to and from the plan

The purpose of requiring a written instrument and an identified fiduciary is so that every employee may, on examining the plan documents, determine what his or her rights are under the plan and may identify those responsible for operating the plan.

Trust Requirement.   With certain exceptions, all assets of an employee benefit plan must be held in trust by one or more trustees pursuant to a written trust instrument. The trustees must be named in the trust instrument or the written plan instrument or be appointed by a named fiduciary. The trustees shall have exclusive authority and discretion to manage and control the assets of the plan unless the plan instrument or trust instrument subjects the trustee to the direction of the named fiduciary, or the authority to manage, dispose, or acquire assets of the plan is delegated to an investment manager.

The primary exceptions to the trust requirement (other than plans that are exempt from Part 4 altogether) are assets of a plan that consist of insurance contracts or policies issued by a qualified insurance company, 403(b) plans, and IRAs.

Plan assets may never inure to the benefit of the employer and must be held for the exclusive purpose of providing benefits to participants and their beneficiaries, and for defraying reasonable expenses of administration. This is the provision that would seem to create a "funded" nonqualified plan for income tax purposes. In the normal nonqualified deferred-compensation plan (see Nonqualified Stock Options in Chapter 15), the benefits are not taxed to the employee if the assets of the plan are subject to the creditors of the corporation. Assets would be irrevocably set aside from the employer's creditors, thus creating a funded plan for income tax purposes when assets are placed into the trust. The formation of the trust alone does not cause taxation, but the required funding of the trust under Part 3 would. Thus, it is crucial when implementing a nonqualified plan that it be designed to fall under the available exemptions to Part 3 and Part 4.

Fiduciary Duties.   A fiduciary must discharge his or her duties solely in the interest of the participants and beneficiaries of the plan, and with the care, skill, prudence, and diligence that under the prevailing circumstances a prudent person would use in the conduct of a like enterprise. In addition, the fiduciary must act for the exclusive purpose of (1) providing benefits to participants and beneficiaries; (2) defraying reasonable expenses of administering the plan; (3) diversifying investments so as to minimize the risk of large losses, unless it is clearly not prudent to do so; and (4) governing the plan in accordance with the documents and instruments of the plan, insofar as such documents and instruments are consistent with the provisions of Title I.

A "fiduciary" is defined as anyone who (1) exercises discretionary authority or control respecting the management of the plan or the management or disposition of its assets; (2) renders investment advice for a fee or other compensation, directly or indirectly, with respect to money or property of the plan or has the authority or responsibility to do so; and (3) has discretionary authority or responsibility in the administration of the plan.

Advisors who provide services to the plan, such as attorneys, accountants, insurance agents, and actuaries, will not be considered fiduciaries merely because they have provided services. However, caution must be used by service providers so that they are not inadvertently considered fiduciaries. If a person is deemed a fiduciary, but is not named a fiduciary, she will only be liable for the aspects of the plan for which she has discretion or control.

Investment Duties.   The ERISA prudence standard affords greater flexibility than the common-law "prudent person" rule, particularly in acknowledging differences in size, nature, liquidity needs, and goals of employee benefit plans. ERISA's prudent person rule requires varying degrees of expertise from fiduciaries, depending on the plan. In order to comply with the prudent person standard, the fiduciary should consider the following three factors:

1. The diversification of the portfolio
2. The liquidity and return on the portfolio to the anticipated cash flow needs of the plan
3. The projected return on plan assets relative to the funding objectives of the plan

The fiduciary must also give "appropriate consideration" to circumstances that, in light of her duties, she knows or should know are relevant to the particular investment or investment course of action. Appropriate consideration includes a determination that a particular investment or investment course of action is reasonably designed to further the purposes of the plan, given the risk of loss and the opportunity for gain associated with the investment or investment course of action.

The prudence standard is measured against the expected performance of the investment or portfolio and the process used to select an investment, not on the actual return on the investment or portfolio. Thus, an investment portfolio that was prudently structured will not cause a breach of fiduciary duty if the portfolio does not perform as expected. The mere fact that there may have been a decline in value of a plan's portfolio does not by itself establish imprudent management. The standard to be applied is that of conduct, tested at the time of the investment decision, rather than the performance, judged from the vantage point of hindsight.

Any fiduciary who breaches her fiduciary duty can be held personally liable to make good any losses to the plan resulting from the breach. The fiduciary is also subject to other equitable or remedial relief as determined by a court, including removal as a fiduciary. The fiduciary will also be subject to a penalty tax, which is levied by DOL, of 20 percent of the recovered amount. The plan, the fiduciary, and the employer should be encouraged to purchase fiduciary liability insurance to cover potential liabilities occurring from a breach of duty.

However, fiduciaries should gain comfort from the DOL's determination that plan sponsors and other fiduciaries are relieved of certain liabilities when a participant exercises control over assets in a participant-directed individual account plan that meets the requirement of ERISA's § 404(c). The requirements are that the plan must offer a broad range of investment alternatives, provide reasonable opportunities to give investment instructions, permit diversification of investments, and provide sufficient information that informed decisions may be made. The financial advisor should help the entrepreneur weigh the cost of all the relevant plan designs, service provider, and communication issues against the benefits of installing and maintaining an ERISA § 404(c) plan.

Prohibited Transactions.   Fiduciaries are prohibited from engaging in certain transactions involving the plan. A "prohibited transaction" occurs if, either directly or indirectly, one of the following five events occurs:

1. A sale, exchange, or leasing of property between the plan and a party in interest
2. The lending of money or extension of credit between the plan and a party in interest
3 The furnishing of goods, services, or facilities between the plan and a party in interest
4 The transfer to, or use by or for the benefit of a party in interest, or any assets of the plan
5. The acquisition or holding, on behalf of the plan, of any employer security or real property in violation of ERISA § 407(a), which relates to the acquisition of employer securities exceeding 10 percent of the plan's assets

A party in interest is defined as:

- Any fiduciary, counsel, or employee of the plan
- A person providing services to the plan
- An employer, and any owner of more than 50 percent of the employer, whose employees are covered by the plan
- Any relative of any of the above
- An employee organization whose members are covered under the plan
- A corporation, partnership, estate, or trust of which 50 percent is owned by any of the preceding persons
- Officers, directors, 10 percent or more shareholders, and employees of any organization previously described or of the employee benefit plan
- A 10 percent or more partner or joint venturer with any person or organization previously described

In addition, a fiduciary cannot lawfully (1) deal with assets of the plan in her own interest or for her own account; (2) act in any capacity, in any transaction involving the plan on behalf of, or representing a party, whose interests are adverse to those of the plan or its participants or beneficiaries; and (3) receive any consideration for her own personal account from any party dealing in connection with a transaction involving the assets of the plan.

A fiduciary who engages in a prohibited transaction is personally liable for any losses to the plan. Any party in interest (sometimes called a "disqualified person") who engages in a prohibited transaction is liable for an excise tax of 15 percent of the amount involved. If the prohibited transaction is not corrected within 90 days of the mailing of a notice of deficiency, an additional excise tax of 100 percent is levied.

Certain statutory exemptions to the prohibited-transaction rules are allowed. For example, loans made by a plan to a party in interest will not be a prohibited transaction if the loans are available to all participants, are made in accordance with specific provisions, do not discriminate in favor of highly compensated employees, bear a reasonable rate of interest, and are adequately secured. In addition to statutory exemptions, certain class exemptions are granted by DOL if the exemption is administratively feasible, in the best interests of the plan, and protective of the rights of participants. DOL may also grant individual exemptions from the prohibited-transaction rules. The requirements for relief under an individual exemption can be found in ERISA Technical Release 85-1 (Jan. 22, 1985). An individual exemption can only be relied on by the party to which the exemption is granted.

Administration and Enforcement

Part 5 contains provisions relating to the enforcement and administration of ERISA through civil enforcement and criminal penalties, by requiring a claims procedure, and by granting investigative authority to DOL.

Criminal Penalties and Civil Enforcement. Any person who willfully violates the reporting and disclosure provisions of Title I can be fined up to $5,000 and imprisoned for up to one year. For an entity the fine can be up to $100,000. In addition, anyone using, or threatening to use, force, violence, coercion, or intimidation to interfere or prevent participants and beneficiaries from exercising their rights under the plan or ERISA can be subject to fines of up to $10,000 and imprisonment of up to one year.

ERISA allows plan participants and beneficiaries to bring civil actions to enforce rights and benefits, to redress violations of fiduciary duty, and for failure to comply with notification requirements. Also, DOL and plan fiduciaries may bring suit for breaches of fiduciary responsibility, to enforce ERISA, or to enforce the terms of the plans.

Investigative Authority. DOL has the power to investigate and determine whether any person has violated, or is about to violate, any provision of Title I, including the ability to require submission of records, to question persons in order to determine the facts, and to enter places of businesses to inspect records. In addition, DOL has the authority to promulgate regulations needed to carry out the provisions of Title I, including, among other things, prescribing forms to be used and defining technical terms used in the provisions.

Claims Procedures. Every employee benefit plan must have a claims procedure. The claims procedure must provide adequate notice, in writing, to any participant or beneficiary whose claim has been denied, and must afford a reasonable opportunity for a full and fair review by the named fiduciary of the decision denying the claim. The claims procedure will be considered reasonable only if the following five provisions are included:

1. The procedures for filing a claim benefits
2. Notification to the claimant of decision
3. The contents of the notice to the claimant
4. A review procedure
5. A decision on review

The claims procedure must be described in the SPD, must not contain any provisions that would inhibit or hamper the initiation or processing of a claim, and must provide for informing participants, in writing and in a timely fashion, of the time limit for processing a claim.

Generally, the plan administrator has no more than 90 days from the date of a claim to either pay benefits or deny the claim. If the claim is denied, the participant or beneficiary must be given a written explanation of the denial. The explanation should contain the following information:

- The specific reason for denial
- The specific reference to the plan provision on which the denial is based
- A description of any additional information needed to decide the claim
- An explanation of the steps to be taken to submit the claim for review

Every participant or beneficiary must be given an opportunity for a full and fair review, by the appropriate named fiduciary, of his or her denied claim for benefits. The participant or beneficiary may have a representative present, and must have the opportunity to review documents and make his or her case in writing. The decision on review must be made within 60 days, must be in writing, and must include the specific reasons for the decision explained in a manner that will be understood by the claimant.

ERISA for Deferred-Compensation Plans

The primary advantages of a nonqualified deferred-compensation plan are the pretax deferral of funds by highly compensated executives, selective participation and vesting by the employers, and only minimal compliance with the provisions of ERISA. Unless the plan is properly structured to avoid ERISA compliance, many or all of the benefits of a nonqualified plan can be lost.

Pension Plan Defined

The required level of ERISA compliance will vary with the type of employee benefit plan. *Pension* plans are more heavily regulated than *welfare* plans. Thus, it is important to determine the category of employee benefit plan to understand which provisions of ERISA apply.

A pension plan is defined as any plan, fund, or program that is established or maintained by an employer, that provides retirement income to its employees, or results in the deferral of income by employees extending to the termination of covered employment or beyond. Consequently, voluntary deferral plans and SERPs will be treated as pension plans for ERISA purposes. Excess benefit plans are also pension plans, but are exempt from all of Title I if they are unfunded.

If a plan is structured in a manner in which the principal effect is the evasion of the standards or purposes of ERISA applicable to pension plans, the payment or arrangement will be treated as a pension plan. Consequently, any attempt to disguise a pension plan as a welfare plan may ultimately prove futile.

It is possible that an agreement to pay deferred compensation benefits as part of an employment contract may not be considered an ERISA plan. In order for ERISA to apply, there must first be "a plan, fund, or program." Whether an offer contained in an employment contract will be a plan, fund, or program under ERISA is to be determined by facts and circumstances. In *Lackey v. Whitehall Corp.*, 704 F. Supp. 201 (D. Kan. 1988), an offer to pay deferred compensation was included in the employment agreements of four key executives of the company. The court found that this did not constitute an ERISA pension plan, but was instead "terms included as part of employment agreements with select individuals. The deferred compensation benefit was never initiated or treated as a general plan for the management team of the employer. It was simply a provision provided to select employees as part of their individual employment agreement."

However, in *Williams v. Wright*, 927 F.2d 1540 (11th Cir. 1991), a one-page letter outlining retirement benefits, a company car, country club dues, continued office space, and insurance coverage based on an agreement that the employee would "gradually alter his work schedule to the retirement status," was held to be an ERISA plan. The employer argued that the letter was intended only to be an employment contract, and not an ERISA plan. The court disagreed, stating that, "it is clear that the letter's arrangement primarily constituted payment of retirement income and was not an employment contract outside the scope of ERISA. These cases suggest that the cautious approach would be to assume ERISA compliance will be required and structure the plan so as to fall under any of the available exemptions.

Exemptions from Compliance

An employee benefit plan that is considered "unfunded and maintained by an employer primarily for the purpose of providing deferred compensation to a select group of management or highly compensated employees" is exempt from Parts 2, 3, and 4 of Title I. This select group of employees is usually referred to as the "top hat" group. If the plan is unfunded, and covers only the top hat group, Part 1 and Part 5 of Title I are all that must be complied with.

Unfunded Plans

DOL has never given definition to the term *unfunded*, and has often stated that facts and circumstances dictate whether or not a plan is considered funded. However, DOL regulations, DOL Advisory Opinions, and court cases provide some guidance. Under the regulations, an exemption (to most of Part 1) is provided to an employee benefit pension plan for which benefits are paid solely from the general assets of the employer; or are provided exclusively through insurance contracts or policies, the premiums for which are paid by the employer from its general assets, and issued by a qualified insurance company.

Several DOL Advisory Opinions have also concluded that a plan would be considered unfunded if the assets used are available to the general creditors of the employer. In Advisory Opinion 90-14A, DOL opined that, while the determination of what is and is not an unfunded plan is based on facts and circumstances, significant weight would be given to the IRS's definition of unfunded for income tax purposes. The IRS considers a plan unfunded if the assets financing the plan are subject to the general creditors of the employer.

Advisory Opinions 91-16A and 92-13A determined that assets held in "rabbi trusts" that complied with IRS requirements would not be considered funded for ERISA purposes. As in Advisory Opinion 90-14A, DOL again states that "in the absence of pertinent legislative history defining 'unfunded' for purposes of Title I of ERISA, the positions adopted by the [Internal Revenue] Service regarding tax consequences to trust beneficiaries should be given significant weight under Title I."

The *rabbi trust* is an effective tool for securing benefits when the concern is a loss of benefits due to takeover of the company, or by current management using assets earmarked for the plan for other purposes.

A rabbi trust is an irrevocable grantor trust that is subject to the claims of the employer's creditors. The trust takes its name from a favorable private letter ruling given to a synagogue for its use of a trust to hold benefits for its rabbi. Since the trust was designed to be subject to the creditors of the synagogue, the rabbi was not considered to be constructively in receipt of plan assets, and was not taxed on deferrals placed into the trust. If this type of trust is properly designed to be subject to the creditors of the plan sponsor, the plan participant will not be taxed on the deferrals placed into the trust.

Since trust assets are still subject to the claims of creditors, protection of trust assets is limited to a change of heart by management. In the event of insolvency, the executive's benefits could be lost. The IRS has issued model trust language, and the format must be followed in order to receive a favorable ruling on the viability of the trust as a rabbi trust (Rev. Proc. 92-64; Rev. Proc. 92-65).

By contrast, a *secular trust* is used when there is concern that the employee will lose benefits due to future insolvency of the company. The secular trust differs from the rabbi trust in that plan assets are not subject to the claims of creditors. The employee is protected from both bankruptcy and takeover of the employer.

The trade-off for this security is immediate taxation of benefits unless there is a substantial risk of forfeiture. When the employee's deferrals become vested, the deferral is immediately taxable to the employee. Since the deferral is immediately taxable, the employer is entitled to take an immediate tax deduction.

However, the employer is not able to deduct earnings on the deferral, which limits the attractiveness of this type of trust. Most voluntary deferral plans provide for 100 percent vesting of deferrals since these amounts are salary that would have been paid to the employee except for the arrangement to defer. Most employees will be unwilling to forgo vesting, and possible loss of benefits, by not meeting stringent requirements, in trade for protection from bankruptcy.

In addition to the unfavorable tax treatment of secular trusts, using a secular trust will most likely result in the plan being considered funded for ERISA purposes. The adverse tax and ERISA consequences associated with secular trusts significantly reduce their utility as a tool for securing deferred compensation benefits.

DOL Advisory Opinion 93-14A, which dealt with a medical and dental benefits plan, provided some detailed guidelines for establishing an unfunded plan. The plan agreement discussed in that opinion stipulated that:

- There was no representation to the participants or beneficiaries that the assets held in the premium trust would be used only to pay premiums.

- The corporation retained all rights of ownership to the premium trust assets, which could be available to pay premiums at the corporation's direction, or to pay claims to the corporation's creditors in the event of its insolvency.
- Neither the plan nor its participants or beneficiaries had a preferential claim against, or beneficial interest in, the assets of the trust.
- Participants and beneficiaries should not look to the assets in the trust as a source of funding for benefits.
- The benefits of the plan were not limited to or governed by the amounts contributed to the trust.
- No contributions from participants to the trust were allowed.

In *Belka v. Rowe Furniture Corp.*, 571 F. Supp. 1249 (D. Md. 1983) the court held that a deferred-compensation plan for key employees was not funded for ERISA purposes. In the facts of the case, insurance policies were paid for by the employer, owned by the employer, and the employer was the beneficiary of the policies. In addition, the deferred-compensation agreement specifically provided that the employee had no rights or claims to the policy.

A similar decision was reached in *Belsky v. First National Life Insurance Company*, 818 F.2d 661 (8th Cir. 1987). In *Belsky*, provisions in the plan agreement separated the use of any assets to fund the plan "informally" from the obligation to pay benefits. The plan agreement stipulated that:

> The rights of the executive or any beneficiary shall be those of an unsecured creditor. If any insurance policy or other assets are acquired in connection with the liabilities assumed by the agreement, such policy or asset shall not be deemed to be held in any trust for the benefit of any executive or to be collateral security for the performance of the obligation of the bank, but shall be a general unpledged, unrestricted asset of the employer.

The court found this paragraph to be particularly significant to its determination that the plan was unfunded. The court confirmed that:

> More importantly, the agreement does not mandate that the employer had or would acquire assets to finance the liabilities assumed in the agreement. While it is evident the employer obtained the insurance policy with the intention that it could be used in funding the Plan, the language of the Plan specifically avoids making a direct tie between the insurance policy and the Plan.

In summary, the inadvertent creation of a funded plan can be avoided. Any assets that are meant to finance a deferred compensation liability should remain subject to the creditors of the employer. In addition, plan documents and any supplementary materials given to the executive should clearly explain that the employee has only an unsecured promise by the employer, and that no assets are securing the plan.

The Top Hat Group

In addition to the requirement that the deferred-compensation plan be unfunded, the plan must be provided only to the so-called top hat group. Yet DOL has never defined what constitutes the top hat group.

In Advisory Opinion 90-14A, DOL described what it believed to be the intention of Congress in creating the top hat exclusion—that certain individuals, by virtue of their position or compensation level, have the ability to substantially influence, through negotiation or otherwise, the design and operation of their deferred compensation plan, taking into consideration any risks attendant to, and therefore, would not need the substantive rights and protections of Title I. Thus, people in the top hat group have the ability to negotiate their benefit packages and have positions within the company that would give them some modicum of control over the design and operation of the benefit package.

The exemption provided for the top hat group is for plans "primarily for the purpose of providing deferred compensation benefits to a select group of management or highly compensated employees." The terms used in the description of the exception have been the subject of debate. DOL has determined that the term *primarily* refers to the fact that the benefits provided must be primarily deferred-compensation benefits. Primarily does not mean that the employees covered must be primarily a select group of highly compensated or management employees, and that other employees can be included in the plan. The use of the word *or* in "management or highly compensated" has also been subject to interpretation. Although DOL has never taken a formal position, it has informally concluded that an employee could be either highly compensated or a manager.

Some commentators feel that an employee should be considered "highly compensated" for ERISA purposes if he or she is considered "highly compensated" for IRS purposes. However, the Treasury Department and DOL concur that the definition of a highly compensated

employee under the IRC is not determinative of highly compensated status under Title I of ERISA.

Given the paucity of regulatory guidance and case law authority, caution must be used in determining who might be eligible for benefits under a deferred-compensation plan. It is entirely possible that if even one employee who is not part of the top hat group is covered under the plan, the plan must comply with all parts of Title I.

When deciding who the top hat group is, care must be taken to ensure that the covered employees are both part of a select group, and either highly compensated or members of management. The group should be small in relation to the total workforce; 4 percent has been considered acceptable, and 19 percent has not. In addition, each covered employee's salary level should be significantly above those of the average employee. Many financial advisors use the Social Security Old Age, Survivors and Disability Insurance (OASDI) wage base as a minimum salary level; salary levels below the wage base may cause additional scrutiny. These executives or highly compensated employees should also have the ability to negotiate their salary and benefit packages.

Required ERISA Compliance

Assuming that the plan falls under the exception for top hat plans, minimal ERISA compliance will be required. If the plan is an unfunded excess benefit plan, that is, if benefits are tied specifically to overcome the limitations placed on qualified plans, no ERISA compliance is required. If the plan is a deferred-compensation plan, and not an excess benefit plan, compliance with Parts 2, 3, and 4 is avoidable.

Although a top hat plan must comply with Part 1, a simplified reporting and disclosure method is allowed. The employer merely must send a brief written statement to DOL within 120 days of plan adoption, and must make the plan documents available at the request of DOL. The written statement must contain the following information:

- The employer's name, address, and tax identification number
- A statement that the employer maintains a plan primarily for providing deferred compensation for a select group of highly compensated or management employees
- A statement of the number of top hat plans maintained by the employer

- The number of employees included in each plan

If the statement is not sent within 120 days of plan establishment, full compliance with Part 1 will be required, which would force the company to make an annual filing of Form 5500, as well as to provide summary plan descriptions, summary annual reports, and all other required disclosures under Part 1.

The claims and enforcement procedures of Part 5 must also be followed in a top hat plan. This means that the plan must have a written claims procedure as described under the Labor Regulations.

ERISA for Split-Dollar and Executive Bonus Plans

Split-dollar plans allow an employer and employee to split the many benefits associated with a life insurance policy by allowing the employer to provide death benefits and cash value growth to valuable employees, while providing for a return of the employer's investment when the agreement terminates.

Under a bonus plan, the employer provides a cash bonus to the employee who invests it in a life insurance policy or other vehicle such as a deferred annuity or mutual fund. The employer can structure the plan to give the employee the option to take the bonus in cash or have it contributed to the selected investment vehicle. Alternatively, the employer can structure the plan so that all bonus amounts are placed directly into the investment vehicle, making the employer the premium payer.

Bonus plans are extremely flexible and can be used in a wide variety of planning applications.

As a Qualified Plan Substitute. A bonus plan can take the place of a qualified plan in situations where a business owner does not want to cover all employees. The bonus plan would allow for selective coverage for key employees, without any of the qualified plan restrictions and with minimal ERISA compliance.

As a Qualified Plan Supplement. Any contributions that cannot be made to a qualified plan due to funding limitations or nondiscrimination requirements can be made to a bonus plan.

When the Corporate Tax Bracket Is Higher than the Individual Tax Bracket. A business owner can effect a tax arbitrage by taking a tax deduction in the higher corporate bracket. For example, a $10,000 tax deduction for a corporation in a 35 percent marginal income tax bracket saves $3,500 in corporate income tax. If the business owner's personal marginal income tax bracket is 15 percent, he pays taxes of only $1,500 on the bonus for an overall tax savings of $2,000.

When Employee Security and Portability Are Primary Objectives. A key employee may not be comfortable with the insolvency risk associated with deferred-compensation plans. A bonus plan is not subject to the employer's creditors, thus giving the employee additional security.

Where the Employer Wishes to Have an Immediate Tax Deduction. Deferred compensation plans are not deductible until benefits are taxed to the employee, usually resulting in delayed tax deductions for the employer. Executive bonus plans give the employer an immediate tax deduction.

Split-dollar and executive bonus plans are treated differently under ERISA than are deferred-compensation plans. When properly structured, split-dollar and bonus plans are considered welfare benefit plans rather than pension plans. In general, the ERISA requirements for welfare plans are less onerous than for pension plans.

Welfare Benefit Plans

An employee welfare benefit plan is any plan, fund, or program that is established or maintained by an employer or an employee organization for the purpose of providing, through insurance or otherwise:

- Medical, surgical, or hospital care
- Benefits in the event of sickness, accident, disability, or death
- Unemployment, vacation, apprenticeship, or training programs
- Day care centers, scholarship funds, or prepaid legal expenses
- Certain plans, other than pension plans, that are described in the Labor-Management Relations Act of 1947 (severance benefits and employee housing)

In order for ERISA to apply, there must first be a plan, fund, or program that does not fall under any of the available exceptions. For instance, bonus programs for work performed by employees are not considered employee benefit plans unless the payments are systematically deferred to the termination of covered employment or beyond, or so as to provide retirement income to employees.

Also, certain employer practices will not be considered a welfare plan:

- Overtime payments and shift, holiday, and weekend premiums
- Payment of an employee's normal compensation from the employer's general assets for periods where the employee is physically or mentally unable to work (that is, sick pay)
- Payment out of the employer's general assets for vacation, holiday, jury duty, or other sorts of non-medical leave
- Unfunded scholarship programs

These types of employee benefits are considered payroll practices, rather than employee benefit plans. One of the deciding factors in whether a benefit is a payroll practice or a welfare plan is if the benefits are paid from the general assets of the employer. Where the benefits are considered funded—as they are when insurance contracts are involved or when a union welfare fund provides the benefits—the plan will likely be considered a welfare plan and not a payroll practice.

Another type of benefit program that is not considered an employee benefit plan is payroll deduction insurance. Such a program will not be considered an employee benefit plan if:

- No contributions are made by the employer
- Participation by employees is entirely voluntary
- The sole function of the employer is to permit the insurer to advertise the program, and to collect and remit the premium payments
- The employer does not receive consideration in connection with the program

It is important with this type of payroll deduction plan that the employer not "endorse" or "sponsor" the plan. If the plan is considered sponsored, it will be a welfare benefit plan.

Severance Plans

If properly designed, a severance pay plan will be treated as a welfare plan, rather than a pension plan. An unfunded severance pay plan will be treated as a welfare plan if (1) the payments are not made contingent on the employee's retirement; (2) payments do not exceed twice the amount of the employee's annual compensation; and (3) payments do not extend more than 24 months beyond the date of employee separation or within

24 or more months of normal retirement in the case of certain limited programs.

If a principal effect of the severance arrangement is the evasion of the standards or purposes of ERISA compliance for pension plans, the plan will be treated as a pension plan.

Exemptions from Compliance

Unless exempted, welfare benefit plans must comply with Parts 1, 4, and 5 of Title I. Thus, a welfare plan must provide for reporting and disclosure, fiduciary responsibility, and a claims procedure. Part 2 (Participation and Vesting) and Part 3 (Funding) of Title I relate to pension plans and do not apply to welfare plans.

In most instances, split-dollar plans are considered welfare benefit plans since their primary purpose is to provide life insurance protection. In DOL Advisory Opinion 77-23, a split-dollar plan was ruled a welfare plan since it was established and maintained by the employer for the purpose of providing death benefits to participants and their beneficiaries through the purchase of insurance.

Assuming the benefit plan is deemed to be a welfare plan, several partial or complete exemptions from compliance are available. These exemptions primarily provide exceptions to the reporting and disclosure provisions under Part 1. In general, compliance with the fiduciary responsibilities and claims procedures of Part 4 and Part 5 will be required for all welfare benefit plans.

One Hundred Percent Owner-Insured

Under a split-dollar agreement that covers only (1) an owner or the spouse of an owner of a business owned 100 percent by the individual and/or the individual's spouse, or (2) a partner in a partnership and/or such partner's spouse, no ERISA compliance is required. A 100 percent business owner or his spouse is not considered an employee for ERISA purposes.

Top Hat Plans

A noncontributory plan that provides benefits only for the top hat group is exempt from virtually all reporting and disclosure requirements. If the plan qualifies as a top hat plan, and all benefits are provided out of the general assets of the employer, the only requirement under Part 1 is to make plan documents available to DOL on request. A split-dollar plan should fall under this exception since benefits are provided from life insurance contracts. Since the benefits must be provided solely from premiums paid out of the general assets of the employer, the split-dollar plan must be noncontributory in order for this exemption to apply.

Plans with Fewer than 100 Participants

A limited exemption is allowed for certain small welfare plans. A small welfare plan is defined as a plan that covers fewer than 100 participants at the beginning of the plan year. The plan must provide benefits solely from the general assets of the employer, from insurance contracts for which premiums are paid directly by the employer, or from insurance contracts for which premiums are paid partly by the employer and partly by contributions by the employees. Thus, contributory split-dollar plans can fall under the small plan exemption.

Where the small plan exemption applies, the plan administrator need not file any of the following four documents with DOL:

1. Plan description
2. Copy of the summary plan description
3. Description of any changes to the terms of the plan or changes to the information required in the plan description
4. Annual report (Form 5500)

Nor is an exempted small plan required to provide participants with a summary plan report or copies of the plan description or annual report. However, the small plan exemption does not relieve the administrator from the requirements of furnishing participants with a summary plan description or from providing DOL with certain documents on their request.

Plans with 100 or More Participants

Unless exempted as a top hat plan, plans with 100 or more participants will be required to comply with all provisions of Part 1, including annual reports, summary plan descriptions, summary annual reports, and those relating to providing certain documents requested by participants.

In summary, split-dollar plans are welfare plans and must comply with Part 4 and Part 5, and possibly all or part of Part 1. Noncontributory split dollar plans with top hat groups are exempted from virtually all of Part 1, whereas small welfare plans are exempted from most of Part 1. If the

Table 14.2 ERISA Requirements for Split-Dollar and Bonus Plans

	Top Hat	Small Plan	100 or More Employees
Reporting and Disclosure			
Annual Report	No	No	Yes
Summary Plan Description	No	Yes	Yes
Summary Annual Report	No	No	Yes
Plan Documents on Request	No	Yes	Yes
Fiduciary Responsibility			
Named Fiduciary	Yes	Yes	Yes
Funding Policy	Yes	Yes	Yes
Allocation of Responsibility	Yes	Yes	Yes
Amendment Procedure	Yes	Yes	Yes
Basis for Payments	Yes	Yes	Yes
Claims Procedure	Yes	Yes	Yes

employer wishes to implement a plan that will not fall under either of these two exemptions, full compliance with Part 1 will be required. The fiduciary responsibilities under Part 4 are not onerous, and generally include naming a fiduciary, allocating fiduciary responsibility, and creating a funding policy. Since the plan is funded with insurance contracts, the trust requirements under Part 4 do not apply.

The rules are summarized in Table 14.2.

Related Issues: Age and Sex Discrimination

In addition to ERISA, employee benefit plans must comply with federal age and gender discrimination laws.

Age Discrimination

In general, the Age Discrimination in Employment Act (ADEA) prohibits discrimination against all covered employees above the age of 40. Under ADEA, it is unlawful for an employer to:

- Fail to or refuse to hire, to discharge, or otherwise discriminate against any individual with respect to compensation, terms, conditions, or privileges of employment because of age

- Limit, segregate, or classify employees in a way that would deprive or tend to deprive any individual employment opportunities or affect his or her status as an employee because of age
- Reduce the wage rate of any employee in order to comply with ADEA

A defense against a discrimination claim is available if certain key elements can be established by the employer:

- A bona fide employee benefit plan exists
- The terms of the plan must be observed
- The action is justified by significant age-related cost considerations
- The plan does not require involuntary retirement based on age

To justify reductions in benefits due to cost considerations, the reductions must not be more than are needed to offset the additional costs of the benefits. In addition, the employer must provide a valid and reasonable comparison of the costs on which the decision is based.

An exception to the involuntary retirement provision is allowed for mandatory retirement of executives of individuals in high policy-making positions. This exception is allowed if executives have been in their respective positions for two years prior to retirement at age 65, and an immediate, nonforfeitable, retirement benefit of at least $44,000 is provided. The retirement benefit must be in the form of a straight life annuity and must come from the general assets of the employer. Therefore, a deferred-compensation plan can be used to pay benefits to senior executives under a mandatory retirement provision.

In summary, employers must generally provide benefits to older employees that are either of equal cost or of equal benefits to those of younger employees. For example, if all employees are required to pay 25 percent of all premiums for a life insurance plan, the plan would not be discriminatory even though older employees must pay higher premiums: all of the employees are paying the same percentage of premium in relation to the benefit, even though the dollar amounts will vary by employee. However, if older employees were required to pay 30 percent of premiums while the younger employees paid 25 percent, the older employees would be paying a higher proportion of the costs, and thus the plan would likely be considered discriminatory.

Sex Discrimination

Employee benefit plans must not discriminate between men and women. Under Title VII of the Civil Rights Act of 1964, sex discrimination is not permitted with respect to an individual's compensation, terms, conditions, or privileges of employment.

CHAPTER 15

Equity-Based Compensation

High-growth companies often find themselves short of working capital and must creatively balance the competing priorities of R&D, marketing, facilities and equipment, and, often most important, top-notch leaders and other key employees. The shrewd entrepreneur recognizes that talented people are indispensable to business success and will design compensation to attract and motivate them without overextending the company's resources. Venture capitalists who finance new and emerging growth companies support noncash, inventive compensation approaches that reward smart and hardworking employees by allowing them to share in the company's success. Thus, equity has become the currency that allows the employer to compete in a marketplace where salaries paid to the best executives are beyond their reach.

For seasoned firms, equity-based compensation serves other purposes. It keeps employees concerned about share value. It reduces cash flow and book expenses. And it minimizes and postpones employers' tax liabilities.

With all its appeal, equity compensation is often expanded outside a company's leadership perhaps covering 20 percent or more of all its employees. And programs can cover different employee groups at different levels without implicating the tough coverage and nondiscrimination compliance ERISA requires of other employee benefit plans.

Stock Options

Stock options are the most popular equity incentives offered by employers. They afford the recipient a right to buy the company's stock at a stated price, the "exercise price," for a specified period of time, the "option term."

Stock options present a win-win for employer and employee alike. The company suffers no charge to earnings, usually realizes positive cash flow when an option is exercised, and gains the benefit of loyal service from participating employees who earn a stake in the long-term success of the company. For their part, employees benefit from an increase in the company's stock price, and their profits are without a ceiling.

Yet, stock option programs are not without their detractors who argue that stock prices may rise or fall for reasons unrelated to company performance. They also note that options will not target the specific accomplishments of executives, but only overall company performance. Finally, stock options, although easy to administer and communicate, are subject to unforgiving SEC and exchange regulations that may limit their flexibility.

Stock options are of two categories, *incentive stock options* (ISOs) and *nonqualified stock options* (NQSOs). Different tax and accounting rules apply to each category.

Incentive Stock Options

ISOs can only be issued after shareholders approve them. IRC Section 422 establishes the following eight criteria to qualify as an ISO:

1. Options may only be granted to employees.
2. Options may not be granted with an exercise price less than the fair market value of the underlying stock on the date of the grant.
3. Options granted to employees who own more than 10 percent of the company's outstanding shares must have an exercise price of at least 110 percent of the underlying shares' fair market value on the date the options are granted, and an exercise period of no more than five years.
4. Options may not have an exercise period of more than 10 years and must be granted within 10 years after the plan is adopted or when it is approved by the shareholders, whichever is earlier.

5. The "grant value"—the number of shares multiplied by the value of the shares at the time the option is granted—is effectively capped through vesting restrictions. The value of shares that can be exercised for the first time by an employee in any year may not exceed $100,000, based on the stock's value at the time the option is granted.
6. Shares received when an option is exercised must be held for at least one year after the exercise or two years after the grant, whichever is longer.
7. Except in the cases of an employee's disability or death, vested options must be forfeited if they are not exercised within three months after a recipient's employment is terminated.
8. Options may not be transferred unless an employee dies.

ISOs enjoy special tax treatment. The employee realizes no taxable income either at the time of the grant or when the option is timely exercised. Gain is generally realized only when the stock is eventually sold, and then capital-gain tax rates apply. However, employees must consider the "spread," the difference between the exercise price and fair market value, in determining whether or not they are liable under the AMT provisions. In addition, if the stock is not held for the required term, a "disqualifying disposition" results, and a portion of the gain will be taxed as ordinary income.

The grant itself is not considered compensation and, consequently, the employee incurs no FICA obligation at the time of grant. Nor are income or FICA taxes withheld upon sale.

The company will not be entitled to an income tax deduction unless employees sell their shares before the end of the ISO holding period. Only under those circumstances may the company claim a tax deduction, limited to the amount of ordinary income recognized by the employee.

Privately held entrepreneurial companies that may go public in a year or more are particularly good candidates for ISOs. Typically, the employees' tax savings are of greater consequence than the company's lost tax deduction. Since share values will likely represent only a fraction of the company stock's IPO price, employees may benefit significantly by exercising ISOs before the company goes public.

One concern in such cases, is the employees' AMT exposure. For that reason many ISO plans adopted by emerging companies include "early exercise" features that allow participating employees to exercise nonvested options. The shares issued upon exercise would be subject to the company's right to repurchase them at the employees' cost if they leave the company before the options would otherwise vest. When the employees exercise their option, they can make an election under IRC Section 83(b) (see Nonqualified Stock Options) and cut both their regular income tax and AMT liability. Although the strategy can be a worthwhile one, the company should be cautioned that an early exercise provision, if not introduced with great care, could inadvertently jeopardize the $100,000 limit and possibly other ISO statutory requirements.

Table 15.1 summarizes the tax attributes of equity-based compensation for ISOs as well as other equity-based compensation plans discussed in this chapter.

Nonqualified Stock Options

NQSOs are not subject to any restrictions on option price or term. Nor is there any cap on the number of options that can be granted or vested in a given year or any constraints on the disposition of stock acquired through the exercise of an option.

Three different categories of NSQOs are:

1. *Fair market value (FMV) options* have an exercise price equal to the FMV of the company's stock on the date of the grant. FMV options are attractive because they are easy to design.
2. *Discounted stock options* have an exercise price below the FMV of the company's stock on the date of the grant. Options discounted more than 50 percent may be deemed to be restricted stock (see Restricted Stock later in this chapter) for tax purposes if exercise is a foregone conclusion. In such a case, the IRS will view the option as a currently taxable transfer of stock.

    Although discounted stock options are more valuable to the recipient when they are granted than FMV options are, they are not universally appreciated. For one thing they require the company to take a charge to earnings equal to the amount of the discount. For another, shareholders may question the merits of such options as performance incentives, instead of disparaging them as bonuses to corporate insiders.
3. *Premium-priced options* have an exercise price above the FMV of the company's stock on the date of the grant. Although shareholders

Table 15.1   Tax Attributes of Equity-Based Compensation Plans

Type of Compensation	Tax Consequences to the Employee	Tax Consequences to the Company	FICA/FUTA Taxes Apply	Accounting Treatment	Withholding Requirements
Incentive Stock Options	Employee recognizes long-term capital gain on the sale of the stock provided specified holding periods are satisfied. Alternative minimum tax implications at exercise.	Company does not get a deduction unless there is a "disqualifying disposition," for example, a failure to satisfy holding period.	No	If the exercise price of the options at least equals FMV of the stock at grant, there may be no charge against earnings; however, disclosures may be required.	No
Nonqualified Stock Options	Employee recognizes ordinary income equal to the spread on exercise of option.	Company is entitled to deduction to the extent employee recognizes income.	Yes, when options are exercised	If the exercise price of the options at least equals FMV of the stock at grant, there may be no charge against earnings; however, disclosures may be required.	No, at grant. Yes, at exercise

(continues)

Table 15.1   Tax Attributes of Equity-Based Compensation Plans (*continued*)

Type of Compensation	Tax Consequences to the Employee	Tax Consequences to the Company	FICA/FUTA Taxes Apply	Accounting Treatment	Withholding Requirements
Restricted Stock	No ordinary income recognition until substantial risks of forfeiture lapse, unless an IRC section 83(b) election is made.	Company is entitled to deduction to the extent employee recognizes income.	When no longer subject to resriction	Compensation expense is measured and charged to earnings over vesting period.	No, at grant (unless 83(b) election made). Yes, when restrictions lapse
Phantom Stock	Employee recognizes ordinary income when phantom stock is paid or made available to employee.	Company is entitled to deduction to the extent employee recognizes income.	When paid or made	Compensation expense is charged to earnings.	No, at grant Yes, when paid or made available
Stock Appreciation Rights	Employee recognizes ordinary income upon exercise.	Company is entitled to deduction to the extent income is recognized by employee.	When exercised	Compensation expense is charged to earnings	No, at grant. Yes, when exercised

may applaud the fact that participating employees must stretch to earn value, employees are apt to see premium-priced options as risky and unmotivating.

Employees do not recognize taxable income when NQSOs are granted. It is the exercise of an option that is a taxable event. For that reason the company is required to withhold taxes on the exercise of an NQSO.

The employee is taxed as ordinary income on the spread between the exercise price and the FMV of the stock, when the option is received. The company is then entitled to a deduction of the amount that is taxed to the employee. All things being equal, companies prefer deductible over nondeductible compensation and thus select NQSOs over ISOs.

One exception applies. If the shares acquired on exercise are both nontransferrable and subject to a substantial risk of forfeiture, both the recognition of any gain and the company's tax deductions are postponed under IRC Section 83 until the shares become transferrable or no longer subject to a substantial risk of forfeiture. The employee can waive the deferral by making an election under Section 83(b).

The benefits of NQSOs can be enhanced by the financial advisor who creatively combines them with other planning techniques. A few examples follow.

Stock Option Gain Deferral

NQSOs can be linked to deferred-compensation arrangements to shelter the taxable gain otherwise incurred when an option is exercised. The employee can have his or her gain credited to a deferred-compensation account as long as the deferred-compensation election is made six months or more before the exercise date and his or her stock has been owned for six months or more. The strategy lets the employee diversify his or her option gain or continue owning his or her company stock (a phantom share, see Phantom Stock Plans and Stock Appreciation Rights later in this chapter), but capture the gain with less risk.

Transferrable Stock Options

As long as the option agreement permits, NQSOs can be gifted to family members (or a family trust) as part of the employee's estate plan. Transferring a vested option is a taxable gift. When an option is exercised, the employee, now a donor, picks up taxable income equal to the spread. When she pays the tax, no taxable gift results, and the donee family member's tax basis in her stock becomes the exercise price plus the compensation income the employee has recognized. The financial advisor should know that, although both the IRS and the SEC allow option plans to be amended to facilitate transfer of options, state law, prior proxy representations, and stock exchange rules may bear on the decision to so amend.

Linking Performance Pay and Stock Options

Compensating employees in a way that reflects their job performance has gained enormous popularity. In other cases, the employer company usually records a compensation expense (which reduces earnings-per-share) for the value of the incentive award, whether in cash or stock, as it is earned. Instead, using this strategy, the company can cap its compensation expense by offsetting performance pay by any growth in share value subject to a transfer option. So limiting the performance plan benefits can altogether wipe out any charge to earnings.

Restricted Stock

The company may award a key employee additional shares, either as bonus compensation or as part of an incentive program. The shares can be restricted—not vested—until the employee reaches her performance objectives or completed a prescribed number of years of service.

The employee will be taxed on the value of those shares when they become freely transferrable or when they are no longer subject to a substantial risk of forfeiture. At that time, the shares' FMV, less any amount the employee may have paid for the shares, will be taxable to her.

Sometimes an employee will prefer to accelerate her tax obligation, and for good reason. An election under IRC Section 83(b) will permit her tax to be measured as of the grant date, even though her shares are then restricted. Such an election will limit her ordinary income to the shares' value on the date of the grant, and any stock appreciation after that date will be subject to more favorable capital-gain tax rates. In the event the employee forfeits her shares, she will then be entitled to a tax deduction for any amount she actually paid for her stock. The company's tax deduction is equal to the amount of income the employee recognized and is available in the tax year that includes the employee's tax date. The employer is also allowed a deduction for any dividends paid on the stock before the stock is taxable to the employee.

IRC Section 83(b) requires the shareholder to file an election within 30 days after the shares have been transferred and another along with her tax return for the year in which the shares were received. A copy of the election must also be submitted to the employer.

The election must contain all the following information:

- Taxpayer's name
- Taxpayer's address
- Taxpayer's identification number
- Description of the property transferred
- Date of the transfer
- Nature of any restrictions which apply
- FMV of the property at the time of the transfer
- Amount paid by the taxpayer at the time of the transfer
- A statement that copies of the election have been furnished as required by law

The financial advisor should be aware of a couple of tax traps:

- An IRC Section 83(b) election is required even when restricted stock is purchased at FMV.
- The employer is permitted a tax deduction only if it withholds on any amount included in the employee's compensation.

Phantom Stock Plans and Stock Appreciation Rights

Phantom stock and stock appreciation rights are not equity interests at all, but forms of deferred compensation.

Phantom stock plans award units, or hypothetical shares of a company's stock, to employees. Units might be awarded with a value based on a bonus pool, equal, for example, to a percentage of pretax income. And the units may vest as stated performance goals are achieved.

Units are valued when they are awarded, and the employee is eventually paid in cash for any growth in the company's stock price (and, possibly, any dividends paid) between the date of the award and some specified future date. That date might be the day the employee retires, dies, or becomes disabled, or it might be a date that is arbitrarily set. The company deducts its cash payment as compensation when the employee receives cash and recognizes taxable income.

A stock appreciation right entitles an employee to receive cash, stock, or both equal to the appreciation in the price of stock from the date of the grant until the date it is exercised. Stock appreciation rights may be coordinated with ISOs or NQSOs and can give the employee a choice to receive cash (by exercising the right) or stock (by exercising the option). Only when the stock appreciation right is exercised will the employee recognize taxable income and the company claim its tax deduction for compensation.

Stock-based compensation is the "best practice" by high-growth companies, and its popularity is likely to expand. The entrepreneur would be well advised to maintain a balanced and cohesive compensation strategy that is sensitive to increasingly complex regulatory issues.

Part Five

Managing Capital Events

16

Buying or Selling an Entrepreneurial Business

Given a professional responsibility to advocate a client's cause vigorously, the financial advisor must first investigate why the client seeks to buy or sell a business. The advisor then can help arrange the purchase or sale so that all the client's objectives are met. For example, if a prospective buyer is driven by an ambition to eliminate a principal competitor, the buyer's advisor should focus on the scope of the seller's covenants not to compete. But if a seller is forced to sell because of unpaid family medical bills, the advisor will avoid sophisticated techniques for deferring taxable gain that also postpone the client's receipt of cash.

The Client's Objectives

Before putting pen to paper, a buyer's financial advisor must be sure of the client's objectives for the acquisition. Although there are many possible goals, 10 common reasons for buying small businesses include:

1. To expand current product lines or diversify into new ones
2. To enter into new geographic markets
3. To procure management or technical personnel

4. To secure new working capital
5. To enlarge channels of distribution or sources of raw materials
6. To gain specific assets such as processes or software
7. To gain the benefit of the seller's plant capacity
8. To improve the buyer's competitive status
9. To create a new outlet for the buyer's products
10. To pick up a potential turn-around business—a financially depressed enterprise—at a fire sale price

The seller's advisor also must sort through the key considerations in a small business disposition. Typically, a client's reasons for selling out involve one or more of the following nine objectives:

1. To realize a profit
2. To become a shareholder in a more secure, publicly held corporation, rather than a closely held one
3. To overcome dissension among owners
4. To respond to adverse business conditions, such as the loss of capital or sources of supply
5. To keep current with technological advances in the industry
6. To insure that the business remains competitive
7. To bring professional management to a business that has become too large for one owner to handle
8. To gain additional capital
9. To join a larger, more profitable enterprise

Once the buyer's financial advisor understands what the client seeks to accomplish, the advisor must direct the investigation toward the business to be acquired. The purchase investigation is an important part of any potential business acquisition and should encompass the following 16 items:

1. Marketability of the product
2. Management personnel
3. Channels of distribution
4. Sources of supply
5. Status of the seller in the industry and in the utilization of technology
6. The industry's future
7. The competition
8. Capital requirements, production capacity, customer credit, and location factors

9. Tax and withholding obligations
10. Contractual commitments and the transferability of assets
11. Legal status of Internet domain names, patents, trademarks, trade names, and copyrights
12. Securities law compliance and related issues
13. Extent of burdensome governmental regulations, including environmental, antitrust, and consumer protection restrictions
14. Extent of employee and labor union plans, other obligations, current negotiations, and proceedings
15. Pending claims and litigation
16. Any other pertinent facts and circumstances relating to the individual business enterprise

Although there may be several reasons why a seller's business should be investigated, the obvious overriding consideration is to determine whether the business should be acquired at all. The investigation process can be expected to yield the information necessary to assess risks, formulate agreements, and to make decisions about the value of the business.

Although computer-assisted analysis has come of age, business valuation remains an art, and it is a major consideration for both buyer and seller in virtually every transfer of a small business. Value has a different meaning for the buyer and seller, with the buyer looking primarily to future value and the seller concentrating on present value. Chapter 11 analyzes the different approaches and methods of valuation from both acquiring and disposing viewpoints.

In most cases, circumstances arise that prevent a buyer from completing an investigation until after a contractual purchase commitment has been entered into. For example, the seller may present certain confidential and sensitive data on a preliminary, tentative basis, consenting to divulge this information only after receiving assurances in the form of an earnest money deposit, a standby letter of credit, or, at a minimum, a binding letter of intent.

A seller should be advised to disclose to the buyer in the early fact-finding stages any current or potential problems that could have a material impact on the business. Candor may diffuse any buyer distrust and inure to the seller's benefit later in the formulation of indemnification provisions. Not surprisingly, financial advisors for both buyers and sellers play important roles in the investigative process, both before a contact of sale is signed and, later, in the closing phase.

Financial Information

A review of the seller's financial statements is of paramount importance in evaluating a potential business acquisition. The balance sheet, or statement of financial condition, describes what is owned and what is owed by a business enterprise as of a given date. Most assets listed in the balance sheet are valued at historic or original cost, less depreciation reserves or deductions if applicable, but some assets such as inventory of finished goods may be reflected on the basis of the lower of cost or current FMV.

Liabilities are set off against asset values to ascertain the net book value, which is simply the result after the assets-less-liabilities computation is made. The net book value represents what should be realized if the business were immediately liquidated.

The utility of a balance sheet may be limited to the purpose for which it was prepared. For example, if a balance sheet has been prepared for the managers of the business, it likely will be wholly unsuitable for use in, or in connection with, a public document such as an annual report. The internal statement would cover matters such as the allocations of resources among divisions or other details of very limited interest.

Although a purchaser of the business may be interested in detailed analysis, the primary concern at the negotiation stage is with the company's overall performance. Moreover, accounting principles used in statements prepared for internal purposes may be misleading for an outsider, as accountants often adopt simplistic compilations when asked to generate quick figures for the management team. Such output is far from the comprehensive audit and analysis needed when it comes to considering purchase terms.

Other short-form or abbreviated financial statements may have been prepared, but for various reasons, they usually will not be helpful. The interpretation of these informal statements is simply too uncertain, even when done by the purchaser's accountant, and it therefore will be advisable to insist on receiving the full-length or long-form financial statements.

Off-balance-sheet items often are found in the financial statements' footnotes or supplementary schedules, depending on the form used by the accountant. The information in these footnotes may include data on stock options, lease commitments, long- and short-term bank debts, warrants, convertible stock provisions, and contingent liabilities.

Income statements or profit-and-loss statements highlight a business's financial performance over a specified period of time. Gross income derived from the sale of goods and services is described along with the expenses and costs required in their production, to net out the amounts actually realized in total sales operations. As accounting treatments of revenues and costs vary in preparing income statements, a careful review of these statements, including determination of the treatments used, is an essential first step in a purchase transaction.

Particularly when closely held small businesses are involved, audited financial statements may not be available. The prospective buyer should, in such cases, negotiate to have the statements prepared at the seller's expense or at least on a shared-cost basis. The cost of an audit, particularly one ordered with a short time deadline, can be large. Whether time permits an audit, or whether the buyer's bargaining power is sufficient to obtain it at the seller's cost, depends in large part on the particular circumstances, but the purchaser should neither act too hastily nor with too few safeguards. A dead deal is usually better than a poor one.

Although audited financial statements generally are regarded as the most essential of all protections in a purchase transaction, the danger of excessive reliance on such data is present and clear in virtually all cases. Not only can the variability of the accounting treatments underlying the data be misleading, even wholly valid historical results can be unreliable as predictors of the future.

Although it is desirable that all relevant data of the target business be reviewed, the purchaser's initial focus should be on financial statements describing operating results of the last five fiscal years. Only by addressing this key information and analyzing the enterprise's overall recent performance can the buyer accurately evaluate its potential future performance.

If the business's financial statements have not been audited within six months of the investigation, the buyer's accountant should be asked to prepare an interim balance sheet and income statement, with prearranged permission to draw on the assistance of the seller's accountant in completing this information. Less satisfactory, but not necessarily unacceptable, especially if the seller's accountant is a well-known accounting firm, is a variation whereby the seller's accountant is primarily in charge of the interim statements' preparation but is requested to make the underlying computations, books, and records available for inspection by the purchaser's accountant. In either case, the current earning power of the business will find its most significant expression, and operating problems warranting further inquiry can be pinpointed. Of course, the assumption that all material information has been fairly disclosed must be treated skeptically and subjected to rigorous audit testing.

Different businesses use varying accounting methods to value inventories, recover the costs of depreciating capital assets, capitalize or expense organizational and other costs, record nonrecurring or extraordinary items, and state net profit or loss. The buyer's accountant needs to examine and evaluate all such items with great care, especially because they may be based on different methodologies chosen by the seller. Variations in accounting assumptions should be determined early in the negotiations so that underlying economic factors affecting the valuation of the business can be properly analyzed and taken into account through the price clause in the contract, including, if the factors so indicate, provisions for price adjustments at or after the closing.

One helpful technique in analyzing financial statements is to compare data of similarly situated companies. When the purchaser and the seller have been in the same business, comparison of statements relating to like economic activities, time periods, and operational functions can bear directly on the overall assessment of the worth of the business. Any data that may differ by reason of variations in accounting methods will need to be adjusted. Even if the seller's accountant certifies that financial statements were prepared in accordance with generally accepted accounting principles consistently applied, the form or significance of the data is by no means standardized. There is simply no avoiding the need to determine which accounting method or methods were used to reach each of the various operational results.

Guidelines for Reviewing Standard Accounting Opinion

Date of Report

In a standard accounting opinion, or audit report, the date of the document reflects the completion of audit work and is therefore, in most cases, the last day of fieldwork at the premises of the client. The date is significant because it establishes the end of the period for which the auditor is responsible to search for material events, thereby excluding from the opinion events that may occur after year's end, and provides a limitation affecting the scope of the audited financial statements.

Scope Paragraph

The scope describes the extent to which an independent auditor's examination of financial statements was made. The standard scope paragraph is worded substantially as follows:

> We have examined the balance sheet of _____ Company as of December 31, 20__, and the related statements of income, retained earnings and changes in financial position for the year then ended. Our examination was made in accordance with the generally accepted auditing standards and, accordingly, included such tests of accounting records and such other auditing procedures as we considered to be necessary in the circumstances.

This wording of the opinion indicates compliance with three general standards of auditing procedure and also three general standards of field-work. The three general standards of auditing procedure are that:

1. The examination was performed by persons having adequate technical training
2. An independent mental attitude was maintained by the auditor
3. Due professional care was exercised in the performance of the examination and preparation of the report

The three compliance with fieldwork standards have the following significance:

1. The work was adequately planned and supervised
2. There was a proper study and evaluation of internal control as a basis for reliance thereon that determined the extent to which tests and auditing procedures were made
3. Sufficient competent evidential matter was obtained through inspection, observation, inquiries, and confirmations to afford a reasonable basis for the opinion given

If any of the six standards above are not met, then the wording for the standard scope paragraph is changed. There are many possible variations from the standard wording, any of which may reflect extensive departures from the normal format.

Opinion Paragraph

The opinion paragraph is beneath the scope paragraph and describes the results of an audit. The standard opinion paragraph is typically worded as follows:

> In our opinion, the financial statements referred to above present fairly the financial position of _____ Company as of December 31, 20__, and the results of its operations and the changes in its financial position for the year then ended, in conformity with generally accepted accounting principles applied on a basis consistent with that of the preceding year.

The wording of a standard opinion paragraph implies compliance with four standards of audit reporting as follows:

1. The financial statements are presented in accordance with generally accepted accounting principles
2. Generally accepted accounting principles were consistently observed in the current period in relation to the preceding period
3. Informative disclosures are reasonably adequate
4. The opinion relates to the financial statements taken as a whole

If any of these statements is not true without qualification, then departures from the standard opinion paragraph are made.

Signature

Every standard report is signed by an independent auditor in the name of the auditor's public accounting firm. Only when the independent auditor is acting as a sole proprietorship does she sign her own name to the opinion. This rule is necessary so that the responsibility for the report extends to the accounting firm as a whole.

Key Words and Phrases

Key words and phrases are found throughout the standard audit report, including "examination," "fair presentation and consistency," "generally accepted auditing standards," "opinion," and "financial statements." Each of these phrases means something special with regard to the auditing procedure. The reader of an audit opinion or set of financial statements should be comfortable with and knowledgeable about the meaning of these words and phrases. For example, "we have examined" means that an audit has been performed, and an audit is not a verification of financial statements but rather an examination. The term *statements* refers to four standard financial statements: the balance sheet, related statements of income, retained earnings, and changes in financial position. The words *generally accepted auditing standards* are guidelines or measures of the quality of an audit. The word *opinion* represents an expression of opinion by an independent auditor; it is neither a casual impression nor a statement of fact. The phrase *fair presentation and consistency* means that the fairness relates to all potential users of financial statements, and the word *consistently* is meant to insure that the comparability of financial statements is not impaired by the inconsistent application of accounting principles.

Contracts and Continuing Obligations

Early in any negotiation, the purchaser's attorney needs to identify and review the seller's contracts that relate to the sale of the business. An existing favorable contract may constitute a major part of the business's value to the purchaser. An unfavorable contract may be avoidable through an asset-purchase type of transaction, but a careful study of this issue may be necessary.

As the well-known *Texaco-Pennzoil* case illustrated, a preexisting stock sale agreement at the shareholder level can present an enormous risk to a purchaser, who by entering into a purchase contract with respect to the same stock can then be held liable for having interfered with the preexisting agreement, even if the former agreement was only a so-called intent letter. The extent of the adjudicated liability in the *Texaco* case was $10.53 billion and, even with a reduction on settlement, reported to be around 75 percent, the final required payment was enormous.

Another landmark case, *Revlon, Inc. v. MacAndrews & Forbes Holdings*, 506 A.2d 173 (Del. 1986), raised the issue of whether an agreement to acquire stock can be legally binding on the seller's board of directors. The Delaware Supreme Court in the case held that once a board of directors opts for a sale of the business, they step into mandatory roles as "auctioneers charged with getting the best price for stockholders." Other observers, however, insist that there are ways to sell a business that may be better than auctions, that there is no legal requirement of creating a level playing field for all potential buyers, and that the board of directors can make binding sale agreements without using the auction procedure.

Although a proposed or actual contract between the selling and buying parties is certainly a highest-priority issue, the ongoing contracts of the seller also can bear importantly on the proposed transaction. Supposedly everyday agreements such as loan contracts, mortgages, leases, security agreements, labor union and employee contracts, customer, supplier, and government contracts can create or increase, decrease, or even destroy the most substantial economic values in any business.

A review of the status of material contracts should be undertaken, including an examination of the business's compliance with contractual obligations, expiration terms, and renewal privileges. For example, if there are arrearages on an equipment loan for machinery that is vital to production, the secured lender may be far along in steps to repossess, regardless of the possible catastrophic impact on the business. A pending equipment lease expiration without a right of renewal could have equally adverse consequences.

Along with the economic impact and status of the seller's ongoing contracts are the issues of their assignability and their restrictions on business or asset sales or business activities. Some contracts may prohibit an assignment or a sale of the business or its assets, whereas others may permit such transfers only with the consent of a third party. Thus, the sale of a business, or substantially all its assets, may founder because the consent of an essential contract party cannot be obtained. Only a careful review of documents and corporate records can lead to a reliable determination in these matters.

The purchaser may incur indirect liability under an ongoing arrangement in an asset-sale type of transaction when no direct contract assignment is made. If a third party has security or other rights in property transferred, the need to retain the property may require the purchaser to take on the obligations of the seller's contract. Restrictive covenants in these agreements sometimes prevent transferring or using property in a way that the buyer intends, and could bring about a default, even when no default previously existed.

With regularity, courts are imposing strict liabilities on asset-acquirers as "successor" companies in regard to products made by the predecessor-manufacturers. Thus, a California court held the purchaser of a business strictly liable for defects in a product made by the seller even though the buyer had discontinued the specific product line before the case arose. The court held:

> Strict products liability is not based upon fault—the successor need not be "morally responsible" for the defect to incur liability. The manner in which the successor company elects to use good will of its predecessor in marketing its products is irrelevant to the issue of whether the costs of injuries sustained as a result of defective products previously manufactured may be spread over society. The general business continued by the manufacturer and its ability to spread these costs must be considered and not merely whether a specific line of products was discontinued.

Another group of jurisdictions predicates strict liability for business purchasers, as to products made by the seller, on the circumstance that the successor holds itself out as a continuation of the predecessor. It should benefit buyers of small businesses to consider the following five scenarios:

1. When goodwill is not acquired, successor liability for defective products made by the seller is not imposed, so if the buyer can avoid taking over Internet domain names, trade names, patents, and customer lists, substantial legal protection may be available.
2. If the acquisition can be limited to avoid covering substantially all the seller's assets, successor liability usually can be avoided.
3. If the distribution of products has been and can be limited to those states not imposing strict liability for defects on successors, the exposure to claims may be avoided.
4. Imposition of successor liability usually can be avoided if the continued existence of a solvent seller is assured. A contractual obligation of the seller to maintain its existence may be very helpful.
5. If successor liability is a possibility, a buyer needs to check out whether existing insurance coverage is adequate or whether additional, specific coverage would be beneficial.

A review of the seller's contracts and continuing obligations should also consider the following areas:

- Contracts and pending bids relating to projects or business transactions over $10,000
- Continuing contracts for the purchase of materials, supplies, and equipment, and other contracts continuing beyond the current year, except minor or routine subscriptions or similar undertakings.
- Employment and labor union contracts.
- Stock bonus, stock-option, profit sharing, retirement, and 401(k) plans, trust agreements, and arrangements.
- Hospitalization, medical reimbursements, disability, sick pay, salary continuation, and similar plans and insurance policies.
- Employees eligible to retire in the next five years by reason of any formal or informal corporate policy or arrangement, with a breakout of unfunded pension benefits and the sources and documents relating to any such pension obligations.

Leases and Properties

If an acquisition includes a transfer of leases or real estate, the buyer's financial advisor must consider a number of important factors. Otherwise, restrictions on activities being carried on or planned for the future may carry over to the new business and thwart the objectives of the transaction.

When real estate is included in the assets of a business being acquired pursuant to a deed, or taken over by an assignment of a lease, the Federal Superfund law, often called CERCLA, is an important consideration. Under CERCLA, officially known as the Comprehensive Environmental Response, Compensation and Liability Act of 1980, an acquiring company will be held liable for the acts of the prior owner of realty if the buyer continues essentially the same operations of the property.

CERCLA imposes potential "absolute" or "strict" liabilities beyond just cleanup for a buyer operating a facility acquired from a seller, or an off-site disposal location, affected by contamination. These liabilities, unless a safe-harbor defense (discussed below) applies, generally tack on to a successor owner in a stock acquisition transaction, and add response costs and damages to natural resources to the cleanup costs. Most states have adopted similar laws, and the state court cases under these laws should receive close scrutiny by a buyer's counsel if industrial facilities are involved in an acquisition.

The safe-harbor defense against strict liability under CERCLA applies if the hazardous substance leakage or leaking was caused by an act of God or war or by an act or omission of a party not having a "close" contractual relationship to the facility operator or owner-tenant, and if there is compliance with the further requirements that the operator exercised due care and took precautions against foreseeable events. A close contractual relationship exists in the context of the sale by a business of its properties unless the purchaser (1) "had no reason to know" that hazardous substances were on the property, and (2) conducted "all appropriate inquiry into the previous ownership and uses of the property consistent with good commercial or customary practice in an effort to minimize liability." To ensure the availability of this safe-harbor defense, a purchaser should document the investigative efforts, with legal counsel providing consultation and supervision. An acquirer of a small business may also be able to gain protection against the carryover of various liabilities, including environmental contamination, by means of indemnification or warranty agreements from the seller, or through escrowing part of the purchase funds for a reasonable period of time.

Title insurance is an essential protection for any acquisition of real estate. A preliminary report of ownership, confirming good and merchantable title subject only to limited liens, covenants, and restrictions that are fully disclosed and understood, should be a contractual condition to be met at or before closing.

To verify that no tax lien or unsatisfied judgments affect properties being acquired, filings at both the county and state levels will need to be checked and search reports obtained from a commercial search organization. Reports of filings of Uniform Commercial Code security interests (or liens) against, or claims against, fixtures permanently attached to, or equipment, inventory, or accounts receivable located at, the real estate, should be included with the tax and judgment searches and reports.

A current survey of real property by a duly licensed surveyor should be required, at seller's expense, at or before closing. Surveys of improved real estate should be "spotted," to show the location, basic type of construction material, and dimensions of all improvements, and they should be closely inspected to see if improvements encroach over onto adjoining property, or if any structures on adjoining property protrude onto the property being acquired.

An acquisition of real estate should be conditioned on compliance with applicable building codes, zoning, land use control and flood control laws, ordinances, regulations, orders, and court decrees. If land being acquired is located in a flood plain, the availability of flood insurance and the amount of the related premiums are preclosing items to check and to provide for in the contractual documents as they may be appropriate in the circumstances.

Consideration should be given to the so-called "public trust" doctrine if land being acquired is proximate to navigable waters. This doctrine has been expanded by the U.S. Supreme Court to hold that state and local governments can impose limitations ex post facto on the uses of land that is *not* adjacent to navigable waters if the land is affected by tides. In effect, the public trust doctrine now means that nonbusiness legal limitations may apply with respect to land either next to navigable waters or affected by tides, and such limitations may be adopted by federal, state, or local government bodies even after a buyer has paid for property planning to put it to a business use. In the *Phillips Petroleum* case, marsh land far distant from any coast or navigable water was held to be subject to this doctrine. *Phillips Petroleum Co. v Mississippi*, 484 U.S. 469 (1988).

At most closings of small business acquisitions, counsel's first priority is to confirm the legal validity and binding effect of the instruments of transfer to real property, whether they be deeds or assignments of leases, as well as to determine the effects of the terms of the instruments and applicable law on the business uses that are planned. Even after the closing, the job of recording of any instruments and obtaining title policies must be assumed by counsel.

Checklist for Reviewing Leases

1. Are there restrictions on the use of the premises that might interfere with the business?
2. Are there restrictions on equipment such as microwave ovens, lasers, or x-ray machines? Will these restrictions adversely affect the business?
3. Are there building or association rules that must be followed?
4. If the lessee is a corporation, or limited-liability company, does the lessor require the officers or members personally to guarantee the payment of rent?
5. Is a deposit required? Will the lessor pay interest?
6. Who pays utility charges?
7. Who pays insurance premiums?
8. Who is responsible for maintenance, upkeep, and repairs to the premises?
9. In the event of glass damage, who is required to pay for replacements?
10. Are there provisions for cleaning services?
11. Are there provisions for signs and listings in directories?
12. Is the lease assignable?
13. Are default provisions reasonable? Is default on the lease tied to default on any other obligation?
14. Is the term sufficiently long?
15. Are rent adjustment provisions understandable so that adjustments can be verified?

Federal Taxes

Tax issues can have major consequences for many deals. A tax-free reorganization under the IRC may enable a selling corporation and its shareholders to avoid recognition of gain or loss on the sale. A buyer, if the transaction is appropriately cast, may inherit favorable tax attributes of the selling corporation, although the law has virtually eliminated any use of the seller's net operating loss carryovers within five years following the acquisition.

The seller's federal income tax returns—particularly those from the previous five years—and the internal working papers, files, and audits of the target business require close scrutiny. Outside audits and proceedings by the IRS, if any, must be examined completely, especially to determine if any settlement or other agreements were made that would survive the sale of the business.

Very often tax issues are resolved administratively by the IRS, which then retains the reports filed by the examining field agents. These reports, if any, should be checked to see what views the IRS may have had concerning the operations and activities of the target business. Verification that correct employer identification numbers, as assigned by the IRS, were consistently used on returns and in connection with any proceedings also may prevent some major postclosing surprises in the form of assessments for additional taxes.

As the acquisition of stock in a corporation will ordinarily result in a carryover of liabilities for unpaid taxes, a close familiarity with the entire tax situation of the acquired corporation must be gained before closing. If the extent of such liabilities appears excessive, an acquisition of assets may be the only feasible alternative. However, the buyer can often obtain sufficient assurances by carefully negotiating an indemnity agreement.

Discrepancies between a seller's tax basis in its assets and the balance sheet figures for the same items often are revealed on examination of tax returns. These differences may be due to the variation of methods used in tax accounting from those used in ordinary financial accounting, to tax provisions for rapid depreciation, to economic conditions that actually increase rather than decrease certain asset values—in recent memory, most real estate has only appreciated—to a combination of such factors. The buyer will prefer high tax bases for depreciable assets so that subsequent depreciation can generate maximum tax deductions and savings in taxes.

In general, the IRS can audit and challenge tax returns for the last three years, the so-called open years. A tax specialist should be requested to ascertain what contingent tax liabilities could affect the open years if a stock purchase is contemplated. A six-year statute of limitations applies, however, if a return failed to reflect any items of gross income, and there is no limitation in cases of fraudulent returns made with intent to evade tax or failure to file any return. Voluntary extensions and suspensions of the statute of limitations caused by 90-day letters ("notices of deficiency") also can affect the "open" time period, so caution must be exercised in determining what fixed and contingent tax liabilities may be hovering over the seller's business.

State and Local Taxes

As the rates of state and local taxes have increased dramatically and cumulatively approximate the federal rate in many areas, income tax returns at these levels should be reviewed as carefully as federal returns. The basic objective is to confirm that the seller has paid all taxes owed to all jurisdictions involved or potentially involved. Particular attention should be given to jurisdictions where no tax was paid or return filed, but whose connections with actual transactions might create tax liability. Any unpaid state and local tax liabilities should be withheld from the purchase price and earmarked in an escrow for that purpose; failure to do so can make the purchaser liable for the taxes. An escrow for state and local taxes also must include all applicable amounts of withholding from the payments of compensation to employees for their state and local income taxes and unemployment compensation insurance, as well as any amounts of currently unpaid sales taxes.

State and local taxes of the target business may be calculated on the basis of taxable income reported on federal returns, or otherwise be modeled on or in some way tack onto the federal tax computations. Whether an acquisition qualifies as a tax-free reorganization usually is consistently determined at the various tax levels, but of course the state and local legislation should be confirmed on this point and the other tax considerations.

In addition to the state and local tax returns, the internal working papers, files, and state audits of the target business should receive attention. Any audits and proceedings by tax authorities should be reviewed, and if tax issues were resolved administratively, the reports should be examined to determine their impact on the prospective operations and activities of the business.

In most states, income taxes are based on the allocation of property, sales, and wages, as among the various states in which business is conducted. If the ratio of these items varies considerably between the buyer and the seller, changes in the allocations of taxable income may result when the two enterprises combine. Whether these changes are advantageous to a particular buyer will depend on the variations in the specific rates among the jurisdictions involved and the weightings of property, sales, and wages required by the respective allocation formulas.

Most states, and some cities and counties, impose some form of sales, gross receipts, or license tax based on gross income. The main factors to be considered with respect to these taxes are the size of the transaction, whether the transaction can be restructured to avoid the taxes, and which party will be required to pay the taxes. If the sale is cast as an asset acquisition, any tangible personal property transferred in the sale, including machinery, equipment, and inventories, may be subject to these taxes. Because the amount of such tax burdens can be considerable, state and local law must be carefully examined.

In many states, sales taxes are not triggered by a bulk transfer of inventory, receivables, and cash, although subsequent sales from inventory will result in sales tax obligations. Another basis of a sales tax exemption for a business sale may be an occasional, incidental, or isolated transaction characterization.

Where sales taxes are concerned, the buyer should pay closest attention to the possibility of stepping into an obligation for unpaid tax liabilities on a carryover basis from the seller. In many states, this carryover obligation results if the buyer does not have a portion of the purchase price set aside in a third-party escrow at the closing, and can result even if preclosing notice is given to the appropriate tax authority. So, determining the correct amount of current sales tax due and setting up the required escrow can be a priority before closing the acquisition of a small business.

Another state-level consideration is the requirement of posting a bond or deposit for worker's compensation insurance. If part of the seller's assets consist of such a bond or deposit, and the asset can be transferred to the buyer, the valuation of such property is not different from that of other items. However, applicable law and any insurance policy should be checked to verify if transfer is possible; otherwise, this asset does not represent actual or potential value to the purchaser and a reduction-adjustment of the purchase price may be in order.

Franchise taxes and license fees are levied in most states, on both domestic corporations and foreign corporations doing business in the state. The formulas for computing these taxes vary, and accordingly the laws of all the states where business is carried on, or where authority to do business has been obtained, must be checked.

Generally, the corporate franchise tax is imposed on the right and privilege of doing business under the corporation's charter. Thus, the tax relates to the privilege, rather than the fact, of doing business in the particular state. Even an inactive corporation is liable for the franchise tax because it is levied solely for the privilege of doing business. An out-of-state corporation, usually referred to as a foreign corporation, that has received a license or authority to do business in a state but has never exercised the privilege, is nevertheless liable for the franchise tax.

Taxes on franchises may be based on valuation, and license fees also may be imposed. Thus, even though the franchise is subject to an ad valorem tax (based on value), this does not prevent a license or occupation tax from being levied. Moreover, it has been held that a corporation's privilege to do business in a state can be taxed in addition to its right to conduct business in the state without constituting double taxation. The corporation itself, as well as its directors and officers, may be held liable if franchise taxes are not paid or if franchise tax reports are not properly and timely filed. Civil and criminal penalties can range, depending on the seriousness of the offense, from small monetary fines to felony convictions calling for imprisonment.

Some states impose a tax on the original issuance of shares or certificates of stock. This tax may be based on the par value of the shares or on their actual value. Usually, tax stamps must be purchased and affixed to the stock certificates to fulfill the applicable legal requirements. A number of states also impose state stamp taxes on the transfer of stock. This tax also may be based on actual or par value. In some states, the tax may be determined by the charter value of the stock instead of by the value printed on the certificates.

Taxes on the original issuance and transfer of stock are excise taxes and have been upheld against challenges that they violate constitutional standards. Although the laws do not apply to out-of-state transfers, the tax may be imposed if the stock is delivered into the taxing state in question, even though the execution of transfer documentation occurred in another state. Payment of the tax is completed when the stamps are affixed to the certificates and then canceled.

Internet Domain Names, Patents, Trademarks, Trade Names, and Copyrights

A list of all of the seller's Internet domain names, patents, trademarks, trade names, and copyrights should be obtained. Their remaining life spans should be determined and their registrations verified.

Domain names can be transferred through the execution of a Registrant Name Change Agreement and following the other requirements found at Network Solutions, Inc.'s website; the URL is *http://www .networksolutions.com.*

Federally registered patents and trademarks are registered in the U.S. Patent and Trademark Office, where assignments must be recorded or registered within three months following any transfer of ownership. Transfers of copyright ownership must be in writing and signed by the copyright owner or the owner's agent, and should be recorded with the Library of Congress, Copyright Office, Documents Recordation Section LM-462, 101 Independence Avenue, S.E., Washington, DC 20559-6000.

Permits, Licenses, and Franchises

Governmental permits or licenses, or public or private franchises, may be required for the business to continue operations after the sale and purchase transaction. Assignment of any such rights is likely to be prohibited or very tightly limited, so that a determination of the buyer's eligibility to have new or assigned rights may be a necessary condition of the closing, from the standpoint of minimum protection for the buyer. If applications must be filed, fees paid, performance bonds, fidelity bonds, or other security provided, inspections conducted, photographs and fingerprints submitted, and other administrative requirements met, the process of obtaining the new or assigned rights may be expensive, burdensome, prolonged, and potentially disruptive to any desired time frame for concluding the transaction.

Liens, Judgments, and Deeds

Evidence of good title can be as essential for items of personal property as for realty, because the total value of equipment, inventory, furniture, and vehicles often exceeds that of land and buildings for a small business. Commercial services are available in most areas, providing lien, judgment, and tax search reports within a few days, or even faster if necessary. Title to property should be subject only to those liens and encumbrances that the purchaser has agreed to assume. Any outstanding judgments against the seller or unpaid taxes can be converted into liens, attachments, foreclosures, or judicial sales, potentially depriving the business of needed assets. Open claims, contingent liabilities, and litigation in process also can ripen into liens, judgments and forced-sale deeds.

In transactions in which the purchaser assumes or can be held involuntarily responsible for liabilities of the seller, the identification and limitation of those liabilities are of great concern. Close attention must be given to open claims, contingent liabilities, pending litigation, unpaid taxes, and outstanding judgments affecting the business or any of its properties, both real and personal.

Employee Benefit Plans

Existing plans that benefit employees of the target business require, in virtually all acquisition transactions, both careful scrutiny and major restructuring efforts, whether the plans will be continued after the closing or terminated. If the target business has sponsored a defined-benefit plan, a termination can generate a statutory "withdrawal liability" for funding deficiencies to a trustee appointed by the PBGC.

Plans that provide health insurance benefits to retirees often contain provisions that the plans will be continued following any sale of the business. Such provisions are important to the purchaser because, even if the seller terminates the entire plan, the termination action may be claimed to be the result of an inducement or interference on the purchaser's part.

The termination of defined-contribution profit-sharing plans and money purchase pension plans, the two most common plans for small businesses, usually involves applying for determination by the IRS that the respective plans were qualified at the time of their termination. However, defined-benefit plans also involve review or approval of termination actions by either or both the PBGC and DOL.

Decisions whether to terminate or continue plans should encompass not only retirement plans, but also ESOP plans, stock option plans, deferred-compensation plans, health or medical expense reimbursement plans, sick pay and disability plans, group term life insurance plans, death benefit plans, legal and financial advisory plans, child care plans, and the entire gamut of employee plans. The assumption of the obligations under one or more plans can be burdensome and expensive for the purchaser, but personnel management problems or poor employee morale may result from their termination.

Unemployment Compensation Rating

Under circumstances that vary from state to state, the purchaser of a business may be able to qualify for continuation of the favorable unemployment compensation rating of the former business. Thus, the preliminary investigation should include a determination of whether a good rating has previously been obtained from the applicable state authority and whether such a rating can be continued after the purchase.

The effect of being able to continue a favorable rating can be a negotiating point for the seller in terms of increasing the purchase price for the business. On the other hand, the lack of such a rating or an ability to continue can justify the purchaser in decreasing the price offered.

Stock Certificates, Options, and Records

In many small businesses, stock transfer books often are not carefully maintained. These books should reflect a chain of title for every share of the corporation, the surrender of certificates transferred, original assignment endorsements on the certificates transferred executed by the prior holders, and the issuance of new certificates to the assignees named in the endorsements. The purchaser's attorney should note any gaps in the chain of title, whether caused by missing endorsements, discrepancies between named assignees and the registered owners of new certificates, lack of documents, or other deficiencies. Because the number of stockholders is limited in a small business, corrective actions usually can be completed before closing.

The existence of outstanding stock options, rights, or warrants should be investigated so that the potential dilution of the purchaser's interests through exercise of any such rights can be determined. Such options, rights, or warrants also may involve securities or corporate law issues, as may class voting rights, preemptive rights, interlocking directorates, and shareholder agreements. These preliminary areas for review should include the matter of whether the seller's directors are qualified to continue in the business, if so desired, and whether they can be considered reliable and loyal as representatives for a new controlling owner.

Corporate minute records should be reviewed to confirm the absence of undisclosed liabilities, the presence of appropriate bylaws, and any necessary actions to authorize the proposed sale transaction and the proper election of current directors and officers. A long-form certificate of good standing should be obtained from the state of incorporation (or, in the case of an LLC, of organization), and a short-form certificate of good standing from each state where the corporation or LLC is qualified to do business. A copy of the articles of incorporation or other charter documents, certified by the appropriate state official of the state of incorporation, should also be obtained.

Checklist for Initial Inquiries

I. Basic organization documents
   A. Charter or articles of incorporation or organization
      1. Certified incorporation or organization instruments and amendments
      2. Capital structure of seller
      3. Preferential rights of shareholder
      4. Restrictions on sale of shares
      5. Qualifications to do business in relevant states
      6. Qualifications of subsidiaries and affiliates
   B. Bylaws
      1. Conformity with applicable laws and charter or articles
      2. Procedures for bylaws amendments
      3. Duties and powers of corporate officers or managers
      4. Election of new officers or managers
      5. Removal of incumbent officers or managers
      6. Qualifications of officers or managers
   C. Minutes
      1. Determine completeness
      2. Subscriptions, payment for, and delivery of shares
      3. Restrictions on transfers of shares
      4. Provisions for committees
      5. Grants of stock options and stock purchase rights
      6. Authorization of employee benefit plans and fringes
      7. Franchise, license, or royalty agreements
      8. Agreements with organizers, subscribers, shareholders, members, directors, managers, officers, employees, or parties related to such persons
      9. Leases and contracts running to or from the corporation
   D. Stock ledger
      1. Record of stock certificates issued, with dates
      2. Certificates surrendered, transferred, or exchanged
      3. Names of holders and numbers of shares by class
      4. Receipts for delivery of shares
      5. Record of replacement certificates, with dates
      6. Treasury shares
      7. Certificates cancelled

E. Claims and litigation
   1. Summonses and complaints received
   2. Claims and threatened actions
   3. In-house litigation files and records
   4. Arbitration files and records
   5. Referral files and correspondence with attorneys
   6. Administrative proceeding files, federal and state
F. Other documents
   1. Annual reports, 10-K, shareholder, state, and so forth
   2. Interim reports, 10-Q, 8-K, and so forth
   3. Business registrations, licenses, and assumed or fictitious name registrations
   4. Tax returns and proceedings
      a) Federal
      b) State
      c) Local
   5. Internal and outside audit reports
   6. Assignment of employer identification numbers
   7. Workers' compensation identification numbers
   8. Unemployment compensation rating and assignability

II. Loans and credit agreements
   1. Restrictions on dividends, issuance of additional securities or debt obligations
   2. Limitations on business activities, mergers, and acquisitions
   3. Rights to require additional security, cross-collateralization, or after-acquired property coverage
   4. Events of default, rights, and remedies
   5. Due-on-sale or other acceleration provisions

III. Real property
A. Real estate owned
   1. Description, locations, and use
   2. Status of titles, mortgage encumbrances, and zoning
   3. Surveys and appraisals
   4. Casualty, title, and flood insurance
   5. Easements and rights of ingress and egress
   6. Encroachments and mechanic's liens
   7. Tax and insurance escrows and tax liens

      8. Availability of utilities, sewers/septic tanks

      9. Party wall agreements and termite inspections

     10. Building code requirements

  B. Real estate leased

      1. Description, location, and use

      2. Lessors

      3. Rent and periods of leases

      4. Net lease obligations

      5. Utilities and services

      6. Business restrictions and events of default

      7. Rights to sublet or assign

IV. Personal property

  A. Tangible assets

      1. Description of equipment, computers, telephone systems, furniture, vehicles, and so forth, owned, leased, or ordered

      2. Encumbrances, chattel mortgages, conditional sale contracts, or liens

  B. Intangible assets

      1. Internet domain names, patents and trademarks, service marks, registrations of trade names

      2. Trade secret agreements and nondisclosure agreements

      3. Business licenses and permits

      4. Other restrictions for entity or its employees

      5. Copyrights

V. Significant agreements

  A. Franchise agreements

      1. Goods or services, territory, term

      2. Termination provisions

  B. Customer contracts

      1. Amount of business in last five years

      2. Exclusivity and termination provisions

      3. Relationships with insiders

  C. Distributorships, dealerships, and supplier contracts

      1. Product supply and servicing

      2. Exclusivity and termination provisions

      3. Relationships with insiders

  D. Government contracts

      1. Amount of business in last five years

    2. Nondiscrimination requirements
    3. Exclusivity and termination provisions
 E. Brokerage agreements
    1. Obligations for commissions
    2. Exclusivity and termination provisions
 F. Insurance
    1. Property and marine insurance
    2. Liability insurance
    3. Health insurance
    4. Life and disability insurance
    5. Self-insured risks
    6. Claims in collection
    7. Claims not yet reported
    8. Director and officer insurance
 G. Noncompetition agreements
    1. Current directors, managers, officers, employees, consultants, agents, and independent contractors
    2. Former directors, managers, and inside or retained personnel, agencies, or contractors
 H. Prepaid items
    1. Insurance premiums
    2. Subscriptions and dues

VI. Employees
    1. Retirement plans
    2. Health and welfare plans
    3. Life insurance plans
    4. Workers' compensation
    5. Unemployment compensation
    6. Discrimination issues
    7. Wage and hour considerations
    8. Accrued vacation time

VII. Liabilities
    1. List of trade and other creditors
    2. Unpaid taxes
    3. Federal payroll and other withholding
    4. State payroll and other withholding
    5. Fixed obligations
    6. Contingent and unliquidated liabilities

17

Succession Planning

Relief from gift and estate taxes, or even their phase out, is currently under consideration by Congress. But for now such *transfer taxes* are imposed on transfers of wealth during one's life or at one's death. Every dollar of value after an exclusion of $675,000 in 2001, ratcheting up to $1 million by 2006, will be taxed by the federal government at a rate as high as 55 percent. This huge tax cost is in addition to any taxes imposed by the state and any administrative and probate costs.

The entrepreneur is hit even harder. With one exception (see Tax-Deferral Opportunities later in this chapter), the federal estate tax is payable within six months of death, often an enormous burden when one's net worth is primarily tied up in a closely held business. The more successful the entrepreneur has been, the more difficult it might be for her survivors to raise cash quickly to pay the tax. The family of the entrepreneur might be left no alternative but to sell or liquidate her business and free up the cash necessary to satisfy the tax obligation.

The entrepreneur owes it to herself, her family, her business, and all those who depend on it to establish a wealth transfer plan that limits and funds the government's take, thereby permitting her business to survive her.

Such a plan is typically a composite, drawing on several compatible strategies. This chapter describes some of the more popular strategies that specifically relate to the transfer of entrepreneurial businesses or interests in them and how they work. (Such strategies will, of course, need to be coordinated with general estate planning techniques, a topic beyond the scope of this book.) But, first, a discussion of the relevant tax rules is in order.

Federal Tax Rules

Before 1977 gifts made during one's lifetime were viewed separately from transfers at death. A gift tax was imposed on each gift in the year it was made, allowing wealthy people to make lifetime gifts at relatively low gift-tax rates and escape the relatively higher estate tax that would otherwise eventually be imposed on them. In 1977 the loophole was shut tight. Since then taxable gifts (excluding those to a spouse, regardless of amount; gifts in excess of $10,000 per recipient from any one donor per year; payments made directly to a school for a person's tuition; those made to a health care provider in payment of a person's medical expenses; and gifts to a qualified charity) are taxed in the year they're made, but then they are added back into the donor's federal estate tax base when she dies. The estate tax is then not only assessed against those taxable transfers made at death, but those taxable gifts made during one's lifetime, subject to a credit for any gift tax that was previously paid.

An annually increasing "unified credit" will, by 2006, allow each taxpayer to transfer, during the person's lifetime or on death, assets of up to $1 million without incurring a gift or estate tax liability. Estates exceeding $1 million are subject to a 5 percent surcharge until the benefit of the unified credit and lower graduated tax brackets has been recaptured, the entire taxable estate then effectively being taxed at 55 percent.

One more tax may also become relevant to the entrepreneur's situation, the generation-skipping transfer tax (GST). The introduction of the GST dulled a planning tool many wealthy people profitably employed. The idea was to pass over one's children and leave assets to grandchildren or even great-grandchildren, perhaps directing their income from those assets to their children so long as they lived, but never technically letting them control the assets. The children, even though benefitting from the gift, would never have their estates taxed as if it was theirs—until GST became law. Now, any property transfer to a beneficiary two or more generations down the family tree from the transferor will be subject to an additional tax, just as if it passed from generation to generation. The GST rate is a flat 55 percent after an exemption of $1 million available to each transferor.

The entrepreneur should not underestimate what powerful tax-savers generation-skipping transfers can still be. Suppose she has an estate that will eventually be taxed at the 55 percent rate. Leaving $1 million to her daughter will thus net her $450,000 after taxes. At the daughter's death, assuming the asset hasn't increased or decreased in value and assuming that a 55 percent tax rate still applies, another $247,500 in taxes will become payable and her son will inherit only $202,500. If the entrepreneur left the $1 million directly to her grandchild, he would net $450,000, after taxes. The savings: $247,500!

Tax-Deferral Opportunities

The entrepreneur's closely held business may be eligible for some estate tax breaks she should understand. The first two may buy her family some critically needed time in paying the estate tax and just might avoid their forced sale or liquidation of the business.

Section 6161 of the IRC permits the IRS to grant a deferral of up to 6 months for gift tax and up to 12 months for estate tax. A request is made through an Application for Extension of Time to File U.S. Estate Tax Return and/or Pay Estate Tax (IRS Form 4768). If an extension is allowed, interest is compounded daily.

Far more important, Section 6166 provides:

> If the value of an interest in a closely held business which is includible in determining the gross estate of a decedent who was (at the time of his death) a citizen or resident of the United States exceeds 35 per cent of the adjusted gross estate, the executor may elect to pay part or all of the [applicable estate tax] in 2 or more (but not exceeding 10) equal installments.

Thanks to the relief Section 6166 affords, whatever fraction of the adjusted gross estate constitutes the closely held business becomes the fraction of the estate tax that can be deferred. And despite the language of the section that indicates that deferred tax can be paid in up to 10 installments, the actual deferral can be spread over 15 years since the first installment on the estate tax payable under the section can usually be deferred for up to five years after the estate tax return is due. One word of caution: Interest is payable annually, even during the first five years when principal is deferred.

Further estate tax relief is available to entrepreneurs and their families by a complex and hard-to-satisfy series of rules that on their face exempt some interests in closely held businesses from the federal estate tax. If an entrepreneur meets the requirements, a husband and wife can pass a business interest valued at up to $1.3 million without incurring estate taxes. Most of the benefit might prove illusory, however, because the $1.3 million exclusion is reduced by the unified credit, which is scheduled to increase to $1 million in 2006.

For what it's worth, these are the requirements:

- The business must be located in the United States.
- The business must constitute at least half the value of the decedent's estate.
- The decedent or a member of her family must have owned the business for five out of the eight years immediately before her death.
- Someone in the family must be active in the business.
- The owner's interest in the business must be left to a spouse or another close relative.
- Her family must own at least 50 percent of the business. Alternatively, the decedent's family must own at least 30 percent of the business, and either 70 percent must be owned by two families or 90 percent must be owned by three families.
- For 10 years following her death, her heir must remain active in the business, the business cannot be sold, her heir must remain a U.S. citizen, and the business must continue to be located principally in the United States.

Valuation Strategies

Probably more fertile territory can be found in the way the IRS values closely held businesses in the first place, and how the entrepreneur can take advantage of the opportunities IRS policy presents.

An entrepreneur's interest in her business may well be her most valuable asset and, consequently, its value may be the biggest determinant of the tax that will eventually be assessed against her estate. Although business valuation is admittedly more art that science (see Chapter 11), the IRS has provided guidelines in valuing a closely held business for federal estate tax purposes. Revenue Ruling 59-60 requires that the following eight factors be considered:

1. The nature of the business and the history of the enterprise from inception
2. The economic outlook in general and condition and outlook of the specific industry in particular

3. The book value of the stock and the financial condition of the business
4. The earnings capacity of the business
5. The dividend-paying capacity of the business
6. Whether the business has goodwill or other intangible value
7. Sales of stock and the size of the block to be valued
8. The market price of stocks of businesses engaged in the same or similar line of businesses, whose stock is publicly traded, either on an exchange or over the counter

Uncharacteristically helpful, the IRS recognizes that the value of closely held businesses should be adjusted to reflect that, unlike publicly traded companies, a privately held concern may enjoy no readily identifiable market for its shares. The difficulty of selling shares in a private business coupled with its relative unattractiveness to purchasers entitles it to a "discount for lack of marketability."

Another adjustment, a "minority interest discount," is also available for interests representing less than 50 percent of a company's equity. This adjustment represents the economic detriment minority owners suffer in having no real voice in management—their retention as employees, the declaration of dividends, or even the sale of the business.

One caveat: The flipside of the minority interest discount is the "control premium," an adjustment frequently made by the IRS to reflect the disproportionate value of shares held by owners of majority interests in closely held businesses.

Income-Shifting Techniques

Possibly the best estate plan is the one that minimizes or even avoids the tax altogether through careful planning. Inasmuch as the tax is measured against the entrepreneur's assets, the careful and deliberate shifting of assets to her spouse, her children or even her grandchildren, whether by gift or by sale, can be the most efficient of planning techniques.

Outright Gifts

The first gifts the entrepreneur might consider are those to her spouse. The unlimited marital deduction permits one spouse to transfer any or all of her assets to the other without any gift or estate tax. For that reason, sufficient assets are usually transferred between spouses to ensure that each will be able to take full advantage of the exclusion that, by 2006, will reach $1 million. The entrepreneur and her spouse will then be able to leave their children up to $2 million in value without any estate tax cost.

Taking further advantage of the marital deduction, the entrepreneur's estate plan is likely to leave assets in excess of her exemption to her spouse when she dies, again free of tax. Once her spouse dies, this inheritance will be added to his other assets and may then be taxable but, in the meantime, the tax can be deferred, and tax deferral is almost always thought to be beneficial.

Other gifts merit consideration, too. The gift of an opportunity should be among the first to explore.

Obvious as it seems, the entrepreneur who owns eight restaurants might simply arrange for the ninth to be owned by her children, and not by herself. (This presupposes, of course, that she has no business co-owners who might object to their being excluded from an opportunity they share with the entrepreneur; see Director and Officer Liability in Chapter 10.) The restaurant's financing can be accomplished by the entrepreneur's pledge of collateral, her guarantee of a bank loan, or both. The result: The new venture will remain outside the entrepreneur's taxable estate since she never owned it.

Every year each of us can give up to $10,000 to any number of recipients, free of gift tax. And a spouse can join in making a gift even if the other spouse actually owns the asset being given away. Gifts need not be in cash; ownership interests in a closely held business clearly qualify for tax-favored gifting. So if the entrepreneur—with her spouse "joining her"—decides to give each of their five children a $20,000 interest in her business each year, $100,000 in total value, plus all the dividends and appreciation it will ultimately represent, can be transferred free of any current gift tax—and free of any future estate tax. Depending on a business's value and the number of children (or grandchildren) who are to be the recipients of the entrepreneur's generosity, a sustained and disciplined gifting program may be enough to shift ownership of her business out of her estate, without any estate tax cost at all.

Other gifts can be tax-efficient, too. The unified credit can be used during one's lifetime to transfer an appreciating business interest. Although the credit, to the extent it is used during her lifetime, won't be available to shelter asset transfers at death, it might nevertheless make sense for the entrepreneur to use it earlier, rather than later. If her business interest is $675,000, she can transfer it to her son, using the credit and paying no tax. If years later the business interest is worth $5 million, he will have kept that value out of his taxable estate and, assuming a 55 percent tax rate, saved his family about $2.75 million in estate taxes.

Even taxable gifts might make sense. Suppose the entrepreneur isn't prepared to tap into her unified credit during her lifetime or, for some other reason, the strategy is unwarranted. If gifting remains an appealing alternative, the tax cost of gifting is at issue, the entrepreneur might consider "net gifts." A net gift of a business interest is really a sale, but for less than FMV. The strategy lets the entrepreneur-seller use sale proceeds to pay the gift tax on the "bargain" element of the sale, the difference between the price she receives and FMV. The amount of gift tax is reduced while a source to pay the tax is created. So, if an LLC interest is valued at $10,000, and a 55 percent gift tax rate applies, the entrepreneur might sell the interest to her daughter for $4,000, resulting in a $6,000 gift that would be taxed at $3,300, easily funded out of the proceeds she receives.

The Family Limited Partnership

A Family Limited Partnership (FLP) is a very popular way to give interests in one's closely held business to her children at a very reduced transfer tax cost—and, at the same time, retain control of her business.

Let's assume that a husband and wife own a growing e-tailing business worth $2.5 million. Although they make gifts of a portion of their business to their children and clearly want to reduce their eventual taxable estates, they insist on maintaining management control over the business.

An FLP strategy will do everything they want it to do. The entrepreneurs can transfer their business to an FLP in exchange for "general partner" interests, which they will retain, and "limited partner" interests, which, using their unified credits, they can give to their children. The general partners will run the business; the limited partners will be passive investors, at least for now.

The gifts by limited partnership interests may be eligible for discounts—for both lack of marketability and lack of control—allowing the unified credit to work even harder. Similarly, they can leverage their $10,000 annual-exclusion gifts, transferring limited partnership interests to their children at discounted values. Not only will the value of the limited partnership interests be excluded from the parents' estates; so will the appreciation on those interests. And, when the time is right, the parents can gradually turn over control of their business by gifting general partner interests, too.

Stock in a closely held business is an ideal asset for an individual to contribute to an FLP. But there is a trap to avoid: One should never transfer voting shares of a controlled corporation—a corporation in which the individual owns (with the application of the family attribution rules) or has the right to vote stock equal to at least 80 percent of the combined voting power of all classes of stock. Transferring such voting stock in a closely held corporation to an FLP and then voting its shares as a general partner of the FLP constitutes retaining enjoyment of the transferred stock—and bring back into her gross estate any limited partnership interests she transferred to the FLP. The solution is to recapitalize the controlled corporation and to transfer only nonvoting stock to the FLP.

Gifting, even net gifting or gifting to an FLP, is rarely sufficient to meet all the objectives of the entrepreneur's wealth transfer plan. For one thing, the value of her business may be too large to give away tax efficiently. For another, giving away business interests might help the entrepreneur solve a tax problem at the expense of maintaining her lifestyle into and through her retirement years.

Sales of Business Interests

Sales of business interests within the family can be very tax efficient, too, and don't deprive the entrepreneur of wealth she may need or prefer to retain. The simplest illustration is the outright sale.

Suppose the entrepreneur owns a metal working corporation that has a fair market value of $1,000,000. By selling to her daughter for $1,000,000, she will, of course, incur an income tax to the extent the price exceeds her "tax basis," usually her cost. (Her profit will be taxed at favorable capital-gain rates.) But the corporation will now be outside her taxable estate and so will any appreciation that may accrue until she dies. If, for example, the entrepreneur dies 10 years later, her estate will be taxed on the $1,000,000 her daughter paid her (or less if she spent it, more if she reinvested it wisely), but the corporation, now worth $5,000,000, altogether escapes the estate tax. So long as the current income tax cost of the sale can be justified by the anticipated estate tax savings, the strategy may make sense.

One question that might arise is how can the daughter best fund her purchase. If she has personal savings or credit in her own right, there may be an easy answer. Otherwise, the entrepreneur might finance the purchase and in fact might thereby defer her income tax liability under the installment sale provisions of the IRC. What should be avoided is any deal design that has the company making distributions to the daughter that she, in turn, pays over to her mother, the entrepreneur. Both the distribution and the payment will be taxable as the benefits of the transactions would understandably be diluted, if not sabotaged.

Companion strategies enhance the tax efficiencies of the sale of business interests to family members: the Installment Sale to an Intentionally Defective Irrevocable Trust, the Grantor Retained Annuity Trust, the Private Annuity, and the Self-Canceling Installment Note.

Installment Sale to an Intentionally Defective Trust

One alternative is the entrepreneur's sale of her business interest to an independently trusteed, intentionally "defective" irrevocable trust, one that is ignored under the so-called grantor trust rules for income-tax purposes. The trust is defective because it empowers the trustee to pay premiums on life insurance on the grantor or her spouse without the consent of an "adverse party"; it empowers the grantor or anyone else in a nonfiduciary capacity to reacquire trust assets by substituting property of equivalent value; or it empowers the trustee to add beneficiaries other than the grantor's after-born or after-adopted children. Again, the concept is one of deferred sale, but here the entrepreneur is permitted to make gift tax-free transfers of her appreciated business interests to her children.

The structure is a tricky one, and an example should help explain it. Suppose the entrepreneur is a 60-year-old woman with significant assets, including a $500,000 Internet-hosting concern operated by her daughter. The entrepreneur expects that her estate will be taxed at the 55 percent rate. She wants to transfer the company to her daughter but her remaining unified credit will shield only $200,000 from gift tax.

Here's what the entrepreneur does: she gives 40 percent of the company to a trust and sells the remaining 60 percent to it in exchange for an installment note of $300,000. The note bears interest at 5.83 percent, the assumed applicable federal rate (under IRC Section 1274(3)) on the date of sale, and requires equal annual principal payments of $30,000. Only any balance due on the note at the entrepreneur's death will be includible in her taxable estate.

Assuming the company generates annual pretax income of 10 percent, the company's value grows at an annual rate of 3 percent, and the entrepreneur dies just after the note matures, she will have transferred an additional $848,957 to her daughter and the transaction will have saved $356,926 in estate taxes.

Why does this strategy work? As long as the business is sold to the trust at FMV—and a valuation expert adequately supports that value—it should not be deemed a gift and the entrepreneur should incur no gift tax or use any of her unified credit by reason of the sale. Nor will there be a gift if the FMV of the business interest equals the FMV of the note so long as it bears interest at the applicable federal rate. On the entrepreneur's death, it is just the outstanding balance on the note that would be included in her gross estate.

But there will be a gift, and it's critical to the viability of the strategy. Should the trust lack the funds it needs to make its installment payments, the IRS could reasonably find that the trust's promise to pay on its note has no substance and, consequently, that the "sale" isn't a sale at all, but a transfer with a retained interest. Such a characterization would result in the "sold" business interest ultimately being included in the entrepreneur's taxable estate. For that reason, the entrepreneur should give cash or property to the trust first, thereby "seeding" it. This gift of seed cash or property would be the only gift to the trust, and it would be gift taxable, or sheltered by the entrepreneur's unified credit.

The trust will be drafted as a "grantor trust" for income-tax purposes, one where the grantor-entrepreneur recognizes all the trust's income, even if it's accumulated or paid to the trust's beneficiaries, presumably the entrepreneur's children or grandchildren. The trust's assets thus grow without any dilution for income-tax payments.

Here's a trick: The entrepreneur's payment of income taxes on trust income isn't a gift to the trust because she is obliged to pay them—yet her recognition of income provides the same estate-tax advantage as would a tax-free gift to the trust each year equal to the income tax liability the trust creates. This tax-free transfer of additional income to the trust is of special benefit to the entrepreneur who consistently uses her $10,000 annual-exclusion gifts, has exhausted her unified credit, but would still be eager to make further tax-free gifts.

One final feature: Property included in one's gross estate receives a new, stepped-up income tax basis equal to the property's FMV, generally as of the decedent's date of death. Since the business interest was sold by the entrepreneur before she died, the trust that purchased it is, of course, denied any step up, and, when the property is sold, the trust's gain will be measured against its cost, not the presumably higher date-of-death value. This result is a bad one and flies in the face of the conventional wisdom that clients should retain title to low-basis property so that when they die their heirs can benefit from a step up.

One might argue that the estate tax exclusion is more valuable than a step up—and one would probably be right. However, one need not make the choice. The trust can exchange its low-basis property for cash or high-basis property. Or, the trust can distribute some of its "assets in kind" to satisfy payment obligations under the note. Either way, the appreciated property can return to the entrepreneur's estate, thereby becoming eligible for an income-tax basis step up, while the estate-tax exclusion is preserved.

Grantor Retained Annuity Trusts

A GRAT is another kind of an independently trusteed, irrevocable trust to which the entrepreneur might transfer a business interest, but where she retains a fixed annuity interest for a number of years (not to exceed her life expectancy), with the remainder interest passing to specific beneficiaries, probably her children. Although the entrepreneur pays a gift tax when the business interest is transferred to the GRAT, no additional tax is payable when the property passes to her beneficiaries as long as she survives the stated term of years. If she doesn't, the property is brought back into the grantor's estate.

Let's go back to our 60-year-old entrepreneur, whose daughter runs her $500,000 Internet-hosting company. Suppose now the entrepreneur transfers the company to a GRAT, but retains a 10 percent annuity interest of $50,000 a year for 10 years, and names her daughter the remainder beneficiary. The taxable value of the gift less the retained annuity interest (assuming a 7 percent IRC Section 7520 rate on the date of the gift) is only $174,585. If the entrepreneur survives the 10-year term, the ownership of the company will pass to her daughter without any further tax bite. If she doesn't the company's value is brought back to her estate, which is credited for any unified credit she used. If the entrepreneur dies just after the 10-year term, she will have transferred an additional $745,152 to her daughter and saved $319,312 in estate taxes.

Thus, if all goes well, the entrepreneur will have transferred her business interest to her daughter at a greatly reduced transfer tax cost and "frozen" its value so that all future appreciation altogether escapes the estate tax. What's more, the opportunities to receive a step up in income tax basis and make gift tax-free transfers equal to the trust's income tax liability—both discussed in the context of the sale to an intentionally defective irrevocable trust—are equally available to GRATs.

The Private Annuity

A private annuity might have the entrepreneur transfer her income-producing, high-growth business interest to her son or daughter in exchange for an unsecured promise to an income stream for the entrepreneur's lifetime, or for a stated term at least equal to her actuarial life expectancy. The strategy is particularly attractive when, owing to ill health, the entrepreneur's life expectancy is shorter than average, and she wants to transfer appreciated property to the next generation. The technique immediately removes the property from the entrepreneur's estate, avoiding gift and estate taxes. Yet, so long as the annuity obligation is unsecured, she realizes taxable gain only as her payments are received; each payment is allocated among basis (the tax-free recovery of her cost), gain (her appreciation on the business interest taxed at capital-gain rates), and interest (taxable as ordinary income). Should the annuity obligation become secured, the entrepreneur will immediately recognize, and be taxed on, all of her gain.

Since the present value of the annuity equals the FMV of the property, the entrepreneur will not have made a gift. And since the annuity payments are never adjusted to reflect any increase in the value of the transferred property, the entrepreneur will have "frozen" the property's value and passed all its future appreciation to the next generation.

Two words of caution: The private annuity works best when the entrepreneur-transferor is in relatively poor health since the annuity tables are generally based on life expectancy tables, and not a guesstimate of her actual life expectancy. However, if the entrepreneur is terminally ill, Treasury Regulations require that her actual life expectancy determine the annuity factor. In that case, a private annuity simply isn't indicated.

Nor is a private annuity recommended where the son or daughter lacks an independent source of income to make annuity payments. Although the business can be reasonably relied on to carry much of the burden, if the business becomes the sole source of the annuity's funding, the IRS might successfully argue that the purported annuity is really a trust arrangement where the trustee retains an interest for life. Under such an arrangement, the transferred business interest would probably be includible in the entrepreneur's taxable estate.

Self-Canceling Installment Notes

A self-canceling installment note (SCIN) is another deferred payment arrangement whereby an entrepreneur can transfer her business interest to her son or daughter, but here it will be for payments over an agreed term. And the promissory note evidencing the debt will "self-cancel" at the transferor's death.

Let's look at a hypothetical fact pattern. Suppose the entrepreneur is a 60-year-old woman who wants to transfer her webmaster business, worth $1 million, to her daughter. She's entertained the possibility of merely leaving the business to her daughter when she dies but believes she can leave more net worth to her through a SCIN since payments contractually stop at death. Both the entrepreneur and her daughter know that, if she lives longer than statistics say she should, her daughter will end up paying more than she should for the business—much more, in fact, because the SCIN must include a "risk premium" to compensate the entrepreneur for the possibility that her death might cancel her daughter's obligation to her.

But the mother's health is relatively poor, and that's the key. Both mother and daughter believe that the daughter will likely pay less than $1 million for her mother's business.

The SCIN arrangement they sign is a tax-year deal. An actuary decides that $80,934 is a reasonable risk premium to add to the business's value, and the daughter signs a $1,080,934 note. If the entrepreneur dies at the end of the second year, the daughter will have paid her mother only $359,951 for the business, and the mother will have successfully extracted the business, its income, and its appreciation from her taxable estate without paying any gift tax.

In fact, so long as the mother dies by the sixth year, her daughter will have paid her less than $1 million. If she lives for the full 10-year term, the daughter will pay her a total of $1,497,095 for the business.

On the surface the SCIN looks much like the private annuity, but each fits better in somewhat different circumstances. On one hand, unlike a private annuity, a SCIN has the advantage of being a secured arrangement without triggering the entrepreneur's immediate recognition of taxable gain. On the other hand, the entrepreneur will be deprived of installment-sale treatment, and thus be better served by a private annuity, and not a SCIN, if she is a dealer in property of the kind transferred, or if she is selling depreciable property or marketable securities.

18

Initial Public Offering

Not every entrepreneur will become a New Economy billionaire but almost all of them eventually give serious thought to going public. As Jeff Bezos, Steve Case, and Paul Allen understand so well, new capital and the currency public stock represents can enormously increase a company's financial leverage and the returns it delivers to its shareholders.

Yet, a public offering doesn't always deliver on its promises to the company or those who built it. An IPO brings with it a new accountability that the entrepreneur and his venture may find uncomfortable, if not stifling.

Public Life

For one thing, founders and other insiders will be forced to forgo all kinds of transactions with their company—sales, leases and management agreements among them—because other shareholders simply might think they're unfair.

No longer will his company be the entrepreneur's alter ego, to treat as his very own; everything he does once the public becomes his partner, even in furtherance of the company's best interests, will scrupulously need to avoid any criticism that he has diverted a corporate opportunity to his own account or otherwise was guilty of a conflict of interest.

Just as the entrepreneur's conduct will be constrained, so will the company's. Governance will now be subject to the approval of the board of directors and the shareholders in a formal and unfamiliar way. To keep shareholders happy, management may be inclined to pursue short-term strategies, calculated to buoy profits and stock prices, at the expense of the long-term goals of the founder, and indeed, the venture.

Once the company goes public, there will be few secrets. Insider information—facts management knows but the general public doesn't—can't be used by insiders to influence their decisions to buy or sell company securities. To enforce the principle, securities laws see to it that any 10-percent shareholder is obliged to disgorge his profits on company stock held less than six months. In addition, SEC Rule 144, promulgated under the Securities Act of 1933, prohibits company insiders from selling shares during a "lock-up" period, usually 180 days after the company goes public.

The company itself can't hold too many secrets either. The SEC requires that key executives' compensation and the company's business plan, among other things, be disclosed when the company goes public and on an ongoing basis.

To make their deals marketable, underwriters will typically permit founders to register only so many of their shares in an IPO, both to ensure that the company receives the lion's share of the offering's proceeds and to counter any impression that the founders are walking away rich and with little incentive to continue to grow the company. Limiting the founders' sale of their own shares could present another problem for them —loss of control. Were a dissident faction to accumulate a significant voting block, the founders' authority—and vision—may effectively be undercut, if not sabotaged.

Finally, a public offering is an expensive proposition. Before the founders begin the process, they will probably need to beef up management. They will also need to introduce new systems and controls to meet financial reporting requirements that haven't existed before.

The offering itself is a cash drain. An underwriter's commission can be as much as 10 percent of the offering price. Legal fees can run $75,000 or more. SEC and state filing fees can represent another $50,000 to $100,000. Audited financials, pro forma and summary financial statistics vary based on the company's size and the audit's complexity, but $20,000 is a minimum, and such services can easily exceed $100,000. Financial printing—for the prospectus, the registration statement, and official notices—might add another $50,000 to $100,000 to the bill. All told, even a small IPO could well cost $500,000 before any proceeds are realized. And, despite the public's voracious appetite for Internet and biotech new issues, and even with the opportunity to raise capital over the Internet, there may be no assurance that the entire offering will be fully sold.

Given these extraordinary concessions costs of risks, why bother? The entrepreneur whose venture is an excellent candidate for an IPO can benefit dramatically from selling shares to the public: He will create a market for the shares he retains; he is likely to realize a better price on the sale of those shares since investors are willing to may more for stock in public companies; and he will gain the advantages of portfolio diversification, once his shares' proceeds are reinvested into other assets.

For the venture, new worlds can open. Since equity, unlike debt, need never be repaid, an IPO can instantly make a company financially healthier. All kinds of debt might be retired, interest payments avoided, and ironically the financial stability that results might well allow the company, when it needs to borrow money, to do so more easily and cheaply than it ever has before.

After a successful IPO, the company's shares (and their owners) might prosper from a vigorous "aftermarket," where more shares can be sold and more capital raised at less and less cost to the company and its owners. The company's stock can become a respected currency. to acquire other businesses and to motivate key employees, through stock options, stock appreciation rights, and stock bonuses. And the company's public status may afford it the attention of customers, suppliers, and others who can help it to continue to succeed.

All these good things come to those who wait—for in IPOs, as in much of life, timing is everything.

Preconditions

First, of course, the venture needs to be ripe. It should probably have revenues of $10 million or more, an annual net income of $1 million or more, a compounded annual growth rate of 25 percent or more, and a strategic business plan that can withstand the foreseeable vicissitudes of life.

Here's another benchmark: The company's financial projections should support a market capitalization of $100 million within three years of going public. Market capitalization is the total number of shares owned by the founders and the public multiplied by the market price of the shares. And market price usually reflects a multiple of a company's earnings, a different multiple from industry to industry.

The entrepreneur should check out the average multiple for his industry by calculating the average price-earnings ratio for publicly traded companies in the same industry and apply that multiple to the earnings he projects for three years after the company goes public, assuming, of course, that the company's net offering proceeds are put to work as planned. Once the $100 million bogie is achieved, the company has a good shot at attracting interest among brokerage firms and institutional investors. Until then, a liquid market for shares is unlikely to develop. And if it looks like it should take much more than three years to reach that goal, a public offering probably doesn't make sense yet.

Management needs to be ready, and some unflinching self-analysis should be urged. Senior executives need to content themselves with their lot as public-company executives, relinquishing their personal privacy, ceding authority to others, and inviting scrutiny of every step they take. And, finally, management needs to exhibit the credibility and leadership to grow along with the company as it will soon be positioned.

The markets need to be hospitable. Unless investors are demonstrably hungry for new offerings, an objectively attractive IPO, even with the best of planning and intentions, won't make sense. And, no matter what, if private sources of capital are more cost-effective, they're probably a better source to tap first. Later, after private money is prudently put to work and adds value to the company's stock, a public offering might make more sense because a higher stock price can command more capital or require that fewer shares be sold.

Registration Team

Assuming all systems are go, the entrepreneur must put together a professional team to shepherd management through the rigorous process of registration. Typically, the team will include legal counsel, a managing underwriter, the underwriter's legal counsel, and independent CPAs.

The underwriter is a key player, and finding the right underwriter is often crucial to an IPO's success. Securities counsel, accountants who represent public companies, and executives at other similar companies that have gone through the process are good sources of leads on competent underwriters.

The underwriter should have experience in the venture's industry and in offerings of the size the company intends to bring to market. And the entrepreneur should understand the underwriter's distribution capability, whether local, regional, or national, and be satisfied that it matches the company's needs.

In selecting an underwriter, management should act deliberatively, neither reacting to the mere mention of a top offering price (most good underwriters will command about the same price under equivalent market conditions), nor looking too narrowly at the underwriting function. Ideally, the company's relationship with its underwriter should be broad and deep, continuing long after the stock is sold. The very best underwriters will let investors know about the company whenever opportunities present them, and will provide ongoing market research and financial advice to the company.

Registration Process

The Securities Act of 1933 governs the sale of securities to the public. (Securities law is a complex practice area; the going-public process, as discussed here, will, of necessity, be simplified and can't be counted on to consider all the variables that might affect any particular company.) The act requires that a "registration statement," setting forth financial and other information about the company and the securities it seeks to sell, be filed with the SEC. Going public usually takes up to 180 days and includes a number of steps. Not surprisingly, the first is planning.

Planning has many aspects. The goal in each case is to test the company's readiness for public ownership. The number and classes of shares should be reviewed and restructured as necessary to meet the goals of the offering. The company's Articles of Incorporation and Bylaws will need to be revamped to anticipate public ownership: the establishment of audit and compensation committees is one typical addition to consider, among many. The company's arrangements with the founders should be revisited; they are almost always sensitive. Executive employment relationships should be documented, and stock option programs implemented. The founders may well entertain an expansion of the company's board of directors to include outsiders, which will inevitably become a requirement in every publicly held company. And targeted management additions should be considered to bring the company's executive lineup to the level it will need to execute all the company's plans successfully.

Another word about the demands of running a public company is in order. Whereas big companies hire financial pros to make deals and work with investors, smaller public companies don't. It's normally left to the CEO to add these new functions to his already daunting portfolio. So, if the entrepreneur who is thinking about taking his company public is a nuts-and-bolts micromanager, he might be well advised to hire a chief financial officer who's operated public companies before and has been through the offering process. That way the boss can do what he does best and keep the company on the profitable track that's made it a reasonable candidate for public money.

The planning also requires a good, hard look at the state of the company's available financial information. For example, the registration statement must include audited financial statements for at least two years. If the company's financials have not been audited—and most are not—the company's management should ascertain whether or not available records are in fact sufficient and auditable.

When the registration team meets, it will be decided who will be responsible for which parts of the registration statement. The team will also consider how the offering should be structured and which specific form of registration statement (depending on the amount of money to be raised) should be used.

Then, an offering timetable and letter of intent between the company and the underwriter (or, if a group of underwriters are retained, as is sometimes the case, a *lead* underwriter) are negotiated and signed. The timetable lays out who is to do what and when. The letter of intent, although a nonbinding document, evidences the company's expectation to hire the underwriter, to sell a certain number of the company's shares at a certain price, and to pay the underwriter an agreed fee for doing so. A contractually binding underwriting agreement is signed later, just before the registration statement takes effect.

The entrepreneur should understand that a "quiet period" starts when the company reaches a general agreement with the underwriter to market the company's securities and ends 90 days after the registration statement becomes effective. During the quiet period, only certain information about the company can be distributed to the public—which, by the way, includes the company's normal advertisements and financial information. The SEC encourages disseminating the kind of information the company has customarily disseminated.

The company can get into trouble when it offers a security before the initial registration is filed. And an *offer* has been construed to mean just about anything that arouses public interest in the company or its securities. So, new kinds of publicity might cause the SEC to delay the effective date of the company's registration statement.

Once the initial registration is on file, the red herring (preliminary prospectus) is a permissible vehicle to elicit investor interest. And so are road shows, where the company's management and the underwriters tell the company's story to institutional investors and financial analysts.

The registration statement must fairly disclose the bad with the good, any unfavorable information that an investor might reasonably require to make an informed investment decision. The statement consists of two parts. Part I, which is also distributed to prospective investors in booklet form, is called the preliminary prospectus, or red herring, before the registration takes effect. It discusses the company, the offering, the anticipated use of offering proceeds, how the offering price was determined, who the sellers are, how the securities will be distributed, and the risks involved.

Part II contains information not required to be included in the prospectus such as the expenses of issuance and distribution and a description of any recent sales by the company of unregistered securities.

The initial registration statement is a collaborative effort of the registration team. The company's legal counsel typically prepares nonfinancial sections. The underwriter and its counsel describe the underwriting arrangement and, frequently, the offering. The company's management, with the help of its CPAs, prepares the required financial statements and disclosures.

After a series of drafts and redrafts, the initial registration is filed with the SEC, the National Association of Securities Dealers, Inc. (NASD), and the securities regulators of all the states in which the securities will be offered. The SEC reviews the filing only to see that the company's disclosures are adequate, but not to bless the merits of the offering. Some states, under their "blue sky laws," may consider whether the offering is "fair, just and equitable." And the NASD will review the reasonableness of the underwriter's compensation. An underwriter will typically charge 1 percent to 2 percent of an issue's value plus commissions of 7 percent to 10 percent of the value of the actual stocks sold—but the NASD will look at all the facts and circumstances in judging whether the compensation is acceptable or excessive.

The SEC and possibly one or more states will then have their say. Comment letters are usually issued within 60 days after the initial filing. They will raise questions about any aspect of the filing that they believe doesn't satisfy regulatory requirements.

The registration team will take any issues raised by the SEC or a state very seriously. The registration will promptly be amended to deal with each and every concern the team deems legitimate. Any others will be negotiated with the regulators until they are fully satisfied. Once everyone on the team approves the amended registration statement, it is filed, and so is a "pricing amendment," disclosing the offering price, the underwriter's compensation, and the net proceeds to the company. In most cases, the SEC will accept the amended registration statement, waive the 20-day waiting period, and declare the registration effective immediately.

The company, at long last, can bring its securities to market. If the underwriter's commitment to the company is "firm," that is, if the underwriter assumes any risk that the securities might not be sold, the closing will usually occur, and the company will usually receive its net proceeds five to seven days after the registration statement becomes effective. If, on the other hand, the underwriter commits only to use its "best efforts" to sell the securities, the company can expect to close on the offering within 120 days after the effective date, as long as the underwriter will by then have sold the minimum allotment of securities specified in the registration statement.

Nontraditional Alternatives

Apart from the traditional IPO, there are a few additional ways a company can go public, ways that might be particularly appealing to some entrepreneurs.

One such approach is "self-underwriting." The idea is for the company to act as its own underwriter, with the help of a local or regional underwriter. Even with some friendly advice from a pro, this alternative is not for the faint of heart.

A second approach is the "small corporate offering registration" or the "uniform limited offering registration", which in many states allows relatively small amounts of capital to be raised through the filing of a Form U-7. When it fits, the process is to be recommended as a way of cutting red tape and saving legal and accounting fees.

A final approach is called a "reverse merger," a strategy recently adopted by motivational speaker Anthony Robbins and, before him, by investment broker Muriel Siebert. The structure has a preexisting, thinly traded public company issue a relatively large number of new shares to the entrepreneur who now controls it. The operating company then sells off its assets to the public company, changes its name, and is ready to do business. The effect of the transaction is to put the entrepreneur's shares in public hands while bypassing the scrutiny of a stock offering. Since the reverse merger does not raise money from outside investors, but merely positions the entrepreneur in the driver's seat of a public company, its application is limited. However, the technique can allow a private company to position itself for the sale of shares to the public within weeks.

Once the venture is a public company, by whatever means, the entrepreneur's life will never be the same. The company will now need to file various forms with the SEC, including Form S-R, to disclose any funds received in exchange for stock and how the company has used them; Form 10-Q, to report the financial performance of the company on a quarterly basis; Form 10-K, to report the financial performance of the company on an annual basis; and, as if that's not enough, Form 8-K, to report any of a host of significant events in the life of the company. All the while management will be on its best behavior to maintain good relations with the company's shareholders and the other constituencies it serves—its customers, its employees, the communities in which it operates, and the public at large.

Index